MOTHERS
and
DAUGHT

The guide
understandin
transforming the
relationship with your
mother

WENDY FRY

Mothers and Daughters

The Guide to Understanding and Transforming the Relationship With Your Mother

Wendy Fry

Foreword by Sharon King

Author's Declaration

ISBN Number: 978-1-910662-36-6

Disclaimer: The information presented herein represents the view of the author as of the date of publication. The book is for informational and educational purposes only to aid and support with emotional wellbeing and personal development. No responsibility can be taken for any results or outcomes from the use of this material.

The ideas represent those of Wendy Fry and not directly those of the founder of EFT, Gary Craig. You are advised to take full responsibility for yourself at all times and to seek the support of a qualified EFT practitioner, doctor, health practitioner or therapist if you have any concerns about your physical health or emotional wellbeing. EFT is a form of acupressure, based on energy medicine techniques from traditional Chinese/Eastern medicine. While every attempt has been made to provide information that is both accurate and effective, the author does not assume any responsibility for the accuracy or use/misuse of this information. The author is not a licensed health professional and offers EFT and The Spotlight Process as an Emotional Health Consultant. In the event you use any of the information, as a constitutional right, the author assumes no responsibility for your actions. If you are suffering from any physical or psychiatric condition, please seek the advice of the appropriately qualified health professional.

Many of the names in the case studies and women's words of wisdom have been changed to protect the identity of the individuals in question.

Copyeditor: Jenny Bardwell

Publisher: Milton & Fry

Orders: If you would like a signed copy of the book and a personalised dedication you can contact me via my website www.mothersanddaughters.solutions

You can also order via www.amazon.co.uk and www.amazon.com

Testimonials

"I know from personal experience that Wendy gives above and beyond to her private clients. Therefore it didn't surprise me that this book is a reflection of that ethos.

Mothers and Daughters is much more than a self-help book; it is like being in a therapy room with Wendy. You are taken by the hand and lovingly guided through a deep exploration of your mother-daughter relationship. It is a roadmap to understanding your mother; your ancestral lines, core beliefs and habits – and importantly, you are given the tools to release what no longer serves you. If you have unresolved issues with your mother or daughter (and who hasn't?) then I urge you to read and use this exceptional book. "

Kate Marillat - Bestselling Author Transform Your Beliefs, Transform Your Life - EFT Tapping Using Matrix Reimprinting and Creativity Coach

"Once again, Wendy Fry has written a powerful and impacting book on relationships. This time she explores one of the most essential relationships that we all experience as women: the relationship with our mothers. Some years ago I worked in the field of emotional health and it became apparent just how many of our programs are set in place by our relationship with our mother. This book not only explores that relationship in depth, but also gives us tools and insights to help us shape that connection into something that is healthier in the present day. Whether your mother is still alive or not, this exceptionally thoughtful and well written book will enable you to deeply impact your relationship with your mother, and rewire your brain to experience it differently. Highly recommended for therapists as well as those who are on a journey of self-growth and healing."

Sasha Allenby - Bestselling Author of Matrix Reimprinting Using EFT, Book Coach, Ghost Writer and Publishing CEO.

"This book is full of deep thought provoking questions which guide the reader to truthfully discover the highs and lows of their mother-daughter relationship and how to heal any damage that might have occurred as a result. Wendy's honesty in sharing her own experiences helps the reader to understand the processes to maximise the benefits of each activity. Women's Words of Wisdom at the end of the book reassures us that we all have different experiences with our mothers."

Curly Martin - Bestselling Author of The Life Coaching Handbook, The Business Coaching Handbook, The Personal Success Handbook and Achievement: Cancer Free For 20 Years.

"The mother-daughter relationship is often a complex one. This straight to the point guide to understanding your mother and transforming your relationship with her offers you the tools and techniques to do just this. Utilising EFT to aid emotional release as an EFT Master I know the power that EFT has to create more effective relationships. Mothers and Daughters will help you to figure out the workings of your relationships and will show you not only how to transform your past but your future too."

Karl Dawson - Bestselling Author of Matrix Reimprinting Using EFT and Transform Your Beliefs, Transform Your Life - EFT Tapping Using Matrix Reimprinting.

"Right from the beginning of reading Wendy's book I was mesmerised. Her comprehensive desires to share and help meant she left no stone unturned. She skilfully used case histories that brought real life and deeper understanding to her reader. Wendy is certainly going to be bridging the gap and may even be closing some gaps completely. Bless you lovely Wendy."

Mary Llewellyn – EFT founding Master Practitioner and Trainer.

"If only our relationship with our mothers and daughters was as good as in the movies. A few years ago I mentioned how Christmas had been delightful until I went to see my mother. I expected a big backlash from people telling me what a terrible daughter I was. Instead I received a flood of messages from people telling me how they'd also had a difficult experience.

Wendy's book gives us a chance to examine the relationship with the person who gave birth to us; a much needed but rarely spoken about subject. Plus a careful reminder that is not always easy and that mother's are not given a book of instructions when they give birth. Many are not perfect and some are well, pretty awful."

Anne Jirsch - Bestselling Author of Instant Intuition, The Future is Yours, Cosmic Energy, Create Your Perfect Future.

"Wendy Fry has written an insightful book about the complex relationship that mothers have with their daughters. It underlines the importance of stepping back and seeing the relationship as it really is, and I particularly like the series of checklist questions and processes that Wendy provides to help us become clear about this. It is so valuable to have an understanding of not just our own relationship with our mother, but also the influences which impacted on their lives, which in turn shaped their parenting skills. As with so many areas of our lives, it is important to unpick the limiting beliefs that we hold, and to take responsibility for our own self-care. It is worth while spending time visiting and re-visiting this book, and working through any negative aspects of our relationship with our mother. As Wendy so rightly says, "It's a universal truth. We all have a mother." This book is for you if you feel you need to change the way you feel about yourself and your relationship with your mother for the better."

Sue Williams - Author of Believe You Can: Face Your Fears and Confidently Claim the Life You Desire.

"As a long term therapist I've seen time and again, the impact of the mother-daughter relationship on forming a woman's identity and shaping her relationships.

In this highly informative book, Wendy Fry captures the mother-daughter relationship beautifully. She teaches the reader to understand the effect of their own mother-daughter relationship on a deeply emotional and psychological level.

What I so love about this book is Wendy's ability to bring across the bigger picture; to step back and help the reader understand her mother as a person. This is a hugely important step in enabling a woman to move past internal conflicts and limiting beliefs that have been getting in the way of her happiness and independence.

And beyond this Mothers and Daughters also offers a number of highly effective tools and strategies to help the reader begin to meet needs which may not have been met in her early years.

The book is a wonderful balance of acceptance for women in all situations and transformative tools to break generational patterns. It's a book about love."

Marléne Rose Shaw - Author of Out Of Fear Into Love: Life doesn't have to be a struggle.

"I am blessed to have a wonderful relationship with my mum, who is my best friend and most ardent supporter, so wondered what I could gain from reading Wendy's book. I have to say it is absolutely fascinating in both its ability to enlighten you to some interesting scientific facts that you may never have come across and totally different perspectives on mothers. Using case studies make it moving and real, I truly connect to that type of approach. I highly

recommend reading it to broaden your knowledge, enhance your feelings and perhaps even change your perspective on mothers. Enjoy!"

Gillian Morris – Author of "EFT for Everyone"

Foreword

Of all the relationships in the world the mother-daughter one, I believe, as women, is the most influential one in our lives. Our mother helps to shape who we are right from the beginning – right from conception. This relationship is the foundation of who we are and how we will show up to mother our own children. It is also an important one in how we perceive and judge our own femininity.

When Wendy asked me to write the forward to this book my first thought was "who am I" to write about such relationships, as my own relationship with my mother was still very much unresolved and I really had no desire at the time to change that. I wanted to stay in my detached, disassociated, protected state with very strong boundaries. I used my work and my busy social live to keep my mother and her over emotions at bay. To me, she felt like a bottomless pit of neediness for love, it felt like no matter how much you love you gave to her it was never enough. It felt like from a very early age I was the parent and she was the child in our relationship. Of course this was her own childhood-mother issues showing up in their full glory.

Even though I have written my own book “Heal Your Birth, Heal Your Life” and previously worked on my own in utero, birth and early childhood traumas, I still felt that our connection was not how ‘others’ describe their relationship with their mothers to be. The irony is I work with clients to help them change their relationship with their mother. I often find that it goes all the way back to their birth and the separation of mother and baby. Well they do say you teach what you best need to learn well “HELLO”, guess where the key to my own mother-daughter relationship was. Yes, my very own birth story.

Whilst I was writing Heal Your Birth, Heal Your Life I asked my mother about my birth story and she told me that the midwife had told her I was coming too quickly and there was a danger my mother would tear so they gave her pethidine to slow down the labour. My mother is very sensitive to any drugs (or alcohol) and as pethidine is a narcotic drug she was pretty much unconscious for the remainder of my birth. She told me she got to hold me for about a minute after I was born then I was taken to the hospital nursery so she could continue to sleep. Bingo there is was. When I checked in with my baby self at that time I could feel the isolation, the resentment of being abandoned, alone and unloved. I found that I attached to the other babies in the room who were also feeling the same way. I even made a vow to help them not to feel so scared. I decided I was on my own and I had to take care of myself. So this is how “Miss Independent”, “I don’t need help or love”, “I’m going to recue others” was shaped in me. The protective barrier around my heart was formed and the inner resentment because my mother wasn’t there for me was created and buried deep inside of my subconscious.

Now, I am eternally grateful to Wendy Fry for asking me to write this forward, as how could I even begin to do so with without healing my own mother-daughter relationship first. I

had to shine a spotlight on my own trauma and take the brave steps to heal our relationship. I am so grateful I did. As I'm writing this forward now my mother has passed away two weeks ago and before she passed I was able to tell her how much I loved her, with my heart wide open, not a protective barrier in sight. I told her I forgave her and explained that it was my baby self that was holding the resentment that had kept us separated all our lives together. She realised that for her too, the delayed bonding experience we had was not as strong as it could have been because of the drugs she was given but also understood and we explored her relationship with her own mother. So that conversation was very healing for us both. Of course there were many other experiences throughout my childhood that needed attention and healing too and I'm sure there are a few still in need of healing but now, I feel a wonderful sense of peace that we finally got that connection.

As an Author, teacher, therapist and a human being I'm so grateful for all the tools we have to bring awareness and transformation to our lives now. In this book "Mother and Daughters" you are going to have many insights and "ah ha" moments. You will be gently and lovingly lead on a deep dive journey into understand who you are, but more importantly who you are not. The first step is to read this book and the second is to give yourself permission to use the tools Wendy is sharing with you. This I promise you will be a journey of a lifetime. Enjoy.

Sharon King - Bestselling author of Heal Your Birth,
Heal Your Life

Dedication

This book is dedicated with gratitude
to my mother Jeanette.

Thank you for giving me the gift of life...

2-11-1943 to 21-10-2015 (71 years young)

Acknowledgements

I would like to acknowledge you the reader. Thank you for allowing me to enter your mind and heart through the sharing of these words.

With loving thanks to my mother Jeanette and father Paul who gave me the gift of life and my brother Colin who taught me how to shape some funky dance moves when the going gets tough. Massive hugs to my wonderful friends especially 'THE HOGS' (Girlfriends with Hearts of Gold) Gill Shaw, Ann Whittaker, Deborah Marshall, Joanna Emmerson, Maaike Vlamm, Lucy Moreton, Lisa Rackham and Caroline Maidment, you are the best!

Special thanks goes to Olive Webb who was like a second mum to me; Olive picked me up many times when I fell down and always with love. Heartfelt gratitude goes out to Margaret Biggs, Helen Stanbridge, Jane Taylor, Curly Martin, Lexie Bebbington, Anne Jirsch, Sasha Allenby and Monica Cafferky. Thank you Sharon King, author of Heal Your Birth, Heal Your Life for sharing insights into mother-daughter relationships and how they first begin in the womb.

To all the people who have caused me pain and discomfort in my life, without the challenges and experiences I had with you, I may never have found the path leading me to do the work I love – so I thank you.

This book would not have been possible without my clients and willing case studies who trusted me enough to be vulnerable. They were comfortable to share even the depths of their own despair and have been willing to work with me to change their lives and relationships for the better. I have learnt so much from you.

I wish to recognise both mothers and daughters the world over, we can learn so much from each other. To all the *'other mothers'*, those special people who find us in our time of need, who love and accept us unconditionally for who we are, I give thanks to you.

CONTENTS

Introduction

Mothers and Daughters: The guide to understanding and transforming the relationship with your mother

It's a universal truth we all have had a mother.

As much as you might like to change your mother, transforming your relationship with her and coming to terms with your past, ultimately begins with you. If you are experiencing familiar emotions like anger, sadness, guilt, blame or shame, please understand that you are not alone in your search for your mother's approval, acceptance and love.

With no *'Dummies Guide'* available to help you make peace with your mother and move on from past pain, I realised the importance of writing an informative and practical self-help guide specifically aimed at daughters to help them find emotional release, gain personal closure and an understanding of how all daughters' lives are shaped through the mother-daughter experience.

I want you to know, that it *is* possible to move beyond the pain you feel inside. It *is* possible to move on from your disappointments, regrets, feeling that you are unappreciated, unloved and misunderstood. It *is* possible to work towards accepting your mother - warts and all and in turn, you will ease the pain of the past and realise you are worth loving.

Each of you reading this will have your own story when it comes to your mother and for mothers reading this, your story about your daughter will be unique to you. Our personal realities are based on what we each individually experience and the perceptions and beliefs we filter through.

It is my intention to help you to bring balance to your thinking, guiding you to react and respond to your mother in a way which serves you better and by doing so; you will understand and transform your relationship at the deepest level.

What does the word 'Mother' mean to you? We will work through the range of emotions you feel when you think of her. I will help you to acknowledge the parts of her you like and love, as well as helping you to cope with the parts of her you do not identify with or find difficult.

When I use the term "mum" or "mother", I refer to your childhood mother, your mother at the time she raised you. This may also include a step mother, foster or adoptive mother or 'other mother figure' that cared for you. Until your 'mother stuff' is understood and healed, the inner and outer conflicts you have or once had remain a burden. I reach out to you and offer to share the strategies which have helped in my relationship with my own mother and also the wonderfully open women I have had the privilege to work with.

Personal circumstances vary enormously; your mother may no longer be with you through death or family break-up; perhaps you are estranged or never knew your birth mother, maybe you were adopted or placed in care for a period of time. It could be you are in a loving relationship but are open to finding new ways to improve communication with your mother – or, you may have decided to simply take some time away from your mother in order to take stock of the relationship.

Through sharing my own story along with the experiences of other daughters worldwide, I aim to make a positive and significant change in how you feel about yourself and in turn your mother.

After reading this book, you may like to take some time out and then come back to it again. There is a considerable amount of content here which will benefit you if you work though it. You can dip in and out of the book or you may wish to or read it from cover to cover.

Not a blame game

What is shared in this book is not up for criticism or judgement. None of us can predict the future and we don't have the foresight to know how we will cope as a mother or daughter until we are living through it ourselves.

Journaling

It can be helpful to buy a journal or notebook where you can record your thoughts and emotions as you read and work through some of the exercises. Later on when you read it back you can chart your progress.

Journey to the self

Self care never felt so good and by taking responsibility to meet your own needs with the grace of an adult, not the grief of a child, you realise just how strong and capable you are.

Whether your mother is with you in body or spirit, I am here to offer you the opportunity to transform not only your relationship with your mother through understanding, compassion, acceptance and forgiveness but to also evolve the relationship you have with yourself and other significant relationships.

The relationship you have with your mother has made you who you are. I will help you to gain strength from the times which have been challenging and upsetting for you, as well as reconnecting you with happier times in your relationship. Together, we will explore your family ancestry, your beliefs about your mother and why your mother was the way she was, as well as leading you to recognise your own limiting beliefs and how they have shaped your life to date. From this point you have the opportunity to consider not only what you would love to have in the relationship with your mother, but also what you would love to have in the rest of your life.

My Story

When nothing is sure, everything is possible - *Margaret Drabble*

My life has been an interesting journey and one which has inspired me to write this book for you. Having been on what has seemed like a never ending quest to please my mother, I know just how overwhelming and draining it can be. At times, you feel you have nothing left to give others, let alone yourself.

My search for my mother's love began in the early days of my childhood as I became sensitive to her moods and my environment. My mum had a short fuse you couldn't predict from one day to the next how she would be. I was a *'mum-o-meter'*, I would gauge, through instinct, when to keep quiet - which was most of the time. I can remember my mother getting angry with me if I woke up at night or, when I couldn't learn things as fast as she wanted me to. I have watched her ripping up one of my dresses and pulling the head off a doll whose hair I was brushing, because she didn't want me to brush it. I saw her kick the dog on more than one occasion for not doing as she asked and I remember getting my legs and butt slapped on a fairly regular basis.

As a result of my experiences with my mother in childhood, I formed many limiting beliefs about myself and what I could do, be or have. I believed 'I wasn't good enough', 'lovable enough', 'intelligent enough' as well as the other limitations which influenced my behaviour such as 'I must keep quiet', believing speaking up and sharing my thoughts and feelings was wrong. This led to further limiting beliefs of 'I don't matter', 'my needs are not important', 'and I must put everyone else's needs before my own'.

My mother's behaviour seemed normal to me growing up; it's all I knew, though in all honesty I was frightened of her and her angry outbursts. A certain look, a wagging finger, a clip round the ear, smacked legs or bottom, berating tone of voice or being sent to my room would leave me feeling shamed, blamed and humiliated. I learnt to respond to my mother, in a childlike way. For much of my adult life I continued to try and care for her every need, trying to be 'The Good Girl'.

How my mother's past has shaped my reality

It was a saddening fact to learn that my mum never wanted to be a mum. I can remember her telling me she only had children because it was my dad's idea. Knowing I wasn't wanted hurt. Like a kick to my stomach, I remember feeling as though all the air had been knocked out of me. I wondered if I would ever recover from the huge rejection I experienced in that moment. I felt guilty for spoiling her life and blamed myself for her unhappiness. I believed I had to make it up to her in some way and spent the rest of her life doing my best to apologise for being here and trying to make her love me.

Having children, meant my mother let go of her dream of being a nurse. She went along with being a mother because she felt she had to. Societal pressures, family influence and her own limiting beliefs all added to the mix of her moulding herself to conform to what she thought was expected of her. In the 1950s, it was the norm for women to get married, have children and stay at home, so that's what she did.

My parents stayed together until I was fifteen. When my father left, I felt totally responsible for my mum. Her self-esteem was at rock bottom so she became withdrawn, lost a lot of weight and chain-smoked. She became suicidal and talked about ending her life by overdosing on medication. I remember locking away her anti-depressants in my jewellery box before I went to school, for fear she would do as she said and "take the lot." My self-imposed responsibility to keep my mum alive was huge. I felt like I had to become an adult before my time.

Mum needed me to support her emotionally. She wanted to discuss the break-up (as did my dad) but as a teenager I knew so little about life, love and relationships. One of the childhood beliefs I formed at the time was, 'I am responsible for my mother's happiness and well-being'. In the barest form, I felt responsible for her survival. This became the ongoing theme (and limiting belief) which I played out, for most of my life.

Nine months before my mother died I began to set boundaries. I was in pain due to a knee injury and I was waiting for an operation for it. When I spoke with my mother about my mobility difficulties, she simply said 'now you know what it's like'. There was no empathy when I told her I could not do her gardening, clean for her or run so many errands until I was better. My mother still asked me to do these tasks but at a slower pace. She didn't seem to hear what I was saying.

A few weeks before my operation in the September, I wrote a letter to my mother stating I would not be able to drive and needed to keep my feet up and rest for two weeks after my operation. I told my mother, how I felt responsible for her well-being and happiness and whilst she may not like to accept help from other people, I could not continue to give her as much time or care over the coming weeks. This letter was no easy task and I feared her response and how she would behave towards me.

The letter I had back was a complete blow. My mother told me she didn't need me for anything and not to bother with her at all. She told me to make my own plans for Christmas and not to see her for her November birthday. She was not able to empathise with my own health problems. Unless I was fulfilling her needs and doing as she wanted, she wasn't interested in seeing me for a social visit. It hurt like hell to read her words though they further indicated to me my mother's narcissism. She never bothered to call after my operation to see how I was. During this time of convalescing, I felt deeply depressed my mother could not show me any love or even make an effort to call me (I was always the one to call her). I felt very lost and alone during this time, emotional hurt outweighed the physical hurt of the operation.

I don't regret writing the letter. My disappointment was to know my mother needed me more to do things for her, rather than actually wanting to be with me as a person. Had I had the opportunity to spend more quality time with her as two adults, I would have loved this. We remained estranged until ten days before she died. Two days before she passed away, I was able to tell her I loved her, she just looked at me and didn't say a word and went back to complaining about the hospital, the staff and all the other things she was unhappy about. From the day I was born right until the day she died, I never heard the words 'I love you'.

I have had to work through the shock of my mother's death, along with other emotions such as anger, grief, guilt, sadness and disappointment. It has not been an easy journey with my mother, but one I am now coming to terms with. I know I can't change my past, but I do know I can create a happier future.

Hands of time – the beginning of understanding my mother

Digging deeper into my mother's past while she was alive, she shared with me how she had never felt confident about anything in her life; she was overweight at school, didn't have many friends, was an only child and felt very much alone.

Exploring further into my family history, it became clear how my Nan had a short temper too. She, like my mum, had mood swings and went into rages pinning my mum into a corner with a chair and giving her a telling off. My mum said she dreaded my Nan's moods and preferred spending time with my granddad or going to a neighbour's home.

When searching for meaning and understanding in your own relationships, you might be surprised by what you discover and how it changes your view about your mother's actions and behaviour towards you. When you explore your blood line and the females who came before you, it opens your mind to understanding what your mother and the women before her went through. You can begin to understand how we learn through inherited experience and the environments our ancestors grew up in.

It was not possible for me to completely change the dynamics of my relationship with my mother in the way I would have liked, before she passed away. I do know however, that in my heart I tried my best to understand her as a person - not only as my mother. I know too, I couldn't have given any more of myself than I did. Now as an adult, after a lot of 'self work', soul searching and learning from my own mistakes, I understand the relationship dynamics of my parents. In turn, I have been able to understand my mother, probably more so now than when I was growing up. I have found peace within myself and realise we are all doing the best we can depending on our experiences, beliefs and perceptions. Forgiveness and coming to terms with my past has been easier than I thought. Forgiving has set me free.

My mother died on 21st October 2015, part way through writing this book. Her life and death have been my greatest teachers.

Chapter 1

Welcome to the Journey of You

When we truly grow up and take full responsibility to heal old wounds and take care of our own needs, our lives change dramatically. Life becomes all we imagined and more - Wendy Fry, excerpt from Find You, Find LOVE

The first relationship we all have is with our mother.

The connection between mothers and daughters affects women greatly at all stages of their lives - from conception to the grave and everything in-between. It is my intention to help you understand the complexity of the mother-daughter relationship and offer insights into your start in the world and how your early life experiences have shaped you. When you comprehend how your birth and childhood experiences have influenced you, it will be possible to move on from the past and create a more positive future - regardless of your early environment.

I invite you to examine some hard truths about the relationship with your mother acknowledging whatever emotions come up, as you are reading; this is an opportunity for healing and personal growth. I will share with you the tools and techniques to help you overcome your conflicts, showing you how to end your inner and outer struggles with your mother. Far too frequently, mothers and daughters fail to understand each other or are willing to work on improving their relationships. This guide offers you the opportunity to do just that. Whether your mother is alive or deceased, it will be possible to change how you feel about her and in doing so, regain a sense of inner peace.

With awareness that it is your responsibility as an adult to understand how your relationship with your mother has evolved, your learning will lead you to accept all of who you are - with or without her love. By applying what is shared in this book, your life will transform. I will be right beside you for the duration of your journey. You owe it to yourself to heal the pain of your past and begin again.

COMING INTO THE WORLD

Every woman who heals herself helps heal all the women who came before her and all those who will come after her - Christine Northrup

Babies seek warmth and nurturance. Ideally we will find that in our mother's arms. It is after we come into the world that we turn to our mothers primarily as a source of support. We seek physical care, nourishment, affection, emotional support and a place we hope we can turn to throughout our childhood and into our adult lives. What we seek is a place called home. A place where we feel sheltered and cared for in our mother's love.

Depending on the culture and beliefs handed down through your family, certain expectations may have been placed on your mother, without fully considering her values, circumstances, wants or needs. Some of the case studies and women's words of wisdom shared in the questionnaires in Chapter Seven indicate many daughters said they wished that their mother had more choices available to her and how they would have liked her to have fulfilled her own ambitions, goals and dreams, as well as being a mother.

How much of your own birth story do you know?

As I explained earlier, I will be asking some difficult questions to help you understand not only your own experiences, but your mother's too. Stay with me and you will be glad you did, as you will learn so much about yourself in the process. The questions I offer will help you to identify the impact of your childhood, as well as your mother's experience of being a mother, from your conception through to adulthood.

If you are a foster child or have been adopted, you may not have the information discussed. Though, if you are in contact with your mother's relatives or wish to find out more about your birth mother, it's never too late to ask these questions. By doing so, you will gain a greater understanding of your mother and of yourself in relation to her. If you do not want to find out about your birth mother, you will still find the information shared helpful, as it could relate to your adoptive mother, foster mother and 'other mothers' who have raised you.

Case Studies and Daughter's Words of Wisdom

Some of the case studies and women's words of wisdom shared in this book are from daughters who were raised by their mothers in the traditional sense, while others were passed into foster care for a variety of reasons and, for some brought up by a step-mother or other family member. Several knew they were unwanted pregnancies and that termination was discussed. Many daughters shared that although they were planned, for a number of reasons, the relationship with their mother has broken down.

All the case studies are from daughters who have willingly communicated their personal histories and experiences. They want you to know that you are not alone. They want to share what they have been through in the hope you begin to understand your mother and gain a deeper acceptance of yourself. As we heal individually, we can heal collectively, creating a space for the daughters who come after us to thrive.

Chapter Six describes the Emotional Freedom Technique (EFT). This is a wonderful tool to release any overwhelming emotions as and when they come up as you are reading through. You may wish to jump to this section now, if you wish to familiarise yourself with this technique ahead of reading.

I will be posing a series of insightful questions throughout these pages. Please be aware these questions are not designed to create blame or judgement of any kind towards your mother, rather they are offered to help you gain information about your mother's life and how her early experiences may have influenced her behaviour and how you relate to one and another.

To gain some further insights into your relationship with your mother, it will be helpful for you to know the following:

- **Were you a planned pregnancy?**
- **Do you know who your father is?**
- **Was a termination discussed at any point during the pregnancy?**
- **Was termination attempted?**
- **Were you conceived through fertility treatment?**
- **What do you know about your birth experience?**
- **Did you or your mother experience any trauma during conception, pregnancy and birth or just after you were born?**
- **How long were you separated from your mother at birth?**
- **What age was your mother when you were conceived?**
- **Was there any illness, mental health problems, family or environmental stressors your mother experienced, which made it difficult or impossible to be the kind of mother you would have liked her to be?**
- **What financial and family support did she have (or lack) whilst raising you?**
- **What information did your mother have in terms of knowing what to expect concerning her pregnancy, giving birth and being a mother?**
- **How responsible were your mother's actions and behaviour towards you during pregnancy, after your birth and during your childhood?**
- **Was your mother hospitalised or on prescribed medications which affected her ability to raise you?**

- **Did your mother have any addictions at the time of conceiving you, during pregnancy or thereafter?**

Despite there being thousands of parenting books out there, few take into account an individual's life experience and how your mother's life circumstances have influenced her role as a mother. Mothers and Daughters will help you gain an understanding of what was going on for your mother emotionally or physically before you came into the world and how the external events and influences she experienced during pregnancy and your childhood, may have impacted you. When you are you able to empathise, understand and relate to her, you will gain an awareness of how her reality has shaped her and her ability to parent.

If you've been feeling your mother was less than perfect, then I don't know a mother who isn't still learning along the way about how to be a 'good enough mother'. Having an insight into your mother's life will support you in beginning to accept why your mother may not have been able to give you what you wanted or needed as a child. How your mother has treated you, will be more about your mother's personal circumstances than it is to do with you. Gaining an understanding and insight into your mother's life, helps to heal the hurt places of yourself and sets you free from the limiting beliefs you've been holding about yourself or your mother.

A mother influences her daughter's development through many stages of her life and ideally, represents a suitable role model for her daughter to learn from. It is hoped she will set clear boundaries yet offer her daughter the flexibility to make her own mistakes and in doing so, learn and grow into a woman in her own right. Many daughters need to have a sense of coming from a loving mother. Having a bond with a mother or mother figure is vital.

In a perfect world, mothers are our protectors, supporters and encouragers. You and I both know we are not living in a perfect world, far from it. Pain is a natural part of growth. Many mothers and daughters have shared with me how distressing some of their early childhood experiences have been. Ultimately, those adverse childhood experiences shape our lives. With understanding and making time to do the inner work, we no longer need to be a prisoner of our past. Each of us can step up with the intention of making the future a happier place to be.

In an ideal situation, all babies would be created as a result of the love of parents who have a shared desire to conceive a child. In interviews with daughters who are also mothers, they have told me that their partner has been resistant to starting a family. For some, sexual intercourse was unprotected resulting in pregnancy, while others shared that their biological clocks were ticking and they wanted to be a mum before it was too late but did not discuss conceiving with the father.

I have known mothers who made the decision to have their daughters adopted or fostered, as they felt unable to cope for a variety of reasons. Some think they may regret their decisions later in life, if they reach a stage when they do feel able to parent. Some of those mothers have contacted their daughters later and were able to build positive relationships. Others were shunned and are now hesitant to reach out again for fear of rejection or reprimand. I've also known that fathers can feel as if they don't have a choice in the decision of child rearing and they too have felt ill equipped to raise a child and so suffer heartache for leaving their daughters - either as a result of leaving the relationship or handing their child over to be raised by another caregiver. Many daughters are left wondering about their mothers, who she is and what she was like. They not only grieve the loss of the physical bond, but also the loss of not knowing where they come from.

In *More Than Just Coincidence,* Julie Wassamer shares her journey - from having her daughter adopted to their reunion in later life. It's a beautiful read and helps us to understand why some mothers feel they are not emotionally equipped to raise a child. This does not mean a mother will never be able to offer love and nurturance to her daughter later on in life, as this true story shows.

I wonder if it is possible for you to recognise where your mother may fit, in being unprepared for motherhood? Perhaps she did not have the inner strength and resilience or external support she needed to raise you, or was completely unprepared for motherhood and doubted she would be a 'good enough mother'. Understanding your mother in a broader sense and with a different perception of her actions (or inaction), you can work towards understanding and forgiving her for her choices. Who you are is so worth loving and with or without your mother's love, it is my aim to guide you to the place within yourself where you can find and keep the love you seek.

CONCEPTION

My mother was my first country. The first place I ever lived - Nayyirah Waheed

Conception and the time spent in the womb is an important stage in our development. Research indicates that babies are far more aware in the womb than we first thought. I am intrigued as to how far research will develop in this area, as some important breakthroughs are being made as the science advances.

Layne Raymond offers amazing insights into our conception, in her wonderful book When the Drummers Were Women. *"it is often said that the first sound we hear in the womb is our mother's heartbeat. Actually, the first sound to vibrate our newly developed hearing apparatus is the pulse of our mother's blood through her veins and arteries. We vibrate to that primordial rhythm even before we have ears to hear.*

Before we were conceived, we existed in part as an egg in our mother's ovary. All the eggs a woman will ever carry come from her ovaries while she is a four-month-old foetus in the womb of her mother.

This means our cellular life as an egg begins in the womb of our grandmother. Each of us spent five months in our grandmother's womb and she in turn formed in the womb of her grandmother. We vibrate to the rhythms of our mother's blood before she herself is born.

And this pulse is the thread of blood that runs all the way back through the grandmothers to the first mother. We all share the blood of the first mother. We are the children of one blood."

When I first read this information, it had a powerful impact on me as I realised how we are connected at such a deep level to our mothers and the woman who came before her, long before our own conception.

In *Heal Your Birth, Heal Your Life*, Sharon King the author and creator of Matrix Birth Reimprinting, shares details of how our mothers live within each of us in the chapter on Consciousness of the Baby, *"even though it is unlikely that you remember the details of your conception, imprints were being formed even then. They were being formed the whole time you were in the womb. And they continued to be formed in the delivery room and beyond."*

A baby senses its environment initially through the mother's womb and after the birth downloads information from the environment through its senses shaping its inner and outer landscapes. Beliefs and perceptions are being formed - although the good news is they can be changed.

Being inside our mother's womb may be the most intimate experience we share with our mothers. This sensory experience does not compare to any sort of physical touch after birth. Growing inside our mother's bodies we are one. Created by her blood and tissue, we are nourished by her and her body responds to our foetal needs. So, regardless of the way we were conceived, or her beliefs and needs, our mothers give us the prize of growing life.

While a child is inside its mother's womb, it is able to experience its mother's feelings. These feelings support a child's self actualisation. In *The Neuroscience of Human Relationships,* Louis Cozolino informs us that it is the right side of the brain which develops first and responds to negative emotional stimuli prior to conscious awareness for survival reasons. A child's brain is wired early on to attend to negative influences, in the same way our predecessors from ancient times would be ready to fight or flee predators. Our early brain formation is influenced by the perception of danger even inside the mother's womb. Her fears and joys become yours.

Additional research in this area indicates that babies pick up a mother's spoken language and how they respond to music, nursery rhymes and stories they hear from inside the womb. The more science advances, the more information we will have about this fascinating subject.

BONDING

Denial of one's needs for others is the most common type of defense against bonding. If people come from a situation, whether growing up or later in life, where good, safe relationships were not available to them, they learn to deny that they even want them. Why want what you can't have? They slowly get rid of their awareness of the need - Henry Cloud

Ideally after a baby is born, it will spend at least the first hour bonding with mother, being laid on her chest and having eye to eye and skin to skin contact with her. Being fully present in this way allows a mother to form a bond and connection with her baby daughter. To a daughter the mother is her entire universe and when the opportunity for further bonding in early years is not available, it can seem like the daughter's world has fallen apart. A baby cannot rationalise why her mother is not around to hear her cries and attend to her needs, this in itself is traumatic.

Following birth, the baby's familiar environment changes from the comforting, warm womb and a sense of safety to a world of external stimuli. If the baby is taken away at birth without the opportunity to bond, it may result in the experience of separation anxiety which can play out again later on in life. The baby may also experience the very opposite of positive mother bonding i.e. the trauma of being touched by others in those first few minutes of birth, or indeed being touched by machines and aids used in childbirth. Birth separation is magnified when mother and daughter are not able to bond at birth. Many of these early birth experiences impact how we will relate to our mothers, other people and the world around us.

As infants, we never question the bond between ourselves and our mothers, it's simply accepted. Intuitively, a child will be aware of conditional love and fear losing the bond if they do not comply with a mother's guidance and direction. The bond can be both positive and negative and may be interchangeable as a child develops and both mother and daughter find themselves moving through periods of change in their relationship.

Some mothers, for a variety of reasons, are not able to bond with their daughters and from an early age the child may be passed to another mother figure or care giver. As a daughter matures, if the bonding process has still not formed, mothers may banish their daughters and expect them to be as independent as possible in caring for their own needs. Many daughters have shared how they were told not to cry, show feelings or ask for needs to be met. They have been embarrassed, shamed or made to feel guilty for wanting nurturance, affection and connection.

There is much pain shared amongst adult daughters, when their early search for love and affection was shunned. Unless healing takes place, the daughter may approach future relationships in the expectation that she will meet with rejection. Such a limiting belief could perpetuate the daughter's ability to thrive in relationships.

She may go on to choose emotionally unavailable partners who unconsciously or consciously remind her of her mother. This becomes her comfort zone. It's not always a happy place to be, but the emotional disconnect seems so familiar, this is the pattern her relationships follow. We can go through our whole lives trying to find a way to fulfil the unmet needs of childhood and even go to our graves believing we are unlovable. Stay with me on this journey of understanding your mother and, you will transform the limiting beliefs you have about yourself.

The daughters who were case studies used in conjunction to this book have shared the following statements with me when they have gone to their mothers for love, affection and support in childhood. The admonishments shared are consistent with mothers who have not been able to bond or who show narcissistic tendencies. You may recognise yourself as being on the receiving end of some of these statements as well as remembering those specific to you and your mother.

• Stop snivelling	• Be a big girl
• Grow up	• I don't have time for this
• Pull yourself together	• I'll give you something to cry about
• Stop crying	• I will lock you in your room until you calm down
• Go to your room, no one wants to see your unhappy face	• Wait until your father gets home
• Stand in the corner and only turn round when you can stop crying	• You should be ashamed of yourself
• You'll have to sort it out yourself	• Don't be selfish
• Tough	• Now you know how it feels
• You don't deserve it	• Look what I've been through
• Stop being a baby	• Shut up or I'll shut you up
	• I'll send you away if you don't stop crying

A mother who is unable to bond or offer support, encouragement or praise may not have had the love and nurturing she needed herself in childhood and may express in her communications exactly what she heard from her own mother. The mother may say and do things which affect her child's self belief and identity and she may have no idea what impact her words have.

Why is my mother able to bond with my sibling and not me?

Older siblings get more total-immersion mentoring with their parents before younger siblings come along. As a result, they get an IQ and linguistic advantage because they are the focus of their parents' attention - Jeffrey Kluger

You might well be wondering why your mother has a better relationship with a sibling or how each of you can have a completely different view of her. Many of the case studies have shared that their mothers appeared to show more love towards a brother or sister, declaring they felt insignificant in the pecking order of who received most love from mum. Every child needs and deserves love and it's interesting to find out how much love was available when there was more than one child who wanted mum's attention.

Siblings often experience their mothers differently. Take into account the following situations, to gain awareness into your personal situation and circumstances:

- **The age of your mother and her experience of motherhood at the time of your conception and thereafter**
- **Her emotional and physical health during and after pregnancies**
- **Variations in her pregnancies (environmental factors as well as personal situation)**
- **Birth traumas and/or separation at birth**
- **The sex of your sibling**
- **The time span between births of each child**
- **Your health and the health of your siblings as baby or child**
- **Whether you and your siblings were planned or unplanned**
- **Your mothers living situation and financial position**
- **The level of support your mother had with child raising**
- **The father of your sibling**
- **Your perception of your mother giving you love, verses the perception of your sibling receiving her love**

If your mother is still alive, it will be interesting to find out how she experienced her pregnancies, how her life circumstances may have been different in each situation and how she felt about herself during the time she carried you and later on raising you, your brothers and sisters or step-family.

The importance of physical touch in childhood

In *Our Mothers Daughters,* Judith Arcana shares with us the importance of physical touch of mother and daughter at birth. This teaches us we are secure, loveable and loved.

Touching between mother and daughter begins the imprinting process and bonds mother and daughter together. Being fed by our mothers from her breast and, or being held close to her when feeding, allows us to associate with the woman who is providing fulfilment, pleasure and sensual gratification.

Babies respond well to touch, warmth, being rocked, soothed, stroked, eye to eye contact, smiles and facial expressions. To a small baby having this intimate connection is pure ecstasy and we continue to look towards our mothers for affection as we mature. Infants who experience closeness of touch in this way during the first few years of their lives are much more secure. For further reading on the importance of human touch and affection at every developmental stage, Ashley Montagu's book, *'Touching'* offers extended reading on this very human need.

Depending on treatments and medications offered to the mother during birth this may delay the bonding process. Using Matrix Birth Reimprinting (see appendix) it's possible to go back to the time of birth and re-create a different kind of bonding experience. This technique created by Sharon King author of Heal Your Birth, Heal Your Life further supports changing your past experiences and beliefs as well as influencing your future more positively.

ATTACHMENT

Secure attachment has been linked to a child's ability to successfully recover and prove resilient in the presence of a traumatic event - Asa Don Brown

Our mothers influence our physical and psychological development. As children we are dependent on our mothers, as well as other caregivers, to help us navigate our way in the world. In a maze of discovery, we seek a mother's nurture, support and encouragement. Our mother is our first love. We are attached to her in the womb and after birth will remain emotionally and physically attached, dependent on her love, nurturing and presence. This dependence remains until the fourth or fifth year according to Freud in his essay *'Female Sexuality'*.

As babies we don't recognise ourselves as separate people from our mothers and this influences our view of ourselves in adulthood.

Some mothers find it difficult to bond with their daughters while for others it comes naturally. A daughter ideally will receive both nurturance and support from her mother to gain autonomy. Forming a healthy bond and attachment with her mother, a daughter will feel close physically and have the emotional support in place for her to develop a healthy sense of self.

John Bolby *(author of Attachment and Loss)* describes in his theories of human attachment, how the survival of our species has depended on the closeness of mother and infant. Generally speaking, without the mother's care, the helpless child cannot exist. With a healthy attachment, a mother ideally responds to her infant's distress, offering nurturance and care as and when it is needed. These set patterns of responding may continue long after a child grows into adulthood depending on the depth of attachment.

Daughters who did not experience a positive bond with their mothers (especially in terms of physical contact) may have a sense of eternal longing to be touched. Intimate touch is not sexual touch, though some daughters may confuse the two later in life. The daughter grows up hungry for love still yearning to be cuddled, bathed and caressed.

On the other hand, daughters who have not experienced loving touch may become touch sensitive and refrain from physical intimacy altogether as it is an unknown experience for them. Kathie Karlson shares more on this theme in the book, *In Her Image* in the chapter related to touch.

However, if mother or daughter becomes overly attached by becoming the centre of the other's universe, this leaves little room for other relationships to prosper. This type of attachment can cause difficulties when a mother turns to her daughter for the love she never received - thus becoming co-dependent. If there is a desire for a mother to dominate and control her child she may demonstrate this by bullying, over protecting, abusing, humiliating, terrifying, suffocating, or over indulging her. When separation eventually occurs the one who is left may fall apart, they have no self identity without the other.

When both mother and daughter strive for emotional intimacy and the desire to have positive mutual attachment, the relationship will flourish. For many daughters having a healthy relationship with their mothers serves them well throughout their adult life. When mother and daughter are independent of each other they are able to connect as friends and adults as well as mother-daughter. In this kind of relationship, the separation process allows both parties to express themselves independently and they do not feel overly responsible for each other.

Through positive attachment, the mother becomes the daughter's role model throughout the daughter's development.

The daughter will grow with her mother until she is ready to move out into the world independently.

HOW WE EXPERIENCE OUR MOTHER AND HOW SHE SHAPES OUR LIVES

Motherly love is not static, to endure it requires change - Evelyn Bassoff

As well as learning from your mother how to express yourself as a female, your mother teaches you about love, parenting, sex and femininity. Her beliefs about how things should be, are handed down to you, with the expectation you will follow in her footsteps. It is important to remember your mother was also a daughter. She has been shaped by her mother and grandmother.

Judith Arcana highlights in *Our Mothers' Daughters,* how we learn the roles of daughter and mother progressively in childhood. The common gender of mother and daughter intensifies the bond. The daughter role is the frame around which our behaviour as a woman is learned. Even in this day and age daughters are generally encouraged to play with dolls and play at being a mother adopting the matriarchal role.

If our mothers are needy and dependent on us, we learn the role of caretaker early on, performing duties out of step with a child's natural development. The responsibility to 'mother' our mother, impacts how we feel about ourselves and as a result we deny our own childhood needs. The role of caretaker becomes the place we operate from, not only in the mother-daughter relationship, but also by caring for siblings, other family members and later on in life in our intimate relationships.

Leanne Case Study

Leanne came to me for support with assertiveness and improving confidence in relationships

Leanne shared with me how she felt she had to give up her own needs to be loved and accepted by her mum. She recognised in our work together she was carrying the pattern of putting other people's needs before her own in friendships and significant other relationships. She felt unable to express her desires as she believed it was selfish to do so and also because she feared criticism or rejection, expecting others to treat her in the way her mother had.

Through exploring her past, her current relationships and her future aims, it became much clearer to Leanne how she was self-sabotaging in her relationships, by not speaking up assertively or setting healthy personal boundaries. Using The Spotlight Process and EFT (Emotional Freedom Technique (see Chapter Six) she was able to resolve much of her frustration in relation to her mother and in doing so improved her confidence to end those relationships which weren't serving her - and to look afresh as to what was possible for her in the future. When Leanne was able to recognise her default behaviours and limiting beliefs, she no longer responded in the same way when others were inconsiderate of her needs and opinions, she became able to voice her point of view assertively and in doing so many of her relationships improved.

Nothing is set in stone or cast in steel. When one person in a relationship changes their default behaviour and responses, others will change too or they will fall away if the relationship no longer serves their needs. This is part of life and learning and as we change so do our relationships.

Much of what we learn about role representation and relationships, specifically significant other relationships, is taught to us by our mothers through witnessing and modelling our behaviours based on their marriage, partnerships and communications with others. Some of our mother's patterns and beliefs may well become our own based on this early conditioning. Mothers and daughters act as mirrors for each other, the mother subconsciously projecting a younger version of herself onto her daughter to share her image and identity. Sometimes however, our mothers show us an image of someone we do not want to be.

Understanding your mother as a woman and as an individual in her own right, recognising that she had her own life experiences as a child, teenager and adult, will help you in uncovering how your mother has shaped your life to date. Gleaning more information about your mother, her hopes and dreams will build up a picture of the real person beyond the blueprint you have of her (and which you may be currently responding to). The knowledge will help you to reframe your experience of her and the meanings you place on her actions and behaviours. When you can look for nuances and clues into your mother's life, before and after you were born then you can identify perhaps with how she felt about her experiences as a daughter and as a woman, not only as your mother.

Much can be learned when you take into account the age in which your mother and your mother's mother were born and how the eras and generations have changed. Further insights are gained when you explore the circumstances and events your mother and grandmother may have gone through. In terms of societal development, women's voting and employment rights, sexual liberation, social and economic freedom to name just a few of the advances your female linage went through before you came into the world.

Binding mothers

Kathie Carlson shares with us in, *In Her Image,* how binding mothers do not have the confidence to live their own lives and to make independent decisions. Over protective mothers gain a sense of self when their daughters make the same choices they did. The mother may firmly believe her happiness can be found through her daughter and may not want to separate and to allow her the freedom to be who she wants to be.

For some daughters who choose to break the mould and not follow in their mother's footsteps or take the advice handed to her, the mother may be forced to re-evaluate her own decisions and values and may not like it. Her daughter's aims in life might make her question her own choices, as well as make her even more aware of her own unfulfilled dreams and ambitions in life, leaving her with a sense of life passing her by.

Conflict can also appear when a successful mother wants her daughter to follow the same path. If the daughter becomes more successful, the mother's self-esteem and identity may be squashed. Or, a daughter might want to go in a different career direction and the mother might feel rejected by the daughter's choices and disappointed that they do not match her ultimate plan. Some mothers hope that their daughters can live out their own unfulfilled dreams. Love becomes conditional on the daughter following her mother's suggestions. I have known many daughters (and mothers) sacrifice their personal dreams, because they thought they had no option but to go along with what they thought was expected of them.

Love has a high price to pay if, as daughters, we continue to do the things we don't really want to do out of guilt or in the belief, that we will be truly loved and approved of when we do them. If we are unable to say 'no' to our mothers, more and more demands are placed on us with the instruction to conform to meet our mother's needs just as she may well have done with her own mother and her mother before her. We become our own worst enemies when the quest for mother's love becomes an endless game of chase. The reward never comes and we exhaust ourselves in the process. Accepting reality helps us to move on from expecting our mothers to change and we can simply change our reactions and behaviours towards her.

Although a daughter may add meaning to a mother's life, it becomes dangerous when the mother believes a daughter is supposed to meet her needs and vice versa. The roles then become an act of servitude and personal sacrifice rather than a healthy mother-daughter relationship. When a mother and daughter are independent adults, taking responsibility and letting go of those previous roles of parent and child we improve the relationships we have with others. This is a win win situation for both women, each standing in her personal power zone, complete, whole and lovable without the need for external approval or validation.

You will realise that in some cultures, to go against family expectations comes with its own difficulties and consequences, in some cases being made an outcast. I have known many women choose to leave their homeland and families to live the life they want. It's not an easy choice to make, though for those of you brave enough to do so, please know you leave a legacy of positive change behind you. As you change, the world changes and daughters everywhere benefit in the long run.

Here are some questions to consider in exploring how your mother has shaped your life to date. As we understand our mothers and the women who came before us, we are able to understand what influenced them and in turn, how our experience of them may have influenced us.

- **How does your mother think a daughter *should* be and do you agree with her views?**

- **What are your mother's beliefs about raising a child, do you agree with her opinion?**
- **What cultural and ethnic influences have played a part in your mother's life and child rearing?**
- **What female roles, duties, beliefs, perceptions and expectations has your mother passed down to you?**
- **What character traits, habits and behaviours do you share with your mother?**
- **What is your mother's parenting style?**
- **If you are a mother, how is your parenting style similar or dissimilar to your mother's?**
- **Did your mother conform to her mother's parenting style, or resist it?**
- **Was your mother a child carer of her siblings or other family members and if so, have you also been required to care for your siblings and family members in the same way?**
- **Was your mother born into an affluent lifestyle or did she and her parents struggle to survive?**
- **How much of a balanced and equal relationship has your mother had with your father and other male role models in her/your life?**
- **How does your mother behave socially, how are you like her/unlike her?**
- **How does your mother act in private? How are you similar or dissimilar to her in this respect?**
- **Was your mother subservient in her relationships, if so have you also been?**

- **Was your mother overbearing or dominant in her relationships, if so how much of your behaviour in relationships is the same?**
- **What repeating patterns in relationships are you aware of, which are the same as your mothers?**
- **How are your partners similar in character and personality to your mother's partners?**
- **What character and personality traits do you share with your mother?** *(positive and negative traits)*

To understand your mother, you need to look beyond yourself and become aware of the influences which shaped her life. There may be many aspects of your mother's character you do not adopt and many of her qualities which you do. In Chapter Four, Mining for Gold, Gifts from Your Mother we look at ways you can learn from your inherited traits and how to keep the more positive behaviours.

As the case studies and women's words of wisdom in Chapter Seven will show we do not have to follow in our mother's footsteps. We can create our own identity purposefully and with the intention not to be like our mothers. Again, no blame here, just the awareness that, we have choices and if our childhood hasn't been a happy experience, we do not need to hold onto limitations or repeat the experience as we bring new life into the world.

Valerie's Words of Wisdom

"It seemed normal to me to grow up, get married, have children and be a stay at home mum, it's all I ever wanted as a teen. I had no ambition other than this. Just like my mother before me, this was the norm. Although my mum never wanted children she said she felt it her 'duty' to do so. The belief passed on to me

was 'to be a woman you have to have children'. Circumstance has meant I do not have a child and it's odd to think I am the last in my female blood line of my mother's heritage who isn't a mother."

Mothers and daughters often have conflicting expectations of each other. Diane Keaton in the film *'Because I Said So'*, tries to fix her daughter Milly up with an ideal man so she will not follow in her footsteps. It's a beautiful and funny film where mothers and daughters begin to understand each other at a deeper level.

BELIEFS ABOUT OURSELVES AND THE WORLD AROUND US

Words, especially yelled in anger, can be very damaging to a child's self-confidence. The child probably already feels bad enough just from seeing the consequences of his or her behaviour. Our sons and daughters don't need more guilt and self-doubt heaped upon their already wounded egos - Jack Canfield

In *My Mother Myself,* Nancy Friday explores the full range of emotions a mother feels when she holds her child in her arms. Fear, anxiety, hate and love are often present. When a child is the same sex, a mother sees *herself*. A Mother's self-esteem will influence the outcomes of a daughter's life - much more so, than what the mother actually wants for her daughter. Our mothers cannot give us a sense of self-esteem they do not possess and a mother's opinion of herself, will be passed onto her daughter in subtle ways.

Beliefs about how a daughter is expected to conform in her role, are set long before she is born. Passing from one generation to the next, ideas about pregnancy, giving birth and raising a child are made up of the mother's beliefs which are handed down through many generations. We are not our mothers; though having come from her it may be at times hard to separate from her and break away from the role we are expected to follow. As adult daughters we are able to change the opinion we have of ourselves through having an awareness of what we learned as a child. As we change we can adapt and set in motion new ideas about our role as daughter. What went before us need not follow after us. When we learn to step more fully into our personal power we are waking up to the fact we can change the conditions handed down to us and begin to live our lives the way we want to and on our terms. We are able to meet our own needs in the modern world and recognise the old ways are no longer appropriate for all mothers or daughters.

The absence of nurturing or validation as a child shapes a daughter's identity and self-belief.

In my work I come across lots of similar examples where daughters have inherited limiting beliefs about themselves. Some of those limiting beliefs are shared here. What limiting beliefs do you identify with? :

- **I'm not acceptable as I am**
- **It's not safe for me to show my feelings**
- **There is something wrong with me**
- **I'm not lovable**
- **I'm bad**
- **I'm unworthy**
- **I'm not good enough**
- **I am responsible for my mother's unhappiness**
- **I am responsible for my mother's happiness and well-being**
- **People can't be trusted**
- **The world is a dangerous place**

If you want to read more about limiting beliefs, go to Chapter Six Recovery and Beyond and in particular, the section on 'Aiding Your Own Recovery - limiting beliefs and how to change them'.

YOUR PERSONAL IDENTITY AS A DAUGHTER

My daughters, your daughters, our daughters deserve safety, protection, and freedom to make their own choices about their personal lives and their physical selves - Carre Otis

Mothers are our primary source for learning the daughter role. A daughter's individual identity depends on her capacity to adopt her mother's characteristics, much of which happens subconsciously.

A daughter's natural inclination is to identify with the same-sex parent. It is from our mothers we build our sense of self, our security and level of competency. Infants thrive well when they are offered nurturance, support and eventually, autonomy. Daughters learn from and are influenced by their mothers, mirroring and matching the behaviours exhibited by her. It is from our mothers in subtle ways as well as spoken ways we learn to deal with stress, illness and unexpected traumas. We look to our mothers to gauge a sense of who we are. Grandmothers, aunts and older female siblings will also have an influence on us if we spend a lot of time with them. Influences on how to be a woman comes by many different means including classic fairy tales such as *Cinderella, Snow White, Sleeping Beauty and Rapunzel.* The characters are beautiful, innocent, subservient, 'good daughters' or victims of their own circumstance who live in the hope one day of being rescued by a knight in shining armour or a fairy godmother.

Before the age of six, we soak up information through our senses from a variety of sources, including our mothers. Female fantasy fiction characters in story books further compound beliefs about mothers, daughters and relationships generally. *"If only life was like a fairytale" we might say to ourselves.* By handing over responsibility to someone else to love, approve of and accept who we are, we are not strengthening the inherent ability we each have to meet our own needs.

The daughter's self-image will start to form at birth and sometimes even before birth, when her mother fantasises about how her daughter will be.

A daughter's self-image and identify is often fourfold

1: How the daughter views her mother

2: What behaviours and beliefs become her own through identifying with and modelling her mother

3: How the mother views her daughter

4: How the daughter responds to her mother based on expectations and/or responding to conditional love

Identity is complex and individual based on these influences. Cultural influence will also play a part in shaping a daughter's identity and beliefs about who she is and who she can be. Daughters not only identify with their mothers (as their mothers did with theirs), they also absorb society's message about women in general being the main person who should meet an infant's needs over and above any other care giver. Many mothers have shared with me that they feel like empty vessels with little time to care for their own needs and are left feeling depleted, angry and drained, with little sense of balance or equality in the parenting roles. Daughters see this and think they have to be similarly self-sacrificing.

Female friendships are also influenced by our mothers. If at any time, we felt abandoned by our mothers, we might find it difficult to form lasting bonds with other women and also experience a lack of trust as to how reliable a friendship can be. We might find ourselves shying away from women who seem like our mothers, before giving friendship the chance to develop.

Helen Case Study

Helen came to work with me initially to manage work stress and to plan returning to work after a period of sick leave

Helen shared with me she hated her female boss and was stressed because of the way the woman treated her. When I asked 'who does she remind you of', Helen broke down and shared it was like being with her mother all over again believing what she did was never good enough which equated to not feeling worthy of love. Although Helen didn't intentionally look to her boss for nurturance she was projecting unmet needs from childhood onto her. This role of mother could not be met by Helen's boss as it was inappropriate and unrealistic.

We used The Spotlight Process and explored the limiting beliefs Helen had formed about herself. We then used EFT to clear past emotions and feelings of not being good enough. Helen realised what seemed like her mother's criticism was really encouragement to help her do well at school and later in life. She was able to re-frame her experience into one which made her feel more confident not only at work but in personal relationships too.

Kathie Karlson highlights the point, *In Her Image,* the primary relationship between mother and daughter is the birthplace of a woman's ego identity where she learns about the world and her sense of security in it. There is often the expectation on both mothers and daughters where mother is martyr and the daughter dutiful. In trying to meet those demands, both mother and daughter deny true aspects of who they are in the process. It's believed a mother *should* be immortal, invincible, loving and giving when we need comfort and security. In reality, mothers can't cope with the demands of motherhood and do abandon and reject their children. How we react to our mothers who are not living up to our expectations impacts not only our personal identify but how we view and identify with our mothers generally. As daughters, even through to adulthood, we may request our mothers to be a certain way making demands of her which she may not want to meet, but feels she has to.

Daughters are sometimes viewed by mothers to have no adult identity of their own, this is especially so when mothers have not been able to separate from their daughters. Even when a daughter becomes a mother herself, the daughter's mother will invariably attempt to pass on her views about parenting even if the daughter doesn't want to parent this way. This will also apply to being raised with step mothers, foster and adoptive mothers. Mother-in-laws may also fall into this category, disagreeing with your style of parenting and preferring their own.

It will be fair to say in childhood a daughter views her mother only as a mother and not a woman with a separate identity. For some, this need for a mother's nurture may continue through to adulthood where the daughter is still trying to get her childhood needs met. Daughters, whose mothers have died during their childhood or been emotionally unavailable, may find the identification process is delayed or indeed they never had the opportunity to mature. Many of those motherless daughters who go on to be raised by another female role model will find the identification process will begin again.

Some daughters may fear turning out like their mothers. This is a very real fear called *Matrophobia*, as Adrienne Rich explains in *Of Women Born*. A daughter who has witnessed her mother's flaws and weaknesses feels helpless believing these shortcomings will become her own. This fear can create intense emotional distress until the dynamics of what has been internalised is worked through.

Pippa Case Study

Pippa came to me seeking support for emotional overwhelm

Pippa was a perfect example of someone with Matrophobia. Feeling emotionally overwhelmed raising two children, running her home and also studying for a degree, she voiced her worst fears; "I'm worried I will get mentally ill like my mother. What if I get so stressed I get angry like my mother? I'm worried I will lose control and harm my children."

Her thought process and fears of becoming like her mother had been concerning her more than bringing up the children. She was in a cycle of fear based thinking, rather than acknowledging how she wasn't like her mother and how well she was doing juggling so many balls, as well as recognising the times when she was loving and responsive to her children. We simply explored new ways of thinking using The Spotlight Process and used EFT to reduce fear and anxiety to help bring her emotions back into balance.

Like Pippa, now might be the perfect time for you to begin to discover who you really are.

Paula Case Study

Paula came to me to work on improving self-esteem

Paula shared with me, how her mother was controlling, interfered in her relationships, career choices and even bringing up her children. There was a constant dialogue of criticism and very little praise or acknowledgement of Paula as a daughter or a mother.

Using EFT, The Spotlight Process and also working through boundary setting by writing a letter to her mother, Paula was able to take back her power and start the relationship with her mother afresh. It took a while and several reminders to her mother, to reinforce her desire for long-term change. Paula is coming on in leaps and bounds in terms of assertiveness and confidence and her mother is now aware of when she becomes controlling which is no longer appropriate in their adult relationship. I later worked with Paula to discuss finding out more about her mother to gain a greater understanding of her behaviour. It turns out her mother never felt loved as a child and would act in a clingy and needy way towards Paula, expecting Paula to fulfil her unmet childhood needs.

Once Paula understood her mother's attempts to make up for her own deficit in love, they planned to spend quality time together and talk things through, This has given Paula's mother a new lease of independence to do new things and to meet new people on her own. With their relationship rebalanced in this way it's been a win, win for both Paula and her mother. They now spend time enjoying each other's company more than ever before. It surprised both of them how much happier they are by creating some distance and yet when they are together they feel all the closer because of it.

Many women want to break free from the old roles of mother and daughter as well as severing ties from the expectations placed on us by society. We want to ditch the need to be 'superwoman' and give up the desire to be liked by our mothers and be accepted as who we are. For many daughters the yearning to be free from her mother's control is paramount if she is to fare well in her life and in the same way, we can set our mothers free from the dutiful mother role and enable her to live her life anew. It might seem like a harsh reality for a mother, that her daughter is fully dependent on her at birth for food, shelter, warmth and nurturance and then no sooner has she moved into her teens, she no longer wants this level of attention and care. Rebelling against what she depended on, can cause conflict in the identities of both daughter and mother. The cry for independence while still wanting a mother's comfort can be confusing for both parties and the balance is difficult to get right on both sides.

The role of mother and daughter ideally adapts over time. As both woman age, the dynamics and expectations change to one of equality and both mother and daughter can meet as adults. With understanding and maturity on both sides, a new kind of relationship emerges when both mother and daughter interact honestly and freely. The defined roles of mother-daughter are no longer necessary when both women are able to act with maturity. Each woman emerges as herself, with her own unique identity.

Questions for Reflection

- **In what way have you developed your identity according to your mother's expectations?**
- **What did your mother teach you about who you could be as a woman, daughter and mother?**
- **What did you learn from your mother about yourself, your body, motherhood, marriage, relationships and how to succeed in life?**
- **What do you have in common with your mother in terms of your personal identity?**
- **What aspects of your identity, personality, the way you look and your life choices has your mother asked you to change?**
- **What are the positive and negative aspects of having your mother as role model?**

- **What elements of her behaviour and sharing of knowledge have not been a positive experience for you?**
- **In what way is your self-image and identity distorted in relation to what you were told about yourself, or the beliefs you have formed based on your experiences? (How do you view yourself?)**
- **Thinking about the last question, are your distortions the same as your mother's view of herself?**
- **What healthy and unhealthy behaviours have you modelled in relation to your mother?**
- **How do those behaviours impact your life positively or negatively?**
- **Describe your mother as a woman, not as your mother**
- **How would your mother describe you as a woman, not as her daughter?**

Reflect on what you have learnt from reading through these questions and in doing so, know this is a further opportunity to understand yourself, your mother and a way of transforming your relationship.

YOUR MOTHER'S PERSONAL IDENTITY

I could not move completely beyond my relationship conflicts with my mother, until I understood her as a person, rather than as my mother - Wendy Fry

Your mother will have her own personal identity based on the stigma of how she believed a mother 'should be' passed down to her by her own mother, family culture and societal influence. Her education, upbringing, family of origin and caregivers all shaped her identity outside of the mother-daughter bond. Even though you might not share or like your mother's personality, traits and behaviours, you began as she did, inside your mother's womb; you share common ground with her, she, just like you, is also a daughter.

Gathering information about who your mother was or is and her mother before her (your biological grandmother) as well as all the women who came before her (as far as you can go back along your female blood line) will be helpful in identifying the patterns of beliefs and behaviours handed down through your ancestral heritage.

If your mother has over identified with you, there may have been occasions when you have acted or behaved in a certain way where she has felt ashamed, embarrassed and judged by others. You may have even heard your mother using the line *"what will people think of me"* because she feels responsible for your actions and behaviours. It's true to say, this may also apply to you, if your mother has behaved in ways which shame you because you have over identified with her and you feel you will be judged because of her behaviour. In the separation process, this phenomenon ideally drops away, as mother and daughter take full responsibility for themselves, simply allowing the other person to be who they are in their own right.

The identifications we make as women, mothers and daughters can and do change over time. Many mothers after pregnancy and sometimes before deny themselves the opportunity to follow their personal dreams and career paths, in order to be the kind of mother society expects. Mothers may lose their self-identity as they mould and shape themselves into what they think they need to be to be acceptable mothers.

When a child flies the nest and leaves home, mothers are often left with a sense of isolation and loneliness. They find themselves not knowing who they are. Many mothers who are also daughters, have shared with me the physical pain they feel when their child leaves home; even if the relationship has been hostile, the sense of loss is still vivid.

If a daughter goes on to live the kind of life the mother would have liked for herself, there can also be jealousy and animosity, because the daughter has what the mother wanted. Daughter envy is something mother's find hard to admit. Mothers are often unaware of the hate they feel towards their daughters. For many mothers who are resentful of their daughter's status, the anger and hate festers within them and overspills into the relationship. When daughters leave home and don't keep in regular contact with their mothers, this can feel like a huge rejection, leaving a void which seems difficult to fill. This is even more apparent, if the mother has no sense of self, personal security or ability to nurture herself or meet her own needs.

Daughters too, may experience the separation process all over again when they decide they want to have complete control over their futures. If the mother has doubts about how well a daughter will fare independently on her own or in relationships, the daughter's confidence may begin to waiver, she may believe she can't make it on her own without her mother. Separating and being independent of each other is a process all mothers and daughters have to go through. More often than not, the separation can be challenging if both party has over identified with the other and the relationship has become enmeshed.

Find out what you can from your mother, her siblings, your father and her friends about her personal history, hopes and dreams. The information shared may offer new insights into aspects of your mother's personality you have never known about. Learning about her, creates self-awareness and offers the opportunity to find new ways to understand your mother and this will bring a deeper understanding of yourself.

Questions for reflection

- **What were your mother's hopes and fears about being a mother?**
- **How many female friends did your mother have while she was growing up?**
- **What era did your mother grow up in?**
- **What era did her mother (your maternal grandmother) grow up in?**
- **Thinking about the era you are in now and the historical changes women have gone through in the last century, what changes have you and your mother lived through as a result of society changing?**
- **What parental influences are now outdated in the 21st century, in comparison to the 1800s-1900s?**
- **How developed was your mother in terms of emotional resilience when she became a mother?**
- **What was/is the quality of her relationship with her mother (your grandmother)?**
- **What have been your mother's greatest life challenges?**
- **What fears did your mother have about bringing a child into the world?**
- **What physical or emotional changes did she go through which were uncomfortable for her during or after pregnancy?**
- **How did your mother feel about herself when she raised you?**
- **How much support did your mother have in raising you?** (emotional and physical support)

- **What behaviours did you exhibit as a child that made your mother think she was being judged as a parent by others?**
- **Who is your mother still holding resentment towards from her childhood or thereafter?**
- **What did your mother feel she had to give up in raising a family?**
- **What surprises did motherhood bring for your mother?**
- **In what ways did your mother feel she changed (for better or worse) after becoming a mother?**
- **Who does your mother identify with? (e.g. her mother or other female role model)**
- **How responsible has your mother been in terms of caring for your well-being as a child?**
- **How bound have you felt towards your mother over the years in being a daughter?**
- **In hindsight, if your mother were able to live her life over what would she have done differently?**
- **In learning about your mother, what do you acknowledge about her which you never knew before?**

Some mothers may have a public façade, acting one way in public and another way behind closed doors. This has become evident in my case studies where Jan said her mother was as sweet as can be in public while at home she was vile, demanding and the complete opposite of her public personae.

A mother's personal identity generally changes once a daughter has grown up and is no longer dependent on her, though for some mothers they may over identify with their daughters and not want to separate away from them. This can be problematic in the relationship, leaving the mother to feed off her daughter, instead of separating into an identity of her own, causing many conflicts unless addressed. It will be worth considering (and even asking) your mother what her fears are around separation and having an identity apart from being your mother.

Both mothers and daughters will react in certain ways when life throws out its challenges. Thinking about your mother:

How often does she/did she show her feelings openly?

- **Reflecting on your own feelings, do you follow the same patterns as your mother, or have you found a way to respond differently in times of conflict or struggle?**
- **Who did your mother learn her personal identity from?** *(Was she raised by your grandmother, another family member or other mother figure?)*
- **What experiences and events do you believe shaped your mother's life and her personal identity?**

Understanding your mother requires you to get curious about who she was before you came along. In taking the time to learn about her, your journey to transformation and healing becomes easier. If you would like some personal support in improving the relationship with your mother or relationships generally, please do make contact to get started www.mothersanddaughters.solutions

PARENTING AND YOUR CIRCLE OF INFLUENCE

As long as a mom or dad satisfy their own needs through their own powers and with each other, they will not use their children to solve their needs - John Bradshaw

Although this book is written for daughters and mothers, it would be unfair not to mention the role of the father and other caregivers who influence a daughter's life. Many women I have known through friendships, work colleagues and also my clients have shared with me they in fact have a closer bond with their fathers. Many felt their male role model understood them to a greater degree.

It is common for various reasons for a mother to spend more time raising her child than the father and they often see their children as extensions of themselves. Fathers although they may play a significant role in childcare, are usually more able to create healthy boundaries with their children. Some fathers however idolise their daughters and unintentionally create conflict and jealousy when mother and daughter both fight for his attention. In other circumstances a daughter may resent the father taking the mother away from her and vice versa. Mother-daughter rivalry comes into play with both women wanting the most attention. This is also common in extended families when the mother has a new relationship and the daughter may not like having to share her mother's time and love and the new partner too can resent the attention given to a daughter.

Some fathers are not around a great deal in a daughter's life due to working outside the home to provide financially for the family. So, in the early stages of child rearing, mothers may take the role of both mother and father in terms of parenting. Some fathers, depending on the era they were born in and considering their own upbringing and beliefs about parenting, may expect their wives and daughters to fulfil a traditional woman's role of minding the home, raising children and being there to fulfil the husband's as well as the children's needs. I've seen many a mother stretch herself to unbelievable lengths to try and keep everyone (except herself) happy. Giving up her career, her hobbies, and her self-identity and conforming to the image she feels she has to portray. Some mothers put the father or step-father first - over and above themselves and their daughter. In some circumstances, the mother will act out the role of mother and 'ideal' parent to keep her husband happy.

In *Motherless Daughters,* Hope Edelman shares in the chapter *'Daddy's Little Girl'* how a daughter will pick up throughout her childhood and adolescence, clues from her father on how to act and behave towards men. He is her first male relationship and becomes her blueprint for the future and later attachments to men.

YOU ARE NOT YOUR MOTHER

We understand how dangerous a mask can be. We become all we pretend to be - Patrick Rothfuss

Every daughter on the planet will at some time question herself as to who she is and what she wants from life. She will review what aspects of her mother's character and behaviour she wants to adopt.

In adolescence generally, as young women we want to experiment with who we are whether it be dying our hair, experimenting sexually, following a certain fashion, hanging out with different friendship groups or expressing ourselves creatively and some mothers do protest as we make these changes. There is a fine line between loving and hating our mothers if we are challenged during this time of transition and transformation from child to adult.

During the separation process, a daughter is searching for her sense of self and a mother is losing her identity as a mother. Both mothers and daughters can go through a crisis of sorts as each attempts to come into their own way of being, both trying to cope with the emotional and physical changes within the relationship. If the separation process is resisted at this stage by you or your mother it's never too late to form your own identity independent of her.

You have a right to set boundaries with your mother and in doing so you will be helping her to loosen her attachment to you and form her own identity. This can be done in a loving way and with consideration as your mother may have fears about not knowing who she is, or what she wants from life. You are handing her an opportunity which may well lead to amazing experiences she has never even thought about.

If you believe you have been abandoned by your mother, rejected, unloved, dismissed or not accepted as a child or adult, you do not have to further punish yourself by dismissing your needs. Both the child and the adult within you deserve to have the identity of your choice. After self-exploration you can go on to create a completely new identity, one which exists independently of the past or your mother's choices. You have the opportunity to do this for yourself as you learn about your needs and how to fulfil them.

You have the power to change your life. By doing so, you become a fine role model for other women, teaching them that it's fine to celebrate their own personal strengths and follow their own dreams. When it comes to picking and choosing behaviours and traits you have learnt from your mother (and deciding on those you wish to display in your life) my advice is *"choose the best and dump the rest".* Separation and then forming your own identity allows both you and your mother to grow as individuals and what could be better than that.

SEPARATION

Are we separate enough to see our mothers whole, as people who are both good and bad? - Nancy Friday

Separation may be one of the hardest experiences mothers and daughters go through.

The intimate attachments formed at birth, are past their sell-by date, as a daughter nears adolescence. The complex love a daughter experiences during the separation process with her mother, may cause confusion, frustration, guilt and sadness. I have known mothers who find the pain of separation too great to bear and they wonder who on earth they are without their daughter.

Many mothers do not feel the need to separate from their sons in the same way they do with their daughters. If they have created a "mini me" this bond is like no other as their daughter represents their sense of self and womanhood.

During infancy, mother and child are very much at one. Time is spent nursing, gazing into the infant's eyes and the sensations of closeness and warmth experienced by mother and daughter continue to bond them together. The child constantly looks for connection, reward and satisfaction, its main aim is survival in a brand new world.

It is common for daughters in their teenage years if not before, to want to separate from their mothers for many reasons. She may feel she can no longer talk to her mother about certain aspects of her life as she develops into a woman and may find herself seeking out alternative mother figures to talk to - whether this be a same sex friend, the mother of a close friend or a stepmother or family relative during the separation process. At this stage of a daughter's life, she may also rebel against authority figures who remind her of her mother. Working recently with a teenager who was in conflict with a teacher at school, when I asked 'who does this teacher remind you of?' the young woman said 'my mother'. We were able to discuss her projections and how she was reacting to the teacher's tone of voice, mannerisms and requests which were similar to her mother's and then to recognise the teacher was in fact a completely different person.

As a daughter moves through childhood into her teens, it's also natural for a mother to re-experience aspects of her own adolescence. Any unresolved emotions and internal conflicts may surface at this time and become part of the complications of separation. Separation covers not just the physical separation of mothers and daughters no longer living under the same roof, but also the desires of daughters to separate emotionally. Both daughters and mothers will need time to adapt to these changes. As adult women, it is unhealthy when the mother or daughter become over dependent on the other for a sense of feeling valued, gaining happiness and self- esteem.

In an ideal world a daughter discovers her own needs independently from her mother. Moving on from infancy she grows and develops her own character, first at nursery followed by school, she makes new friends and finds personal interests. Some adult daughters still provide for their mothers unmet needs (and vice versa) in terms of conversational intimacy, affection, attention and closeness. If neither mother nor daughter have close external relationships outside their bond it is even harder for them to part. In this dynamic, they become the centre of each other's world, enmeshed and each expecting the other to fill the role of soul mate, mini-mother, sister, friend and husband.

Generally, though not always, the more a mother clings to a daughter the more the daughter will struggle to break free. In my work, it's become apparent that the adult separation process often begins in a moment of conflict when the daughter may have been trying to assert her views and opinions without her mother's approval. It might take a disagreement or several squabbles of this kind for the mother to realise her daughter is growing into adulthood and wants her independence. Some mothers may also take the daughter's wish to become autonomous as a personal attack. As mirrors of each other, a daughter too may feel rejected when a mother wants to move on from her traditional role.

Mothers can sometimes become overly attached as to how their daughters turn out. This can have both positive and negative connotations. If there is an element of unhealthy narcissism, the over binding attachment can be damaging to a daughter as some mothers do not want see their daughters as being separate. They are unable to love and accept their daughters in their own right because the mother's focus is inward and their motivation is one of control and dominance. Self-centred mothers are mostly concerned with personal gain and keeping the daughter for as long as possible. Narcissistic mothers are unable to fully let go and allow the separation process to complete, this frequently leaves the daughter feeling like she doesn't know her own mind and 'mum knows best'. There is often internalised anger, frustration and rage for those who feel powerless against their mothers. The behaviour loop of the mother demanding and the daughter giving into her mother's demands sets up a chain reaction and only one person's needs are being met, namely the mother's.

As a result of this, daughters may go on throughout their lives to have a series of limiting beliefs and fears such as:

- **It's not OK to be me**
- **My feelings don't matter**
- **I don't know what I want**
- **I'm scared I'll make the wrong decision**
- **No one will love me unless I do as they say**
- **It's not safe for me to leave this relationship**
- **No one listens to me**
- **I feel small and insignificant**
- **I can't stand up for myself**
- **I don't matter**
- **I'm powerless**
- **I can't get it right**
- **I'm trapped**

- **I'm invisible**
- **I have no control**

Millie's Words of Wisdom

"I carry my mother's voice around inside my head, berating myself as if she were right beside me. I have to catch myself when I'm going into her judgements and criticisms of me. Although she is no longer on this earthly plain, her voice, her view of things, her mannerisms and behaviours are still a part of me. I just need to turn her voice down and turn mine up."

In the same way a daughter may be eager to separate from her mother, many mothers may long for this separation too. Others may not want to lose their daughters and will become reluctant to let her go or vice versa. Generally, a daughter may feel safe in her early years, being like her mother and having a solid bond with her. In the case of conditional love, many daughters may fear separation as the underlying beliefs are 'love will be taken away', 'I will be disapproved of' or 'I will make mummy angry'. Many of these beliefs have not been tested out for accuracy but still run in our thought loops as we are projecting our past into our future and imagining our worst fears. Utilising The Spotlight Process (Chapter Six), you will be able to uncover where your limiting beliefs come from and gain an opportunity to examine your thoughts, re-directing them and in doing so, find a more balanced approach when it comes to letting your mother go.

When a daughter develops into her teenage years, moving through puberty and towards forming sexual relationships of her own, it can be a trying time for both mothers and daughters, each having their own ideas about what's acceptable behaviour and what isn't. This can relate to what the daughter chooses to wear, who her friends are, what time she comes home - as well as her choice of partner. Mothers might see this as the final rejection as their daughter becomes a woman and replaces her need for a mother with the need for a partner.

Evelyn Bassoff, shares in *Mothers and Daughters, Loving and Letting Go,* how as a mother's child turns outwards and away from her, the mother faces a void which forces the mother to reorganise herself emotionally. For many mothers, losing the exclusive relationship can create a physiological crisis with mild and transitory depressive symptoms, while for others there is a feeling of relief as they anticipate new found freedom releasing themselves from obligations and childrearing.

The mother might find she is unable to cope with letting her 'little girl' go. She may find herself reacting negatively to her daughter's choices and becoming a critical and controlling parent, wanting to be the one who makes the final decision about how her daughter should live her life. This may be because a mother sees herself in her daughter and might not like what she sees. She may be envious of her daughter or dependent on her daughter to meet her own childhood needs. Her own sense of self, identity and self-esteem are tangled up in this relationship with no beginning and no end.

Daughters may regress back to childhood when their mothers become controlling and demanding. If these types of demands come into play the daughter will act out the earlier role of being a dutiful daughter much younger than her years or may report back to a moody teenager and throw a tantrum when the mother becomes overbearing. When boundaries between mother and daughter aren't clear, it's an unknown quantity for a daughter to comprehend what is her own experience and what is her mother's. This will change when a daughter is confident in her identity and strong enough not to react from the hurt parts of her younger self then she will be able to pull away from the need to please her mother and accept her mother's beliefs and ideals are no longer hers.

Ideally, an adolescent daughter will form a separate identity from her mother and in doing so, become a unique individual with a firm sense of self, who she is and what she wants from life. Separation at whatever age comes about when mother and daughter recognise themselves as two different people and they understand their identities do not have to be merged. Separation includes forming one's own beliefs and value systems, as well as having the freedom to choose one's own hopes and dreams. Mothers with a healthy view of this division will promote their daughter's separation, allowing them to make their own choices while still keeping a connection as an individual. The separation process may happen many times over before mother and daughter can be together as equals. Ideally, this process will happen during a daughter's adolescence, allowing a girl to blossom into a self-confident, autonomous and independent woman.

Depending on the age of your mother after the separation process has taken place (whether you still live with her or not) she may learn to enjoy the extra time she has for herself and look forward to pursuing her career and personal passions. Sadly for many mothers, that time may never come, if she feels unable to let her children stand on their own two feet, is frightened of not having a purpose, or is needy in her own behaviours and fears being alone. It's natural for both mother and daughter to want to be mothered at times and a healthy relationship can allow for this, each woman nurturing the other with willingness, expecting nothing in return.

Separation can occur at different stages of a daughter's life dependent on her personal situation.

- **Separation during childhood/teens/adulthood**
- **Separation through adoption, fostering or going into care**
- **Family separation, divorce or re-marriage**

- **Separation through personal trauma**
- **Separation through illness, emotional or physical unavailability**
- **Separation through estrangement**
- **Separation through death**

My wish for you, is that you experience the gift of separation. In doing so, you will understand yourself as a unique and beautiful individual, not only a daughter but also a woman. If you have not already separated from your mother, make this something which you strive for and in doing so, you set her and yourself free from the chains which bind you.

It *is* possible to have a more positive relationship with your mother, once you have both adjusted to living your lives differently. Setting boundaries about what is acceptable or not, and meeting your own needs, strengthens your relationship - even if the relationship doesn't turn out to be the way you expected.

It may only be after the death of your mother that you wake up to the fact that you are now an individual in your own right. You may feel hesitant at first as to how to express yourself, how to reconsider your life and what you want from it. Separation through death gives you back your own life, enabling you to live it on your terms without the need for your mother's love or approval.

It is my hope, having read this far, you are now beginning to understand the complexity of your mother-daughter relationship and have learned new things about your mother and yourself. Reflecting on what has resonated with you so far, take a moment and acknowledge your progress.

Chapter 2

Learning About Life

LEARNING ABOUT LIFE

The mother daughter relationship is the most complex - Wynonna Judd

We are all constantly learning about life. From the time of conception through until the day we die, learning is a continuous process. By discovering more about your family dynamics you will begin to understand yourself at a deeper level. Acknowledging that all relationships have ups and downs, you can choose to let go of a victim mentality and free yourself from past hurts and fears.

Understanding how your past experiences have affected you as a daughter and also learning about your mother's younger days, will be helpful and will go a long way towards healing your childhood traumas. For more deeply seated childhood traumas you may wish to contact me or seek the help of an experienced professional to support you in resolving past emotional pain (See appendix) It's through healing your past and overcoming self-sabotage, you can eventually move on from self defeating behaviours to take charge of your life and put your needs first, taking responsibility to become a healthy adult and looking after your own needs, both emotionally and physically.

Recognising conflicts you may have caused, or made worse directly or indirectly and owning up to the times when you may have said hurtful words, lashed out or given your mother the silent treatment, you can begin to forgive yourself once you acknowledge as mothers and daughters we are doing the best we can with the knowledge, wisdom and ability available to us at any one time.

TRAUMA IN CHILDHOOD

There are wounds that never show on the body that are deeper and more hurtful than anything that bleeds - Laurell K. Hamilton

Trauma in childhood covers a range of issues. Trauma will mean different things to different people. What may have traumatised you may not have had the same impact on a sibling or other family members. Shocks and ordeals can happen to any of us at any age, how we react and respond to new upsetting events is often based on the original blueprint we have created when something in our past has been traumatic for us.

Our individual emotional or physical wounds could be as a result of being abandoned or neglected as a child, witnessing or engaging in family conflicts, parents divorcing, mental health issues within the family and physical, verbal or sexual abuse and violence. Being exposed to Adverse Childhood Experiences (ACEs) impacts how a child develops and how they survive and thrive in the world.

If you experienced anguish in childhood, you may have formed limiting beliefs about yourself, other people and the world around you as well as the expectation additional suffering and trauma will follow. The memory of the trauma lives on long after the actual event is over. We become hyper vigilant - responding in fight, flight or freeze mode to any perceived danger whether the threat is real or imagined.

What we believe to be true, may in fact be a protection mechanism the mind creates to keep us safe from further perceived threats. These self defeating beliefs are made up when trauma occurs, to protect us from our worst nightmares. We may find ourselves responding to a situation when a memory which seems like the original trauma surfaces, though in reality it is completely different. Our filters can easily become our default responses and our behaviours reflect the imagined scenario.

These reactions more often than not limit our potential in so many ways.

Over time as most people fail the survivor's exacting test of trustworthiness, she tends to withdraw from relationships. The isolation of the survivor thus persists even after she is free - Judith Louis Herman, Trauma and Recovery

The subject of trauma requires a separate book to do it justice. I have covered in brief some key points for your understanding. If you have an interest in childhood trauma, you may wish to explore research in the area of Adverse Childhood Experiences (ACE study). This is one of the largest research studies ever conducted, to assess associations between maltreatment in childhood and health and well-being in later life, if you are an ACE sufferer, the good news is you can make changes for the future, learning what contributes to raising a child effectively. More on this topic will be covered in Chapter Five, as well as links to the study in the appendix.

More advances in research are being gained in the areas of adverse childhood experiences, the impacts of stress and how those stressors can alter the structural development of neural networks and the biochemistry and neuroendocrine systems. Research shows how early ACEs have long-term effects on the body, including speeding up the process of disease and ageing and compromising immune systems.

The study indicates epigenetic transition may occur due to stress during pregnancy or during interactions between mother and newborns; this will include not being able to bond with the infant for many reasons. Infants are aware of maternal stress and depression in the mother. There are also indications that partner violence may have epigenetic effects on infants. Traumatic childhood experiences are major risk factors leading to poor quality of life, illness and death.

Chapter Five includes the family and community protective factors of the Ace Study which contribute to raising a well-balanced child. To date, more than 50 scientific articles have been published on this study. The initial study was conducted at Kaiser Permanente from 1995 to 1997, with more than 17,000 participants completing a standard physical examination.

Individual Risk Factors

- **Children under four years of age**
- **Children with special needs**

The medical status of the baseline participants was measured and the ACEs tested were for:

Physical abuse

Sexual abuse

Emotional abuse

Physical neglect

Emotional neglect

Violence towards the mother

Household substance abuse

Household mental illness

Parental separation

Incarcerated household member

Some of the risk factors associated with Adverse Childhood Experiences, are shared here:

- **Parents' lack of understanding of a child's needs**
- **Parental characteristics such as young age, low education, single parent, large number of dependent children and low income**

- **Parents' history of childhood maltreatment in family of origin**
- **Parents thoughts and emotions which tend to support and justify maltreatment behaviours**
- **Substance abuse and or mental health issues including depression**
- **Non-biological, transient caregivers in the home** *(e.g. mother's partner)*

Family Risk Factors

- **Family disorganisation, dissolution and violence including intimate partner violence**
- **Social isolation**
- **Parenting stress, negative interactions and poor parent-child relationships**

Community Risk Factors

- **Community violence**
- **Concentrated neighbourhood disadvantages (***e.g. high unemployment rates, high density alcohol outlets, history of poverty, residential instability, poor social connections)*

Further research into early childhood trauma, indicates that if a mother dies through tragic death, is absent physically or emotionally or is unavailable due to abandonment or early adoption etc, the daughter may have no memory at all of her mother or only a fleeting one. For other daughters, their mothers can seem dead to them due to a lack of bonding and the daughter will go on to mourn for an experience she never had. Accepting the reality of our childhood traumas becomes easier with understanding. It is possible to overcome the hurtful parts of your past, using the tools and techniques I will be sharing with you.

Understanding our adverse childhood experiences and working through the range of emotions using EFT and The Spotlight Process as shown in Chapter Six, aids further healing, bringing relief from the complex mother-daughter relationship.

ABANDONMENT

I'd like to see much more understanding of emotional issues around hurt, abandonment, disappointment, longing, failure and shame, where they stem from and how they drive people and policies brought into public disclosure - Susie Orbach

There are people who stay in life and people, who go. Sometimes, it's our mothers who can't be there for us.

Being abandoned at birth or later on in childhood by your own mother is one of the most devastating experiences you might be forced to go through. Being physically or emotionally neglected by your mother for whatever reason, on a short or long term basis, may have a lasting effect on you until you are able to understand why your mother made the choices she did.

Daughters who have been abandoned by their mothers, or who have a perception of being rejected, may go on to form an 'ideal' of a wonderful mother who they have never met, in the hope that one day they will be re-united with an auspicious and loving mother image. Frequently living on false hopes and dreams which do not come to fruition, the search for mother love can be a painful one. Many daughters in this situation have shared with me that they have so many unanswered questions. They don't know who their mother is in relation to themselves.

In *Motherless Daughters*, Hope Edelman talks about the subject of being abandoned by our mothers leaving unanswered questions:

- **Who was she?**
- **What was/is she like?**
- **Where is she now?**
- **Why did she leave?**

I will pose these further questions, in addition to the above:

- **Who am I?**
- **What's wrong with me?**
- **What did I do wrong?**
- **Why didn't she love me?**
- **Why didn't she want me?**
- **What could I have done to make her keep me?**

For daughters whose mothers leave through physical or emotional abandonment (rather than death), they may feel rejected and worthless. Some daughters may suffer from depressive symptoms - a sense of emptiness, lack of empathy for others and without addressing these symptoms, they may go on to form addictions and have problems with expressing anger or become over angry because they are unable to mourn the loss of their mother.

When a mother dies naturally, it is somehow easier for the daughter to understand as this was beyond the control of mother or daughter. Both examples of loss involve the grieving process, which may last for a few years or, for daughters whose mothers are alive but unavailable, the grieving can last a lifetime.

It is worth noting at this point that unless we actually know our mother's story and what led her to the choices she made, we do not have full understanding. We are imagining stories which may have no truth, stories we tell ourselves can be hurtful and mean we always feel abandoned. When mothers choose to have their baby daughter adopted because they think they cannot give her a good start in life, this could be regarded as an act of love rather than rejection.

Birth mothers choose life, and a family, for their child. But this choice is rarely celebrated. Women routinely face family, friends and even health-care providers who think that adoption equals abandonment, according to researchers and conversations from birth mothers - Nina Easton

If you have the belief that you have been abandoned by your mother you might imagine you have something fundamentally wrong with you. Your thinking gets stuck in a cycle of negative thoughts, impacting your relationships and life generally. Once you begin to understand your mother's reasons for adoption (for instance, allowing another family to raise you because she is not able to mother you) you can begin to rebuild your identity on firmer foundations.

In my work and the information shared from the case studies included, it is clear mothers left their daughters emotionally or physically because they could not bond with them or they could not provide for them. Some young mothers were forced by their parents to give their child up as was the case of one daughter I worked with, who fell pregnant under the age of 16.

Daughters who have been abandoned (or feel they have been) can suffer low self-esteem and fear of rejection. They carry around the idea they are flawed or something is wrong with them and the belief they are unworthy of love. Abandoned daughters may also endure verbal and/or physical violence in relationships rather than end the relationship and feel alone.

Ponder the following questions in relation to your experience, making notes of any emotions which surface as you read through. Whatever emotions you might find yourself experiencing as a result of your loss, you will be able to find comfort using EFT to release the emotional charge.

- **For those of you who have been abandoned by your mothers how does this influence your ability to trust others?**
- **How stable do you feel in your capacity to form positive and lasting relationships?**
- **How often do you find yourself being overly responsible for others and in doing so neglect your own needs?**
- **How able are you to discern and make distinctions of when abandonment is real or when it's a memory of rejection being re-triggered?**
- **In what areas of your life are you unable to say no and create healthy boundaries with others?**
- **How often do you find yourself putting up with poor behaviour in relationships for fear of desertion?**
- **How frequently do you find yourself fearing abandonment or rejection in friendships and relationships?**
- **In what situations do you most need someone to rescue you?**
- **What emotions have you freely expressed to your mother or others in relation to being abandoned?**
- **What emotions linger for you that would benefit from expression in order to heal your wounds?**
- **How well have you coped with other losses in your life?**
- **How easy do you find it to ask for help and support?**
- **In what circumstances do you find yourself wanting to control a situation in order to feel safe and secure?**
- **When have you ended a relationship because of your fear of being left, you leave first?**

- **Knowing it is possible to move beyond fear of abandonment, imagine how your life will be different when you have resolved your fear?**
- **What inner resources do you already have to overcome your fear of abandonment?**
- **What additional resources might you need in addition to the above?**

Sally's Words of Wisdom

"Although my mother never abandoned me in the physical sense, I never felt noticed by her in comparison to my sisters. She never showed me affection or offered me emotional support. When it came to making decisions or celebrating my achievements she wasn't able to guide me or offer any praise. I felt abandoned by her because I never felt loved."

Taking the time to work through your emotions using the processes shared will not only support you now as an adult it will also offer the child inside you the solace, love and comfort needed.

FLIGHT-FIGHT-FREEZE RESPONSE - HOW YOUR BODY REMEMBERS TRAUMA

The ability to delude yourself may be an important survival tool - Jane Wagner

Many of you will have heard of the fight and flight response though not everyone is aware of the freeze response. We are animalistic creatures and when we think there is a threat of danger (real or imagined) our bodies naturally go into fight, flight or freeze response.

It was helpful to operate from a fight, flight and freeze response when we were cave men and women, as our lives depended on heightened senses. We would either stay and fight or run from attack though if the fear is too great and if we weren't able to run or fight, we would freeze instead (like a rabbit caught in the headlights of a car). While in 'freeze' response we might pass out and disassociate from our bodies, we may also experience having no sensation of pain and sometimes no memory of the event at all.

You may find yourself going into fight, flight and freeze response daily, if you find yourself into situations which trigger you. We can also trigger ourselves by thinking about the original event. These responses release chemical and emotional reactions in the body which re-traumatise the system all over again, as if the original fear and threat to survival was actually happening. If you would like to understand more about the fight, flight and freeze responses, you might like to discover the works of Dr Robert Scaer, author of *The Body Bears the Burden: Trauma, Dissociation and Disease,* which goes into more detail about these responses.

EFT helps to release the flight, fight, freeze response and in turn, will help you to transform these emotions. You can read more about this technique in Chapter Six and the appendix, along with The Spotlight Process, which will help you to work out where your thinking may be limited or stuck and will support you in moving on from negative beliefs about yourself and your mother.

MEMORY CLUSTERS AND HOW WE STORE MEMORIES

Each day of our lives we make deposits in the memory banks of our children - Charles R. Swindoll

In this section we will explore how we store information through our senses and place meanings on our experiences.

Many years ago I studied NLP (Neuro Linguistic Programming) which is an approach to communication, personal development and psychotherapy, created by Richard Bandler and John Grindler. Learning about NLP, helped me understand the way the mind works, how we store and retrieve information and how we communicate. The mind is amazing. It's a storehouse of information which we filter. We are judge new experiences through an old lens. We distort, delete and generalise experiences, based on what has happened in previous events in our lives. We may remember these as blueprints which we experience through our senses. Predicting how something will end, even when we have no evidence, means we replay the old movie which is similar in some way to the new experience. We judge our experiences through comparison with the record we already have.

Our past experiences influence how we react to others and the world around us

We may get things confused and what is actually happening to us may not be processed and we jump into default mode, where we are basing current experiences on similar ones experienced in the past. It will be helpful to note when you find yourself doing this and to question are you reacting to a new experience with a new response – or are you on auto pilot and responding in the old way?

Our storehouse of sensory information

- **Visual** (what we see outwardly, including how someone may look at us)
- **Auditory** (what we hear, including sounds, the words we hear and the way words are spoken by others, including tone and pitch)
- **Kinaesthetic** (what we feel internally inside our bodies, or externally via touch, including the texture of something and level of pressure felt physically)

- **Gustatory** (taste)
- **Olfactory** (smell)

Deletion: When we delete information, we may be paying attention only to certain aspects of a situation and wipe out facts overlooking, ignoring and omitting sensory information coming into us. We edit our current reality in this way as there is so much information coming to us. If we didn't delete, we would experience too much sensory stimulation (information overload).

Distortion: It's easy to misrepresent reality. What is actually happening in an experience can be distorted and we can perceive things incorrectly. We distort, creating imaginary futures which limit us in a negative way.

Generalisation: We make up and form our beliefs based solely on one or two experiences. We absorb information and make assumptions about what the information means, comparing it to the information we have already stored. Sometimes our assumptions are incorrect.

Use these questions to reveal what you may be distorting, generalising and deleting, as you process information in connection with your mother.

- **What aspects of your relationship do you delete?** E.g. perhaps your mother looks after your children or picks your dry cleaning up, but doesn't say "I love you". Many mothers show their love through acts of service such as cooking for you, running errands and keeping a clean and tidy home. Spend time noticing what your mother does for you now or did for you in childhood which indicates how much she cares for you.
- **How do you distort information you are receiving in your relationship with your mother?** E.g. your mother wants to go away with friends and does not invite you or

tell you what she is doing until after the event. Do you feel rejected or pleased for her?

- **When do you generalise negatively about your relationship with your mother?** E.g. "she will never change", "she will always let me down", "she isn't worth it" etc.

RULES, CONDITIONS AND BELIEFS

It is our interpretation of the past, our limiting beliefs, and our undigested pain that stops us from being able to move forward with clear direction - Debbie Ford

The way a mother communicates, holds her child, tucks the bed corners in, cuts a sandwich or removes a stain will probably have been learned from her mother. We may continue to do things our mother taught us which are not helpful. As well as the practical teachings we also learn from her how to be a mother, daughter, sister, woman and caregiver. We may choose to follow her parenting style or completely go against it.

Almost half of the daughters who volunteered as case studies, had mothers who were expected to help raise siblings as part of their duties as children. The unspoken message was there was something very selfish and impure about you if you did not want to be a hard-working wife and mother. Women who have broken away from the traditional daughter role have been frowned upon. Those daughters who chose to have careers and to stay single were cruelly called 'old maids' further impacting the beliefs about being a woman and who or what you could be or couldn't be.

This highlights the changes in generations when women born in the early 1900s had much larger families and daughters were expected to help their mothers create a happy home for their fathers to return to. Quite often a, woman put a man's needs first, before her own or, indeed her children's. It is helpful to be aware how you may have learnt to put others ahead of yourself, believing that it's wrong to make time for you, or say no to others' demands.

Beverley Case Study

Beverley came to me for support with ill health, stress and exhaustion

Beverley shared with me she felt too guilty to sit down if things needed doing around the home, even after being at work all day it felt wrong for her to relax and take a breather. She spent no money on herself instead, buying lots for her children to somehow try and make up for the time she spent at work. Her mother had stayed at home so Beverley believed it was wrong to work outside the home although as a single mother she had to work for money. This conflict caused her extreme anguish and she questioned her ability to be a 'good enough' mother.

When we explored Beverley's beliefs, she realised she was being unrealistic and quite hard on herself. Her father had provided financially for her family when she was a child and her mother had the help of herself and her older siblings to care for the younger family members. Beverley was now living in a different era with very little support from the father of her child or from family or friends and it was not possible for her to provide for her children in the same ways.

In our work together, Beverley was able to reframe her beliefs about how much of herself she could realistically give to her family. Beverley realised in comparison, her mother's family was much larger than her own and were on hand to offer help, her mother also had financial support from her father and the support from women in the extended neighbourhood as well as siblings caring for each other. She was able to cut herself some slack by creating new beliefs about her role as a mother and also as a woman independent of her children. She was able to enjoy life more and looked forward to taking some regular time out to rest and relax. In addition to our work together, Beverley learnt to ask for the help of her family to babysit and joined new groups where other single mothers talked over their concerns and also offer each other emotional and practical support. Beverley also invested in some after- school and holiday play schemes, when she was able to take time out away from her family, have time for herself and her personal interests.

Exploring your beliefs as Beverley did, understanding why they were formed, where they come from and how they might be hindering you rather than helping you, will serve you well. Updating your beliefs to those which are more realistic will support you further. Just because your mother had certain beliefs and may have done things in a particular way, doesn't mean you have to follow in her footsteps.

Questioning your limiting beliefs will be one of the best methods of healing you can give to yourself. When you find a limiting belief popping into your head or out of your mouth, ask yourself the following:

- **What is it I believe to be true in this situation?**
- **Is this my belief or one which was handed down to me?**
- **How far back along my female timeline does this belief go?**
- **How does this belief help me achieve my goals?**
- **Up to now, how has having the belief limited me?**
- **If this belief isn't helpful, how can I change it to one which serves me better?**

- **Knowing I can change any of my beliefs about myself, my mother and how to live my life, what else am I choosing to change?**
- **Recognising my actions and behaviours which support these beliefs, what do I need to start doing, stop doing, or do differently?**
- **What's the one thing I can do today which supports new and healthy beliefs?**

Elizabeth's Words of Wisdom

"I'm not certain my mother enjoyed her role as mother; she never indicated this to be true. Like her mother before her she was obsessed with cleaning. There were so many rules and conditions around keeping things clean and tidy and it took the fun out of playing. In fact I don't remember playing with my mother at all. Creativity and play is important as a child and I regret not having more freedom to have fun with my mother. There's nothing I enjoy more than playing with mud pies with my children, getting dirt between our toes and laughing at the tops of our voices."

WHAT ABOUT LOVE?

The hunger for love is much more difficult to remove than the hunger for bread - Mother Teresa

It is possible, when a mother has experienced her own traumas that she is unable to love or give her child what is required 'in the moment.' As a child there may have been times when you felt rejected or unloved. Although love means different things to different people, it's recognising how a mother can generally only give as much love as she has experienced herself. Her lack of love is not about you, but about her and who she believes herself to be. Although some mothers are physically present during and after childbirth, she may go missing emotionally by way of psychiatric issues, addiction, depression, grief and not having the ability to cope with a newborn child. Lack of bonding, attention, love and nurturing may be impacted because of childbirth itself, accident, illness and poverty or family circumstance.

A mother's ill health, absence of family support, mental illness, stress levels, financial insecurity, as well as her confidence in mothering, all impacts a child's experience. Some mothers are loving, nurturing and caring homemakers and provide us with food, clothing and keep us clean. If a mother has not been shown how to do these things, it may not come naturally to her.

For many daughters, there is a deep sense of yearning for mother love if this experience was missing in childhood. Left unaddressed, this yearning can last a lifetime. On the other hand, many daughters I have spoken with, who felt they were not loved or mothered adequately, have found love from other mother figures. They have used their experiences to avoid these patterns of behaviours fearing they may turn into their mothers.

Working with women from large families where food and love was scarce, for those daughters a sense of deprivation remains. Even when food and love is plentiful later on, the old belief remains and the fear of supplies running out becomes the focus. There is so much to consider when we talk about love and we will each perhaps have our own take on what love means, depending on our life experience. The aching hole of emptiness when we miss a mother's love is sometimes filled up with over-eating, jumping from one relationship to another, over spending, drug abuse, alcoholism or over achieving.

Rather than following destructive paths, it would be far healthier to address the root cause of the problem instead of reaching out for something to fill the void. If you would like one-to-one support with any of these issues, please contact me for support. www.mothersanddaughters.solutions

UNMET CHILDHOOD NEEDS

A deep sense of love and belonging is an irreducible need of all people. We are biologically, cognitively, physically, and spiritually wired to love, to be loved, and to belong. When those needs are not met, we don't function as well as we are meant to. We break. We fall apart. We numb. We ache. We hurt others. We get sick - Brené Brown

Suzanne's Words of Wisdom

"I have ruined many a promising relationship when I've constantly questioned 'but what if you leave me', 'what if you stop loving me'. It didn't matter what my partners said or did, I didn't trust they would stay with me. I realised my belief was my partners would reject me just like my mum did when she gave me up for adoption. I'm pleased I now have the awareness of an adult and how my limiting beliefs from childhood were jeopardising my own relationship success. I still have to catch myself when I project the past into the future but at least now I'm aware of it."

Emotional support is something which goes hand in hand with the physical needs of a child. Not having this emotional support means the infant will attempt to find an alternative source of nurturing or try to parent themselves from an early age with no role model to learn from.

If a child has become independent from an early age, it might be difficult for her to be open in adulthood for fear of being let down. If the daughter felt emotionally or physically abandoned, she may find herself keeping others at a distance if her needs were not met at a time in her life when she needed nurturance most - she will do whatever she can to keep herself free from harm, real or imagined.

Marie's Words of Wisdom

"I've always sacrificed my own needs and plans choosing to prioritise my mother's. I realise now in my attempt at doing everything she required of me, this was really my attempt to win her love."

Children need at least one consistent person in their lives to fulfil their most basic needs and this may not always be the mother.

Mothers are nearly always doing the best they can, parenting, working and running a household as well as dealing with life's unexpected challenges. Many do not mean to push their children away; they are simply busy or preoccupied. However, many daughters have shared with me how they felt discounted and unheard when they were told:

- **Don't make a fuss**
- **Be a good girl**
- **Don't cry**
- **Shut up**
- **I'll give you something to cry about**
- **Be quiet**
- **Don't say another word**

Words can harm as well as heal.

What every child ideally needs to hear, instead of the above is:

• Talk to me • I'm listening • What's wrong • It's ok to be upset • I heard you say how you feel and that's great • I'm here for you • How can we work through this? • I love hearing your words • You are important to me • I love you • I believe in you • You're amazing	• I'm sorry • I forgive you • I'm proud of you • You must have been practicing you're almost there • You can do it • Congratulations • I knew you could do it • You've got what it takes • You have great ideas • I like how you think • You did it! • Well done!

Thinking about your own communications with children or indeed in your significant other relationships, do you come across as an encourager or criticiser?

FIGHTING FOR ACCEPTANCE, LOVE, APPROVAL AND ONENESS

The mother-child relationship is paradoxical and, in a sense, tragic. It requires the most intense love on the mother's side, yet this very love must help the child grow away from the mother, and become fully independent - Eric Fromm

Our hunger for our mother's love can be all encompassing. Many daughters have shared with me that they will do anything to feel loved by their mothers.

Dancing between the need to please our mothers and the need to please ourselves, one minute seeking love and approval and at the same time fearing abandonment and rejection, we constantly try out new steps to find different ways to appease our mothers. We expect our mothers to take care of us and to be there for us come what may, not just in our childhood years but in later life too. The frustration begins when our mother isn't able to meet our needs. We may experience her unavailability as personal rejection. It will be helpful to explore how realistic your needs as an adult and to reflect on why your mother may not have been there for you when you needed her most as a child.

It's true to say some mothers do not fit the mould of what an 'ideal' mother is. She may be cruel, inconsiderate, abusive and unavailable. In the variety of case studies shared I hope to offer insights into the various experiences daughters have suffered at the hands of their mothers, when ideal parenting hasn't been part of the mother- daughter package. We discuss too, why in some cases, mothers were simply unable to cope with their own tragic pasts and unable to raise a daughter in the ideal way because of unresolved traumas. Each mother-daughter relationship is unique, even amongst female siblings the experience your mother, will vary. The relationship itself will determine how mother and daughter view themselves.

Danna's Words of Wisdom

"All I ever wanted was to be listened to, respected and understood. I needed my mother to show me how to be positive and confident about myself and to teach me how to respond differently when people let me down. I guess she never really knew how to do that for herself, so how was she going to be able to show me."

EMOTIONALLY UNAVAILALE MOTHERS

Your family is unavoidable. You cannot escape them or trade them in for another family. You also can't change them...but you can change your response to them - Jami Attenberg

It's ok to admit there may be things about your mother you don't like and find hard to accept. In the same way she too might not agree with, respect or like certain aspects of your personality or behaviours. None of us are perfect and it's having the ability to look beyond the imperfections and accept what we can't change which gives us a greater sense of freedom.

Not always, but sometimes mothers might desire to shape us into carbon copies of themselves, or put pressure on us to achieve the things they didn't, in order to feel fulfilled. Some mothers desire to mould us into the idea of who she thought she should have been. It's as though our mothers want to live through us and make a better go of things second time around.

Understanding why your mother couldn't be there for you

There are many factors to consider as to why a mother might be emotionally or physically unavailable. Some of the reasons may be connected with but not always the following:

- **Depression** *(including post natal)*
- **Illness** *(her own or other family members)*
- **Emotionally overwhelmed with mother/daughter/ womanly duties**
- **Caring for other family members**
- **Personal trauma**
- **Stress**
- **Domestic violence**

- **Parental separation**
- **Alcohol, drug or substance abuse**
- **Prescribed medications**
- **A personal career or study**
- **Secondment**
- **Mental illness**
- **Hospitalisation**
- **Criminality** *(e.g. sentence to prison)*

Depending on these factors, your mother's ability to parent you, may have been out of her conscious control. Your mother, too, may have been trying to come to terms with her own experiences, unwanted events and trying to find ways to fulfil her own unmet needs alongside raising you.

Sandra's Words of Wisdom

"What I wanted from my mother was unconditional love, to be wanted, listened to. I wanted her unconditional acceptance, her physical and emotional presence, her attention and admiration; sadly she wasn't able to meet my needs."

ANCESTRAL PATTERNING

To unlock the Mother Myths and the secrets to life, we look to the forces that shaped our lives, of the woman who came before us - Patricia Commins

Reaching back into your personal ancestry can be revealing in terms of the conscious and unconscious patterns of behaviour which run through generations of your female timeline. We will discuss not only learned behaviours from our predecessors, but also ancestral memory which is very subtle.

The expectations of a daughter are made up of generational beliefs about how a daughter should be. A mother naturally wants her daughter to become like her or wants her to fulfil roles she never had an opportunity for. Often as daughters, we do not question what's handed down to us until we find we are hurting or our relationships aren't working and want to understand why this is so.

As detailed in the previous chapter, scientific research shows that the egg you came from was formed inside the ovary in the first few weeks of your mother's life, while she began her gestation inside the body of her mother (your grandmother). The cell you came from was once inside your mother's foetus inside your grandmother's womb. This means the egg you came from was in your grandmother's body for months and then in your mother's body for years. Gaining greater insights into the women who came before you and how your own beliefs, behaviours and responses have been formed, will help you to deal with your own emotions in relation to your mother and with relationships in general.

Nothing influences children more than the silent facts in the background - Karl Jung

"The child is so much a part of the psychological atmosphere of the parents that the secret of unresolved problems between them can influence its health profoundly. The participation mystique...causes the child to feel the conflicts of the parents and to suffer from them as if they were its own. It is hardly ever open conflict or the manifest difficulty that has such a poisonous effect, but almost always parental problems that have been kept hidden or allowed to become unconscious" Psychology and Education, C.G.Jung

The enmeshment which can happen within intimate relationships stays within the family tree and gets passed down the generations when an individual doesn't do the inner-work to heal their unconscious pain. This is what Jung *calls "participation mystique".* The inner work you choose to do now and as you read through the contents of this book, will allow you to move through your ancestors' archaic suffering. Past wounds will no longer be passed down and those who follow you will benefit.

Ancestral Memory

Walking, I am listening to a deeper way. Suddenly all my ancestors are behind me. Be still they say. Watch and listen. You are the result of the love of thousands - Linda Hogan

With advances in research, many theories discuss epigenetic, ancestral and biological memory traces being passed on through DNA. One such study lead by Rachel Yehuda, a research team at New York's Mount Sinai Hospital on Holocaust survivors indicates an association of parental preconception trauma. Epigenetic alterations are evident in both exposed parents and offspring; the intergenerational effects of psycho physiological trauma make for interesting reading. I would personally love to see more research developing in this area.

Inherited memory is a fascinating subject, when we begin to understand it is possible to be influenced by the collective suffering passed down through generations. These memories are not memories of actual events but formed of instinctive behaviour patterns as a result of the circumstances of our ancestors. It is worth considering how our ancestral memory in addition to our early learning, form beliefs about ourselves and the world around us. We may find ourselves making connections in new situations.

From childhood through to adulthood our subconscious drive is to seek security, it would have been the same for those who came before us. We seek out the situation which will model what security looks like, feels, like and sounds like based on our early learning. We have a deep compulsion in our relationships to re-create what we subconsciously believe to be normal. If we have experienced pain, neglect or abandonment in childhood we may subconsciously set ourselves up for the exact same thing to happen. This influence runs from birth through to the day we die, unless we are able to explore our patterns of behaviour and make changes to our perceptions and beliefs. Swiss psychiatrist Carl Jung used the phrase 'collective unconscious', while others may call ancestral memory 'genetic memory' or 'inherited memory'. If you have a specific interest in the area of ancestral memory, Terence Watts offers additional insights in his book *Warriors, Settlers, Nomads: Discovering who we are and what we can be.* He shares revealing information about the skills and psychological attitudes we have inherited from our ancestors.

Your mother is the origin of you, the intricate bond between generations, your source and your blood-line. Through her, you are connected with the female blood line and all the women who went before her. To understand ourselves, we need to explore the experiences which shaped our mothers' lives. Although each of our mothers had her own unique experiences and life story, we carry a portion of our mother's DNA and her life blood within us. We may also share similar looks and features, mannerisms, behaviours, beliefs and even aspirations. We may even have the same hopes and fears, the same health conditions and complaints.

We deepen the connection with our own lives when we reach out to others who knew our mothers. Perhaps, you too, will find similarities between your mother, her mother and their predecessors. By asking your mother's family, friends, neighbours and colleagues to share their memories of your mother, you may be able to see her through fresh eyes and learn things about her you never knew. You will gain a greater understanding of your mother when you are able to voice your questions and gather information shared about her. For example, if your mother has been critical of you, you might find out that your grandmother behaved in this way towards her or, she may have been self-critical, based on her own lack of confidence. When you are able to talk to your mother's peers, you will not only establish ties with other women, you also gain awareness about who your mother was and where you come from.

By understanding yourself, your mother and your family tree, you will find a way to acknowledge your mother's life and also recognise the child inside you who is searching for a mother's love, approval, recognition and acceptance. You may even discover what you wanted was there all along, you just didn't realise or recognise it. Perspective is everything and the more we know about our mothers, the more we understand ourselves. I for one now understand my mother's depression and low moods, she had given up who she wanted to become to do what other people and society expected of her, it comes as no surprise now why she was depressed.

Claire's Words of Wisdom

Claire shared with me that it wasn't until the day of her mum's funeral when she met up with her mother's neighbour, she was told how proud her mother had been of her. From an era where too much direct praise for a child was frowned upon, Claire's mother secretly shared with her neighbour how much she loved her daughter and how proud of her she was, but found it difficult to tell her in case she became self- centred. Although Claire regretted not hearing this from her mother's lips, it left her with a deep sense of comfort. Knowing her mother did care, even if she never voiced it on personally she was able to attend her mother's funeral with an even greater sense of love.

Historically it's been hard for mothers and daughters to see themselves as unique individuals independent of each other and whole in their own right. Depending on the culture we grow up in, I know for many women this is proving to be a challenge, though with persistence we can to break away from the cultural norm. With diplomacy and willingness for each of us to live our lives on our terms and appropriate to our individual needs, daughters are gradually changing old paradigms.

Pushpa Case Study

Pushpa sought intervention for assertiveness and anger management

Whilst working with Pushpa, although she felt some emotional release of anger and frustration using EFT, she explained she felt she had to follow the cultural expectations laid out for her as a daughter, wife and mother. She was in fear of speaking up and became anxious at the thought of doing so. It took courage for her to be assertive and to stand up to her family, husband and in-laws stating she wanted to continue her studies as well as be a mother. This didn't go without argument and a whole barrage of abuse stating it was her duty to look after her husband, home and children and not have any career ambitions of her own.

After some confidence and assertiveness training and discussion, Pushpa was setting clear boundaries and not backing down. She gave up on her need to please others and fit to the cultural norm. Pushpa shared with her family her career aspirations, she let them know clearly that without fulfilling her dream, her life would not be complete and she would feel resentful having to live under someone else's rules and conditions. This story has a happy ending, as both families and the husband rallied round to help with childcare and eventually respected Pushpa's decisions to fulfil her personal goals of becoming a solicitor and the family are in fact very proud of their daughter and her achievements. Cultural traditions do not have to stay the same as we have seen in Pushpa's example.

Learning about your mother's life

What date was your mother's birth? Take into account the generational and societal changes women have gone through over the years.

- **How might the era your mother grew up in, shaped her and in turn her ability to nurture and express love?**
- **What changes have become apparent to you about the role of parenting from the time of her childhood to yours?**
- **What societal or cultural influences have impacted your mother's behaviours?**
- **What have you learned directly from your mother's parenting style?** *(both positive and negative)*
- **How is your parenting style different to your mothers?**
- **If you are not yet a mother what do you imagine your parenting style will be?**

It is my belief that you and I are here right now in this time and space to create positive change in the world and to shape a different reality for the daughters who come after us. We do not have to copy learnt behaviours and patterns. History can be a teacher and improvements made and in turn, beliefs about how women and daughters 'should be' will change.

Discovering the women in your blood line:

- **What was the size of your mother's family and that of your grandmother and great-grandmother?**

- **Were your female relatives married, widowed, divorced, co-habiting or single?**
- **What hardships did the women in your blood-line suffer?**
- **At what age did they die?**
- **What was the cause of death?**
- **How many siblings did each of those women have?** *(Did they all live through childhood?)*
- **How many of the females in your blood line worked outside the home?** *(If so what was their job title)*
- **Where did they live?**
- **How many other people shared the living space?**
- **What additional information can you find out about the lives of the women who came before you?**

Within each of us we carry our mother just as she carried us. There might be times when you think 'mum would be really proud of me', or 'mum would go mad at me'. Echoes of her voice, behaviours, mannerisms, moods, hopes, joys and fears all reside within. It's deciding what aspects of your personal ancestry, behaviours and beliefs you wish to continue with as an individual or as a mother.

Author's Notes

"I frequently wonder about my own female heritage and the epigenetic emotional impact passed down through my time-line. My grandmother's mother was a wife, mother and widow all in the same year".

Bruce Lipton PhD, cell biologist and author of *Biology of Belief,* is leading the way in researching energy fields and the impact of epigenetic inheritance.

THE DISEASE TO PLEASE

I was the problem and the solution - Abby Norman

The disease to please begins early in life when as daughters we learn about what makes our mothers happy or unhappy. We learn to respond to her rules and conditions because our main desire is to gain her love. Some of those expectations we can fulfil while others may be impossible to meet. We are two different people with different values, rules and conditions. We live through our own unique experiences and may also have opposing aims in life.

Communication between mothers and daughters will break down if there isn't the opportunity to talk adult-to-adult in the relationship once a daughter is a woman. If neither mother nor daughters are willing to speak about what's not working in their relationship and how they want to improve it in a calm, non-blaming and assertive manner, things will stay the same or build up and get worse. Many daughters invest much time and energy trying to please their mothers, without having any clear direction of what it is they are trying to achieve.

Yvonne Case Study

Yvonne came to me asking for help in the area of careers and feeling unfulfilled

Yvonne shared with me she was trying to live the life her mother never had. Yvonne didn't want to be an actress, but because her mother gave up her own acting career to raise her and then

spent a small fortune on sending her to acting school, she felt she at least owed it to her mum to follow in her footsteps and fulfil the career her mother never completed. After sticking out acting college and getting just a few small parts in plays, Yvonne knew acting wasn't in her heart and apologised to her mother for not making it.

Using The Spotlight Process, Yvonne became aware of the beliefs connected with her relationship with her mother. She had picked up the limiting belief 'I have to live your dream' after hearing her mother tell her as a child 'I gave up everything I had to have you'. In turn, she formed the belief 'I have to give up the life I want to live because you gave up yours to have me'. After much discussion, tears, EFT tapping and a fresh conversation about what her mother really meant, what came to light was that the choice her mother had made to have Yvonne had been a willing one. Tracing back to the original argument where she thought her mother was angry at her, this unconscious stream of words were what shaped Yvonne's beliefs about her mother and who she thought she needed to be in order to win her mother's love.

I love working in the area of relationships as it is so rewarding when daughters are able to understand why they formed the beliefs they did and how to transform them. Yvonne now works as an educator and speaker. So although she isn't a professional actress, she formally uses her acting and presentation skills and has become a sought-after speaker, working all over the globe.

I have known many one-sided relationships where, for the sake of a quiet life, the daughter complies with her mother's expectations. The same goes for mothers, too, who struggle with being a daughter and a mother at the same time. How frequently do you find yourself saying 'yes' to things, when all you really want to say is 'no'? If this becomes a pattern for too long, it becomes harder to make changes and create new behaviours in your relationship.

Perhaps in reality, your mother isn't who you want her to be. Accepting her as she is, will bring a sense of closure. It's like agreeing to disagree. When you are able to accept yourself and understand she can't meet your needs for whatever reason, there is no longer the need to keep searching for something which can't be found. Your need to reach agreement and gain approval, acceptance or validation will disappear. Then, the energy you would have spent looking for those things, can be invested elsewhere.

Becoming your own 'inner mother' as an adult daughter is paramount in your ongoing self-care. When you take responsibility to heal your hurts, whether by seeking professional help or working through your experiences through reading, talking with trusted friends or joining a support group, you stop the self-defeating patterns in your relationship and put your needs first. It is not selfish to put one's needs first, in fact by caring for yourself first, will enable you to care for others more effectively as you will not be 'running on empty'.

By taking personal responsibility to meet our own needs, we change our negative patterns and behaviours and in doing so, we no longer have to blame our mothers for our life circumstances. We begin to understand her and the hand we have played in our relationship with her. With this awareness, we become self-fulfilled, happier and more confident in our abilities; we no longer need her to define who we are.

By taking responsibility to 'mother' ourselves and commit to healing our hurts, we can make the rest of our lives the best of our lives.

The Rescuer

I think there's a tremendous amount of guilt that goes on between mothers and daughters, no matter how good or bad their relationships are - Ellen Page

More than three-quarters of the case studies shared, indicate daughters feel like an emotional rescuer in relation to their mothers. Whether it is trying to keep the peace and not upset her, listening to her talk about her worries and fears and trying to find solutions to her problems, many daughters share their mothers seem incapable of dealing with life which has left them with an overwhelming responsibility to parent their mothers. As well as daughter, they take on the role of 'fixer'.

Perhaps you, too, recognise yourself as a rescuer?

Author's Notes

"My mum re-married just three months after meeting my step-father. It wasn't until after she married him, she realised he had problems with managing his anger and alcohol intake, as well as gambling and sexual perversions. I can remember sitting in a solicitor's office in 1982, aged 16, asking what I could do to stop him hitting my mum. It seemed like she didn't have the strength or know how to break away from this relationship. She would tell me what was happening to her; sometimes I would hear it or witness it. One evening I confronted my stepfather telling him to hit me instead of my mum; I knew if he did, I would go to the police. My mum begged me not to speak to him in this way, saying he couldn't help it.

It took strength on my part to let my mum know legally what she could do, but unless she was going to press charges or take out an injunction against my stepfather, it seemed there was nothing I could do as a child. I felt responsible for my mother's life and well-being, but I didn't want to go against her wishes because I feared losing her love and approval. I indirectly fed into this loop of her behaviour and his, by not taking further action. It makes me sad to realise I didn't have the guts to stop the abuse inflicted on her because I feared losing my mother's love. It felt like I couldn't win either way."

What does my experience bring up for you? Have you, too, reflected on the past wishing you'd taken different actions? Perhaps you can identify where you have unconsciously behaved in a way to try and keep your mother's love. Perhaps some of you have experienced or witnessed domestic violence. Whatever this brings up for you, it is a wonderful opportunity to further heal the hurt within.

- **What do you hunger for in relation to your mother?**
- **What is the driving force behind responding in the way you do towards her?**
- **How does your mother treat you?** *As an adult, teenager or child?*
- **How do you respond to your mother?** *(From the child, teenager or adult part of yourself?)*
- **In what situations have you found yourself stepping in to take care of your mother emotionally or physically?**
- **How long have you been acting as mother or emotional rescuer to your mother?** *(How old were you when this way of behaving began?)*
- **How often do you give into your mother's wishes for fear of losing her love, acceptance or approval?**
- **What are your greatest fears in relation to stopping your default responses and behaviours in relation to your mother?**

For many daughters there is an engulfing fear of being cut off from the main source of love, namely our mothers. This fear goes back to the basic survival instincts where as babies we looked towards our mothers to keep us safe, protected and nurtured. A child is not able to provide these things for themselves and within our adult mind remains the memory of the fearful child, looking to its mother as a means of survival. Beliefs are an important factor to consider as to why mothers and daughters behave the way they do. For more information about beliefs, see Chapter Six Recovery and Beyond and in particular the section on 'Aiding Your Own Recovery - Limiting Beliefs and How to Change Them'.

REPEATING RELATIONSHIP PATTERNS

You're going to go through tough times - that's life. But I say 'Nothing happens to you, it happens for you'. Joel Osteen

How often do you find yourself repeating relationship patterns and regretting later the choices you've made? In this chapter, we will explore how and why we do this. In my work with daughters who are in conflict with their husbands, significant others, bosses, co-workers and friends, it is often interesting to note, that when I ask the question, 'who does this person remind you of', they surprise themselves and say 'he/she is just like my mother!'

Instead of detaching from our mothers through natural separation, a daughter may find herself projecting her co-dependency, unmet needs and expectations onto the adults she comes into contact with. Unconsciously, she selects partners who respond to her in the way her mother did. We don't always consciously choose relationships with others, who are like our mothers, but subconsciously we may choose someone whose character, behaviour traits and demeanour is similar.

The concept of a daughter's relationship with her mother, determining subsequent relationships is not a new one. Freud in his 1931 essay *Female Sexuality,* wrote *"We see then that the later phase of exclusive attachment to the mother...is far more important in the woman than it can claim to be for men...Many a woman who takes her father as the model for her choice of husband...repeats with her husband her bad relationships with her mother...The mother-relation was the original one, upon which the father-relation was built up."*

What we aren't able to resolve in our childhood relationships, we may find ourselves projecting into our adult relationships by searching for the validation we never received from our mothers and going the extra mile to win the praise, affection and attention missing in our childhood. The feelings we have towards our mothers are often the same feelings we have towards our partners. Some questions to pose at this point are:

- **What did you want from your mother which you never received?**
- **How many of your unmet needs from childhood are you are trying to find in your current relationship?**
- **How often have you projected your unmet childhood needs onto your partner to fulfil?**
- **What happens when your partner can't meet your needs, how do you respond?**
- **How often do you find yourself reacting to your partner in the same way you react to your mother?**
- **Who in your current or past relationships reminds you of your mother?**
- **Do you have your own identity outside of your relationship with your mother or significant other? If no, what are the consequences of not having your own identity independent of another?**
- **How well do you know yourself, who you are and what you like and dislike etc?**

When our mothers have not been emotionally available or had an inability to provide for our needs, it may mean we go into relationships wearing blinkers. The unconscious drive and the aim of our relationships is to see what we can get from the other person and we find ourselves reaching out to replicate either the connection we had with our mothers, or one we *wished* we had, in an attempt to receive the nurturing elsewhere.

Our desire for the ideal mother is the driving force behind our choices. We hope our selection of partner will fulfil this ideal though in reality, we are faced with those needs being ignored time and time again. On the rare occasion they are satisfied, we do not believe what is on offer and will question if the love will last.

A daughter without the secure foundation of a constant, positive and loving base in childhood, may find herself desperate in relationships and likely to settle for unsuitable partners. If she feels "second rate" it's likely she will choose "second rate" partners if her underlying belief is that she deserves no better. Many daughters go on to date men who abuse them physically or emotionally as their mothers have done, not believing themselves worthy of better treatment. A daughter's yearning for love outweighs any rational thinking.

For daughters who have experienced domineering mothers of the kind who say *"no one will ever love you as much as I do"*, this may set up a self-fulfilling prophecy and so no one quite measures up to mother! They may go on to choose possessive, arrogant and jealous partners who remind them of being swamped by mum. When this becomes too much to bear, the daughter will want to run away and rebel as the relationship reminds her too much of her dominating mother.

Take note too that for many daughters not in a relationship, it may be because this feels safer than being in one. We may find ourselves having brief relationships, which we end ourselves, before we can be abandoned. If we have experienced a lack of mothering in childhood whether physically or emotionally, the fear of being deserted again gets carried into your adult relationships. There may be underlying fears connected with relationships not lasting and not putting your trust in someone, when you've been previously let down.

If we've learnt to survive independently as children, we might close off our needs and our message to the world is *'I don't need anyone', 'I'm fine on my own', 'I'm capable of managing my own life' or 'keep your distance'* and *'I don't trust you'.* We could come across as cold, distant, controlling, intimidating and aggressive. Although a relationship might be desired at a deeper level, some daughters avoid relationships altogether, as the thought of losing love all over again is too great to bear.

Real life is far from the fairy tale of a knight in shining armour or the fairy godmother rescuing us from our distress; we can do this for ourselves, once we understand why and how we make the wrong choices.

If you've experienced trauma growing up or had any negative beliefs about being unlovable reinforced, the chances are you might still believe you're unworthy of love and a loving relationship. You may go on to devalue yourself, sabotage yourself and your relationships, as well as continue the pattern of choosing relationships which are hurtful and unhealthy. It is important to do the inner work and use the processes shared in Chapter Six, to make positive and lasting change.

Jayne's Words of Wisdom

"The one thing I wish my mother could have given me is an example of a woman in a healthy loving relationship with a man. I saw instead a woman who loved a man who did not love her back; she tried as hard as she could but never received the love she desired. In many ways, my own relationship experience

reflects hers. I keep choosing partners who, for whatever reason, just can't love me in the way I need to be loved."

To recognise whether you are falling into a pattern of repeated behaviour, consider that to do something once is an event, twice a coincidence and three times a behaviour. Understanding your limiting beliefs and why they have been in place up till now, will give your new relationships the opportunity to flourish.

If we believe we have lacked love in our early years, had an experience where love is confused (physical, sexual or emotional abuse), or if our relationships have been narcissistic, or we experienced love as being conditional, then we have no healthy blueprint for unconditional love. The good news is, that with awareness, we can change our behaviours, perceptions and beliefs and in doing so have healthier relationships.

Alice Miller, shares in *For Your Own Good,* how those who have felt victimised are not fully able to understand their past sufferings and may try to hurt themselves or others again. They indirectly repeat the hurt they were made to endure. Frequently, those wounded in childhood, demonstrate destructive repetitions of behaviours. In a misguided way, they act out their past experiences in an effort to heal past hurts.

Carrying anger and resentment from your past experiences, may mean you unwittingly attract a person who also needs aspects of their past to be healed. Two needy people with unresolved issues in a relationship can be a recipe for disaster and you may find yourself playing out your childhood unmet needs. Another aspect to consider is how we might take on our mother's role in relationships – either copying her parenting style or doing the opposite.

Daughters who find they constantly give to others, acting out what they believe to be the 'ideal mother role' may feel used when little comes back in return. Better to practice self nurturance and self care, giving love to ourselves first and foremost. Trying to find our ideal mother in our partner is not advised. When an external source of love is not available, we are no longer thrown back into the 'needy child' part of ourselves and instead, we are able to meet our own needs, regardless. Working with our inner child in this way has so many benefits.

Although it is in many ways deemed acceptable for a woman to depend on a man, or for a man to need a mother figure to care for him, the same underlying compulsions are at hand. If we have found ourselves taking on the parental role at a young age, we might look to our partners to care for us to make up for this. Or, once again, we become "the fixer" in relationships and find our partners have the same expectations towards us as our mothers.

Daughters who have been fixers or whose mothers have been unavailable may go on to work in caring professions where they give to others the nurturance, time and care they never received as children. Such professions may include nursing, animal care, teaching, therapy, care workers, healing professions, emergency services staff etc. Although these roles can be rewarding, all daughters who find themselves in caring roles, also benefit from making time for themselves.

Liz Case Study

Liz came to me for support in improving 'significant other' relationships with men

Liz repeatedly chose men who were uncommunicative, emotionally and physically distant and who criticised her looks, job, the way she spoke, how she ate, as well as criticising her friends etc. She felt she could never say or do the right thing. In our work together, Liz came to realise she was choosing partners who represented her mother. In both actions, words and deeds, she was re-living her childhood all over again in these unhealthy relationships. In her search for validation, recognition and love she had lost her identity and didn't know who she was outside of the relationship. Using The Spotlight Process (Chapter Six) Liz was able to redefine the kind of relationship she wanted and was able to recognise straight away if any potential partner reminded her of what was familiar to her from childhood. She chose not to take those relationships further and instead, spent time, getting to know someone before she became intimate with them. She opened herself up to being treated with respect, love and care and eventually went on to value herself and the new relationship experiences she was having. Bumping into Liz recently, she shared that she is now happy and settled in a loving relationship and is pleased to have left the ghosts of her past behind.

The refusal to mourn the disappointments and losses of childhood, to bury them once and for all, condemns us to live in their shadows - Sheldon. B. Kopp

Self-love is the healing road to recovery. When we are able to let go of our need for our mother's love, approval, acceptance and acknowledgement, we stop looking for her in potential partners. Instead of looking outside ourselves for love, we look inside.

Whether self-care and self-love is making time to take a bubble bath, listening to our favourite music, reading a book, spending time in nature or going for a run, when we can give ourselves love, time and care, we become richer for the experience. For you, self-love might be connecting with friends, going to a dance or exercise class, seeing a movie or stage play, treating yourself to a spa day or a beautiful outfit. You could also try simply looking in the mirror every morning and saying to yourself *'I am enough'.*

Think about those things which make you feel loved, special and cherished and give them to yourself. Self-love doesn't mean you aren't taking responsibility to fulfil other areas of your life.

Balance is important and making time for you as well as others, creates a healthy balance. You might have a family, a career and other commitments which take your time, but making quality time for you, will be time well invested. You are the only one who can change your current reality. This begins with self-awareness, self-respect and that all important self-love.

Present day relationships, including those with your own children, siblings, significant others, colleagues, friends and lovers are defined by your past relationship experiences. If your relationships aren't working then it's worth exploring, in depth your beliefs about relationships and work towards updating those beliefs to better serve you.

Something good can come out of your suffering. When you have the awareness of what you don't want for yourself, your children and your personal relationships, you can turn those "don't wants" into "do wants" communicating clearly and assertively your ideals (see Chapter Five) The Beginning of You, and the section Who Am I, What Do I Want? By breaking the loop and ending the repeating patterns and behaviours which no longer serve us, we create something entirely new.

COMMUNICATION STYLES

To effectively communicate, we must realize that we are all different in the way we perceive the world and use this as a guide to understanding our communication with others - Tony Robbins

How are you relating?

How you relate, will be the direct result of what you have learnt about communication from birth until now. Your experience of how you have been related to in the past and the meanings and perceptions you have placed on previous relationships, will be filtering into this present time. Relating is all about communicating and includes how we relate to others and how we relate to ourselves. As well as tone and pitch of voice, relating also includes our various communication styles, our body language and the content of what we say and how we say it.

Sometimes we think we are communicating effectively though at times, what we want to say and what we actually say, are two very different things. Take a look at the information offered here and explore the various communication styles to see which you tend to adopt. Use the information to bring your relating style back into balance, if you feel there is any room for improvement.

ASSERTIVE: Standing at an appropriate distance from another with an upright, still, relaxed and open body posture, making eye contact. Communication is direct, positive, responsible, honest and accepting.

PASSIVE: Weak body language, avoiding eye contact, fiddling with clothes or hair, quiet tone of voice, apologetic, moaning, helpless communication style.

INDIRECT AGGRESSION: Rolling eyes, mean looks, looking away from the other person, physically turning away from them. Communication style is controlling, sly, deceiving and manipulative.

DIRECT AGGRESSION: Challenging eye contact, hands on hips, invades personal space moving body too close to another's, wringing of hands. Communication style is bossy, impatient and overbearing.

Think of a negative and upsetting conversation you've had with your mother. Consider how you were relating (communicating) by answering the questions below:

- **What were you relating?**
- **Why were you relating?**

- **How were you relating?**
- **Where were you relating?**
- **When were you relating?**
- **What happened when you were relating?**

What you think is being said (what you think you can hear) and what *is* actually being said may be two different things. Think before you react and examine your perception of what you *think* is being said asking for clarification to get an accurate meaning. Sometimes we can get things totally wrong and find ourselves reacting from the past when we felt similar emotions to ones we experience in a current moment. Improving your relating style is important if you wish to build, transform and create loving relationships.

My belief is that communication is the best way to create strong relationships - Jada Pinkett Smith

Putting the relate back into relationships

Once we are aware of our relating style, we can make changes to our style of communication for improvement. We can learn to master different and more effective relating styles.

Tanya Case Study

Tanya sought my support to understand why her relationships were failing

Tanya had become pregnant at the age of fifteen and admitted she wasn't coping well with being a mother, trying to find work as well as childcare and managing the whirlwind of emotions she experienced daily. Tanya had moved to and from different family members' homes with her daughter, but still didn't have the feeling of anywhere being home, she felt she didn't have the ability and confidence to parent her daughter in the way she wanted. Tanya went back home to her parents two years after her daughter was born where she was exposed to the fights between her mother and step-father, both of whom were regularly drunk and would involve her in their arguments.

I worked with Tanya using The Spotlight Process (Chapter Six) and we discussed and explored her past relationships in depth. The theme running throughout was being on the receiving end of angry communication styles. This way of communicating she realised belonged to her mother, her grandmother, various male characters in her life, relationship partners and also belonging to the voice of bullies she was the target of at school. As a teen, Tanya had experienced many unhappy times trying to fit in, she had been expelled from school on numerous occasions and had gained a reputation as a trouble maker. Tanya wasn't able to express her emotions constructively and clearly, she would explode when her frustration and anger built up to boiling point, not even knowing at times what had caused it.

Tanya made great progress in our work together, once she realised she had been communicating in ways which weren't helpful for her. She understood how the way she responded to others made the situation worse. After some soul searching and working with Tanya to find the way back to herself she realised she was beautiful, lovable and worthy, despite how others behaved around her. For the first time she started to believe not all future relationships would be hostile, angry or cause her heartache. We used EFT to reduce anger, sadness, frustration and despair leaving Tanya in a much better place emotionally. Tanya went on to leave her parents' home and formed a loving relationship with a single dad. To this day, she, her partner and their mutual children are doing well, her partner and the children use EFT when emotions run high and find they can easily communicate how they are feeling.

Once you are aware of how your past experiences influence you negatively, you can make changes in your life.

SELF-SABOTAGE IN INTIMATE RELATIONSHIPS

There are two basic motivating forces: fear and love. When we are afraid, we pull back from life. When we are in love, we are open to all that life has to offer passion, excitement, and acceptance. We need to learn to love ourselves first... in all our glory and our imperfections. If we cannot love ourselves, we cannot love others or our potential to create - John Lennon

We all do it at some point in our lives, unwittingly sabotage ourselves, as the fear of the unknown can be greater than the fear of what actually is. Staying in a comfort zone is one of the biggest culprits preventing us from positive change. Your personal comfort zone in intimate relationships could include any of the following. It will be different for each of you reading.

QUESTIONS FOR REFLECTION

How often do you:

- **Tell yourself it's better to stay single?**
- **Find yourself being passive in relationships?**
- **Convince yourself future relationships will be like the past?**
- **Move from one partner to another without making a commitment to a lasting relationship?**
- **End a relationship so they don't end it first?**
- **Tell your partner you're busy even when you're not?**
- **Expect your partner to be able to meet all your needs?**

- **Look for evidence your relationships aren't working?**
- **Discount the positive in your relationships?**
- **Choose not to believe words of love and affirmation?**
- **Criticise your partner inwardly or outwardly but still stay with them?**
- **Use aggression or the silent treatment to communicate your needs?**
- **Turn away from your partner without talking things through?**
- **Find yourself avoiding physical contact and intimacy?**
- **Close down or walk out when an argument or disagreement is brewing?**
- **Find yourself running from relationships before they've had a chance to blossom?**
- **Reacting to your partner when their actions and behaviours remind you of your mother?**
- **Acting as a moody child or angry teenager in communications with your partner?**
- **Giving into your partner and not stating your own needs?**
- **Expect your partner to mind read what you want them to do, say or be?**
- **Put up with disrespectful behaviour from your partner?**
- **Avoid talking through your emotions, thoughts and feelings?**

Comfort Zone

Our comfort zone includes all the things we are comfortable and familiar with - even if we don't like them. When we are in this zone we take no risks, we are stagnating, we are not growing or evolving, we are just getting by. Our comfort zone operates as a self-protective mechanism and although we say we want positive change, we still stay in this zone. This can be compared to being trapped inside a cage, too frightened to move out of it, even if the cage door is open.

Consequently, the love we search for is slower to obtain, or there is no change at all if we stay stuck where we are. It's as though this invisible comfort zone is made up of a million voices telling us why we shouldn't, mustn't, ought not to, daren't, don't want to do whatever it is we say we really want to do!

Are you staying in your comfort zone?

When something outside this zone appears scary, risky or dangerous our survival instincts kick in. Fear and excitement are similar emotions in the way we experience them. This means, we may be uncertain whether we are excited or frightened and so talk ourselves out of doing certain things. It is perfectly natural to feel apprehensive when trying new things but unless we take action, nothing will change.

Mistakes, or rather the fear of making them and not getting things 100% right, create a comfort zone. A comfort zone consists of mental conditioning which may not always be based on facts but has been made up from our perceptions and the meanings we have placed on things and people. If we feel we have taken risks before and those risks have not worked in our favour, we may be hesitant to take risks again, in case it all goes wrong.

Creating our own prisons

The truth is however that if we stay within the boundaries of the self-imposed walls we build up around ourselves, change won't happen - we'll be doing what we always did and getting the same results, feeling stuck, uncertain and afraid. By thinking and doing the same things, we get the same results.

Moving on from the past and creating the future of our dreams

So, it is time to join me and the hundreds of women I have worked with and form a united army moving on from the past and creating the future of our dreams. Focus on all the things which could go right and take those first steps towards achievement.

What we learn about life and the meaning we place on things ultimately shapes our character. I have known many daughters turn into a clown thinking they need to be the entertainer with a laugh and joke while underneath this facade they are crying. Instead of revealing who they are, they pretend to be someone they are not. They are afraid if they reveal the hurt parts of themselves, they will not be accepted.

I have known other daughters who become serious, controlled, unforgiving, harsh, sarcastic and punishing as a result of their early relationship experiences. Underneath is the fear of being manipulated or controlled by others and to avoid this, their mask is one of 'don't mess with me'. This stops the softer, more playful side of their personality coming out and in turn, can impact relationships because their behaviour is too regimented and confined.

Life begins at the end of your comfort zone - Neale Donald Walsch

Love and Relationship Inventory	**YES**	**NO**
I have a preconceived vision of love and relationships and how they 'should' be		
Love needs to be a certain way for me to be happy		
I offer love based on conditions		
I believe love can only be experienced by receiving it from another		

I think it is selfish to love myself. It is my mother's (or another's) responsibility to love me		
I question and judge the actions of others instead of being in the flow of love		
I spend time worrying I'm not getting enough love		
I believe the past will repeat itself and I'm scared of getting hurt		
I put love outside of myself rather than taking responsibility to give love to myself		
I believe if I love someone, their love may be stolen or taken away from me		
I believe I am unlovable or unworthy of love		
I lose my self identity when I'm in a relationship		
I fear being rejected in relationships		
I expect love to be like one of the fairy tales I read as a child		
I gain my self-worth and value through others' validation of me		
My sense of security is only present when I'm in a relationship		
I am dependent on others for love		
Other people have better relationships than me		
I don't know how to love myself		
I end relationships before I have given them a chance to blossom		
I sabotage my future hopes by not having a relationship and 'playing safe'		
I put other people's feelings ahead of my own		
I need to be loved to feel complete		
I want to be close to someone, but I'm afraid of being vulnerable		

It feels scary to open up to another person and be intimate		
It feels safer to be out of a relationship than in one		
I don't know who I am outside of a relationship		
My happiness depends on being in a relationship		
My emotional wellbeing depends on another person's validation of me		
I feel like a 'nobody' unless somebody loves me		
I am desperate to be loved		
I will close off my love, unless I get 100% love back from the other person		
When I don't get what I want from a relationship, I feel cheated and let down		
I try to change the people I am in a relationship with		
When a relationship ends, I feel like a failure		
When I'm by myself I don't feel like a complete person		
I feel empty and alone when I'm not in a loving relationship		
I am preoccupied with negative relationships from the past		
Without a relationship, my life would be empty and meaningless		
I'm frightened of being alone for the rest of my life		
I can't stand on my own two feet without someone to lean on		
If I'm in a relationship I'm on alert and expect things to go wrong		
I have never got what I wanted from relationships		
I look for evidence that I'm unlovable		

When I'm in a love relationship, I look for all the flaws in my partner and the relationship itself		
I cling to hopes and dreams of a relationship working out, even though I know it's best for me to leave		
I don't seem to exist outside of a relationship		
I go into relationships blindly, it's better to be in one than alone		
I feel alone and unhappy when I'm in a relationship		
I look for signs my relationships will not work out		
It feels unsafe for me to be totally myself and share all of myself in a relationship		
I drift from relationship to relationship, I have never spent time alone		
In relationships I become totally dependent on the other person to provide my happiness		
I go into relationships for the wrong reasons		
There must be something wrong with me if I'm not in a relationship		
I constantly think about negative experiences in previous relationships		
I feel like I can't move on from negative relationships from the past		
I put all my energy into my relationship and leave nothing for me		
I'm afraid I will never be loved		
I feel insignificant and worthless outside of a relationship		
Life only has meaning if I'm in a relationship		
I feel more real in a relationship		
I need someone else to complete me		
I feel incomplete or off-balance when I'm not in a relationship		

I don't trust anyone enough to share my feelings openly		
I am afraid of being honest or assertive in relationships		
I avoid having a relationship because I fear the physical or verbal violence they sometimes bring		
I am afraid I will have to give up my family, career, hobbies etc if I have a relationship		
I put my own needs last in a relationship		
I find it hard to communicate my needs in a relationship		
I don't know who I am or what I want in a relationship		
I put up with unacceptable behaviour and hope the other person will change		
I hide who I am in a relationship, in case I am not accepted, disapproved of or rejected		

Read through your answers. For every yes, reflect on where your beliefs come from, how old you were when you formed this belief, how does having this belief limit you in adulthood? What thoughts, actions, beliefs and behaviours can you alter to change your future outcomes. Deeper work may be required for those of you who have marked mostly yes and it is recommended you find a reputable therapist to support you in understanding your behaviours and beliefs. Please see appendix for additional support or contact me direct at www.mothersanddaughters.solutions

PROJECTION IN YOUR PERSONAL RELATIONSHIPS

Words are singularly the most powerful force available to humanity. We can choose to use this force constructively with words of encouragement, or destructively using words

of despair. Words have energy and power with the ability to help, to heal, to hinder, to hurt, to harm, to humiliate and to humble - Yehuda Berg

Inside every daughter is a longing for a place which feels like home.

Without the safety and security of a home, whether it be purely an emotional home where you can share your true self, or a physical home in a place where you feel whole, many of you may have a sense of feeling adrift in the world, un-tethered, empty, lost and alone. With the feeling of uncertainty, we might project false beliefs into our relationships, believing they are not quite right. We may feel something is missing and ask for more than can realistically be given.

Many daughters have shared with me they go from relationship to relationship, the next being just like the last. They feel isolated, lonely and not considered. The yearning to be loved continues along with a deep river of fear of not being loved, running under every relationship interaction. Perhaps you've found yourself repeating patterns and falling in love with the wrong type, attracting significant others who reflect your own unmet needs or who are similar to our mother in terms of behaviour, personality and manner.

Some daughters prefer to be single rather than risk being vulnerable in a relationship. Others may project their unmet needs onto bosses, friends, co-workers and colleagues. Many do not recognise they are doing this by trying to get their needs met from other sources. In many cases, it can be our bosses, friends and colleagues who match how our mothers respond to us and the relationship cycle of not getting our needs met filters into all life areas. For others, it is those very friends, co-workers and associates who make up for lack of mother love.

It's difficult for daughters who feel unloved, to sooth and comfort themselves if they have been lacking in the mother love department. It's not until we are able to mother ourselves and meet our own needs, we find ourselves no longer choosing the wrong relationships or sabotaging the ones we have.

Don't take anything personally. Nothing others do is because of you. What others do and say is a projection of their own reality, their own dream. When you are immune to the opinions and actions of others, you won't be the victim of needless suffering - Don Miguel Ruiz

Chapter 3

Getting Naked With Your Feelings

GETTING NAKED WITH YOUR FEELINGS

The more we idealise the past...and refuse to acknowledge our childhood sufferings, the more we pass them on unconsciously to the next generation - Alice Miller

Millions of women's voices are never heard. If there ever was a time to get naked with your feelings, this is it!

Deep inside you there is a child who yearns for expression. You might hear her voice as a whisper, a gentle call or, at times, a powerful roar. Keeping your inner child's voice suppressed, does not serve you. Whatever your internal voice sounds like now is the time to let it out and in doing so, fully express all of who you are.

Allow yourself to be un-censored, un-masked, de-robed, and totally outspoken and together, we will get down to the bare bones of discovering who you really are behind the emotional baggage you have been carrying around up till now.

Your feelings are your in-built guidance system, designed to let you know when something isn't a good fit for you and also to motivate you towards or away from certain experiences. Getting naked with your feelings is an opportunity to free yourself from the past and in doing so, create a brighter future.

This chapter is designed to encourage free expression. A place where daughters everywhere can share their experiences and the range of emotions within the mother-daughter relationship. Whether it's a yearning for the relationship you idealised and never had, dealing with feelings of abandonment or simply coming to terms with accepting your mother as she is. When you give the younger you a voice to release pent-up emotion, within the safety of the processes shared in this book, you will only wish you had done it sooner.

Many of the case studies shared how they felt guilty, ashamed, unkind, rude and unloving to talk about their mothers in such a way. They had never voiced their innermost thoughts and feelings in this way. Many still fear upsetting their mothers and risking further conflicts by speaking the truth. Unless, as daughters we change inside, its unlikely external changes will take place in our relationships. Without finding some means of self-expression and emotional release, we are prisoners of our own making.

It is with the help of those daughters who have come forward to share their stories which turns this book into a useful resource. It is my hope you will know you are never alone in how you feel. Let us connect together as daughters across the globe and share honestly how we feel in relation to our mothers. Now is the time to welcome and openly acknowledge every layer of unexpressed emotion, knowing this is a safe space to do so.

Many women I have worked with, share the belief, that it's not OK to talk about their mothers, let alone express anger or cry. Often our attempts at speaking out and revealing our feelings were thwarted in childhood. Women learn this, not only from their own families and cultural, educational, religious frameworks but also in their marriages, workplaces and friendships.

You may have heard expressions like *'children should be seen and not heard', 'keep a stiff upper lip', 'be a brave girl,', 'don't cry', 'pull yourself together', 'don't embarrass me'* and *'respect your elders'.* These are just a few of the possible phrases you may have been told in relation to expressing your thoughts, feelings and emotions in childhood and you still operate from these beliefs today. When we push down the negative emotions we feel in relation to our mothers and experiences growing up, they fester deep inside and appear in other ways which only limit us. We stay trapped in the negativity of the past.

Unexpressed emotion means we regress back to the child who first experienced self- doubt, not knowing how to deal with the limiting beliefs we have formed about ourselves. We have learnt sharing how we feel is wrong. In all honesty, we aren't serving ourselves if we can't find a healthy way to release our pent-up emotions, they need to go somewhere. The Emotional Freedom Technique (EFT for short) is the perfect method to find expression and emotional release. See Chapter Six for the EFT tapping points and full process. It is only you who suffers when you continue to drag around old, outdated 'mother-daughter baggage'. There is no blame here. It is not until we are mothers ourselves, or when we gain a sense of maturity, that we begin to understand some of our mother's fears and insecurities, as well as gaining awareness as to why she may have behaved in the way she has.

In Louise L. Hay's book *You Can Heal Your Life,* Louise shares that if we are willing to do the mental work, almost anything can be healed and I agree with her!

The diversity of the mother-daughter relationship and the full range of emotions it embraces, goes way beyond what I have included in this chapter, though what I share is based on the case studies and information gained from my clients.

Getting naked with your feelings may well be the best outcome you could wish for. In addition to the tools and techniques shared in the book you will find a range of downloadable MP3's on my website www.mothersanddaughters.solutions to guide you through releasing negative emotions. You can listen to these audios in the comfort of your own home to help you let go of the past and feel better in the present. If, as you read through this chapter, you feel you would benefit from one-to-one therapeutic support, please do check out my services on my website.

REPRESSION - WHAT HAPPENS WHEN WE CAN'T EXPRESS HOW WE FEEL

Unexpressed emotions will never die. They are buried alive and come forth in uglier ways - Sigmund Freud

Negative emotions aren't just stored in the head, they are stored throughout the body and we may unconsciously repress them in our organs, tissues, muscles and the walls of our cells, without even knowing what we are doing. When we ignore our feelings, our lives become stressful, we are frustrated and this eventually leads to low mood, low energy and possible depression. Having the ability to welcome all emotions, means we can respond to them and heal what remains unresolved.

Depression is sometimes classed as *'anger turned inwards'*, otherwise known as *'imploding'*. This happens when we keep our thoughts and emotions inside. Stress, anxiety and panic symptoms are common when denial of our feelings or self expression is marred or there is fear connected with acknowledging how we feel or speaking up and expressing ourselves. We learn from parental conditioning to keep our thoughts and feelings inside as a way of managing our worlds. If we've had an experience of speaking up and it hasn't been well received, if we've been punished, embarrassed or judged wrongly when we have attempted to have our have your say, it's natural not to want to risk this happening again. We retreat back into our comfort zones where nothing changes.

As children, we see our mothers only as we want to see them. In the early years of childhood we deem our mothers to be all powerful and perfect. When we grow up and mature, we realise how untrue and unfair this perception of our mothers is. She is human just like us and for different reasons may not be the mother we wanted her to be. Although the umbilical cord is cut at birth, there remains a sense of hope that your mother will remain connected to you and will always be there for you unconditionally. As much as we might desire and crave our mother's love, attention, approval or acceptance, when we face the fact that what we want from her may well never come, we gain acceptance of what is.

If you are interested in exploring more in this area, Jenbella Nova, shares in *The Meaning of Negative Emotions A-Z*, the full meanings of negative emotions.

ANGER

If you carry around a lot of suppressed or repressed anger (anger you have unconsciously buried) you may lash out at people, blaming or punishing them for something someone did a long time ago. Because you were unwilling or unable to express how you felt in the past, you may overreact in the present, damaging a relationship - Beverly Engel

Personal enlightenment comes when we are able to embrace the full range of human emotions.

Although anger has a bad reputation, it's natural to feel this emotion at some point in your life. Fear of expressing your anger can have more negative energy than the anger itself. When you are able to vent your emotions in healthy ways, you are able to reduce many related emotions such as stress, anxiety and depression. What may appear as anger, may actually be a cry for love. You may find yourself using one emotion to hide another. Being able to welcome, acknowledge and release the anger you feel in healthy ways, creates an emotional shift in your life.

When an unhealed child's wounds come to the fore, anger can surface at the least expected times. Anger can be experienced as a feeling, a thought or a combination of both. For some daughters, anger may be expressed using no words at all. They find themselves releasing the emotional build-up through crying, throwing things, stomping feet, hitting, punching or shouting out and for some self harming and using various substances, to release what they feel inside.

I want you to know it *is* ok to feel anger towards your mother. All daughters the world over have felt anger towards their mothers at some time in their lives and vice versa. It's a natural part of life to feel angry when our needs aren't met, if things aren't going the way we want them to, or circumstances are inflicted upon us against our will.

Find a safe place in your home, alone, where you can release your pent up anger and put your feelings into words or sounds to unburden yourself. Venting your anger in healthy ways, will help you to separate from the negative aspects of your mother and support you in reducing anxiety, low mood and depression and will raise your mood.

Anger check-in

- **Think about your body. When you feel angry, where in your body do you have the sensation of anger the most?**
- **On a scale of 1 to 10, 10 being intense, how high is your anger score?**
- **What's the temperature of your anger?** *(cold, warm, hot, boiling)*
- **If your anger had a colour what would it be?**
- **If your anger has a texture what's it made from?**
- **What shape is your anger?**
- **What does your anger smell like?**
- **What does your anger taste of?**
- **Draw your anger, what does it look like?**

- **Use EFT as detailed in Chapter Six, to work through your anger**
- **Write about your anger in a journal**
- **When anger builds up take physical exercise**
- **Use creative art work to express your anger**

Daughters are frequently angry with their mothers when they do not feel listened to, understood, loved, acknowledged, accepted or praised. Daughters are not alone in feeling this way and if you are a mother reading this, I am sure you too, have felt this way towards your daughter and your own mother. It's all too easy in mother-daughter relationships to allow miscommunication to prevent relationships from blossoming into ones where clear, assertive communication reigns.

Your anger might remind your mother too much of her own repressed anger and what you share with her, may bring to the surface the un-healed parts of herself. She may not want to deal with this and will turn away from you if the pain she experiences of her own emotions, is too great to bear. Your mother may have found it easier to find fault with you, your siblings, father, neighbours, society and the world in general, rather than allow herself to actually experience her emotions freely and give voice to the wounded child inside.

When you think of your mother rejecting your expression and range of emotions - get curious and wonder what parts of her own experience she may be avoiding? Not meeting another half-way, or misunderstanding each other's communications, actions and behaviours, can lead to many an angry outburst on either side. This is natural and in many ways normal in a mother-daughter relationship and can be worked with to create a healthy compromise.

Anger often covers the deep need for love we craved as children. If our love towards our mother was shunned, we might think that 'to love is dangerous'. This echo's many women who have shared with me, beliefs which have spilled over from childhood into adulthood *such as, 'I'm unlovable', or 'everyone I love leaves or rejects me'.* We are filtering through old models and are preventing ourselves from gaining love from other sources. We think we are not worth loving – a feeling based on only part of our experience and the unmet needs of the desperate child.

Without full expression, pent-up anger leads to unhealthy addictive behaviours such as over consumption of alcohol, drugs, food, risky sexual behaviours and overspending etc. Addictions may be sought to escape the pain hiding inside.

When we grow in maturity and understand ourselves better, we are able to welcome and face our anger acknowledging why we feel the way we do, without blame. Simply owning our anger and finding healthy ways to release it, is the key to understanding ourselves and understanding our mothers.

Judy's words of wisdom

"Losing my mum emotionally at such an early age distorted my ability to trust in relationships. I did not have the love and affection of my dad because he left when I was a child and then I felt abandoned all over again when my mum died. Even though she wasn't emotionally available to me growing up, not having her physically in my life came as feeling of numbness and a sense of her death not being real. The feeling of not belonging to anyone or anything was a shock for me.

Soon after mum passed away and we buried her, I felt so much anger to the point of rage. I was impatient with people at work and strangers in the street, in the supermarket or driving my car. I felt close to losing it on many occasions and had visions of having trolley rage, hitting someone or screaming until I couldn't scream anymore. Gone was my role of dutiful daughter, all round do-gooder and when she went, so did my identity to a degree. I began to question, who am I without her?

For the first time in my life I felt free to express all which had laid dormant inside. It shocked and surprised me how angry I felt and I seriously needed to let rip. I'm angry at myself for having got myself into this situation. I was my mum's emotional rescuer simply because I didn't know any better and was angry at her and my dad for feeling like I had no choice but to mother my mum. Caring for her emotionally and later on physically, has felt much like a prison sentence for most of my life. My role was taken from me when she died. As much as it came as a relief for my duty to be over, with it came a sense of powerlessness and a reminder of all the previous times I felt out of control.

For a while I went through my life in a daze. I comfort ate, drank too much, declined meeting with friends and in many ways I was frightened to express my anger and hatred towards my mother. I did not expect to experience this after her death and it was a shock to me when I didn't know what to do with my temper as I'd never been allowed to express it.

I wasn't aware anger is part of the grief cycle. I'm pleased I've found new ways to unburden myself, using EFT. I've also joined a kickboxing class, I go jogging, I talk openly and honestly to friends and I also write a heap of stuff which I end up ripping up and throwing out, but it helps me to express what remains inside. I also did a massive splatter painting with some old paint on a sheet I don't use and totally let out all the years of pent-up anger I'd kept within. My pressure cooker of anger which was set to burst is now on a gentle simmer. I'm so glad I've found new ways to manage my feelings and all I can say is, thank goodness for EFT."

ANGER AND BEREAVEMENT

We bereaved are not alone. We belong to the largest company in the world, the company of those who have known suffering - Helen Keller

It's natural to feel anger as part of the bereavement cycle. Giving yourself time to work through bereavement and all associated losses, will serve you well. Anger during the grief cycle can be unpredictable, you may feel fine one day and not the next. Remind yourself that *'this, too, will pass'* and soon you will notice yourself having more good days than bad.

In my experience, it is by working through our emotions, and facing our fears, communicating our experiences and being willing to heal the past, which allows us to reflect on our relationships with our mothers differently. No longer are we being victims of our own circumstances, we are free to move on from the past and make our futures all we want them to be.

One of the best books I have read on the subject of parental bereavement (or preparing yourself for eventual loss) is *Losing a Parent* by Fiona Marshall.

Explore your memories of anger

When you are able to welcome and accept you have a right be angry you are not denying your feelings, you acknowledge all aspects of yourself.

In the same way you would embrace an old friend, welcome and acknowledge your anger and then let it go.

- **Welcome and accept your anger as you would an old friend**
- **Dig deep and explore why it's there**
- **Recognise anger as being a healthy emotion indicating an opportunity for further healing**

- **Think about what made you angry and how you responded**
- **What is your earliest memory of feeling angry in this way?**
- **What unexpressed anger may you have from a previous time which impacts your life now?**

In terms of your experience with your mother and her anger

- **What are your mother's beliefs about expression of anger?**
- **How often did she express anger towards you?**
- **In what ways may your mother have buried her own anger?**
- **Under what circumstances were you able to show your own anger towards your mother or others?**
- **What did you believe about yourself and your mother as a result of her anger or your own anger?**

Moving beyond anger

- **Work through your anger by expressing it in healthy ways** *(for guidance, download the MP3 on releasing anger on my website)*
- **Use EFT** *(Chapter Six)* **to release anger**
- **Allow your anger creative expression through writing, art, drama etc**
- **Choose a form of physical exercise to release pent-up anger**
- **Talk about your anger with a friend or therapist**

Angela's Words of Wisdom

"I spent most of my life trying to make my mother happy, so afraid was I of her angry outbursts, I became ultra-sensitive to her mood and could almost feel her anger brewing up. I never expressed my own anger; to me it seemed destructive, I was scared of its power. Now, after my mother's passing, my anger has well and truly come out of hiding. I'm angry at her selfishness. Angry she never hugged me when I needed it. Angry she wouldn't listen when I wanted support. Angry she couldn't be there for me emotionally. I'm angry that for most of my life it never felt ok to be me. Most of all, I am angry she had never told me 'I love you'. I never thought I'd get over the hurt of what my mother inflicted on me, but instead of continuing to carry my bitterness and anger towards her, I became a stronger person as a result of my experiences. My mother taught me everything I don't want to be."

YOUR MOTHER'S ANGER

Consider the negative events of your mother's life and how her experience may have led to her own, unresolved emotions of anger:

- **What experiences from your mother's past are you aware of which may have made her angry?**
- **How does she express her anger?**
- **Is it possible there are things from your mother's past you don't fully know about? She may not have shared with you in detail the challenges she suffered, or may not want you to know** *(she could be frightened of her own expression of anger, or may be trying to protect you in some way)*

- **From whom did she learn about anger and the expression or non-expression of it?**
- **What are the possible benefits if you were able to ask her more about her past, in order to understand your own anger and hers?**
- **What area of your life do you keep private from her in fear of her expressing anger towards you?**
- **What evidence is there, that if you told her why she sometimes makes you angry she would not welcome this?**
- **Do you know if your mother had an abortion, miscarriage, stillbirth, lost a sibling or her own parents - which may have put her into a bereavement, loss and anger cycle?**
- **What were the choices your mother was forced to make in her past which may have made her angry?**
- **What are the traumas she has experienced or witnessed which have left a residue of anger?**
- **Has your mother suffered physical, emotional or sexual abuse?**
- **Has your mother had any physical, mental or emotional health problems?**
- **Has she been divorced, separated or widowed?**
- **Thinking about the latter questions (all of which would have been traumatic) how might these experiences have shaped her life and her ability to show love?**

By sharing openly with each other and finding out more about your mother's past and what has made her angry whether it has been expressed or not, gives both mother and daughter an opportunity to heal. It's time to end the war against anger by welcoming it and expressing it in safe ways.

FEAR

Everything you want is on the other side of fear - Jack Canfield

Fear is often at the root of all other feelings. When you are unable to meet your own needs, or those you depended on as a child couldn't meet theirs, a deep sense of insecurity may leave you feeling scared and unsafe in the world.

Having the belief something is dangerous (even when it isn't) can make us fearful. A fear only has to be acknowledged to be transformed. Fear is a healthy emotion and used wisely lets us know we need to take action and take care of ourselves and those we care about.

Fear-based thinking and the associated feelings which go with it, can become a habit. We might find ourselves responding automatically, reacting to something in the present moment which reminds us of a past experience. Becoming aware of your internal dialogue is the first step towards stopping automatic fearful thinking. By having an awareness that not all thoughts are based on current reality, you are able to re-frame your current perceptions. Fear can be used as a motivating force. It helps us to move beyond personal limitations and aids us in developing coping strategies to overcome real or imagined fears.

The emotion of fear is very closely linked to anxiety. If we are anxious about something, our fear escalates. Fear is a natural impulse when we feel our survival is threatened. Frequently our childhood fears are carried through into adulthood, until we are able to gather enough information to realise there is nothing to fear. Like finding out there were no monsters living under the bed, ghouls or gremlins loitering inside the cupboards, we can change beliefs when the evidence is contrary. Children are afraid of many things. Some of their fears are very real and remain under the surface of conscious awareness. We carry around many limiting beliefs based on childhood fears.

What childhood fears were true for you?

Fear of monsters, the dark, scary movies, shadows on walls or the whistling wind? Other fears might include the fear of expressing your emotions, upsetting your mother, fear of being left alone, fear of rejection and criticism, blame or judgement. Fear of showing love, not being loved and also fear of being emotionally smothered may also have been true for you? Were you afraid of your mother's anger, being smacked or physically reprimanded, getting things wrong, being shouted at, or being sent to your room for punishment? Fear may also include deep concerns about survival, health and poverty such as not having a home to live in, not having enough to eat etc. Safety and trust issues as well as physical or emotional health problems are all things we (and our mothers) may have feared at some time in our lives. How many of those fears are true for you now as an adult?

Their mothers had finally caught up with them and been proven right. There were consequences after all but they were the consequences to things you didn't even know you'd done - Margaret Atwood

As a child, what did you fear the most in relation to your mother?

Add your own fears to the list

- **Fear of being hit, slapped, pushed etc**
- **Fear of being sent to your room alone**
- **Fear of not being fed**
- **Fear of being locked away or sent away**
- **Fear of your mother's anger and rage**
- **Fear of verbal attack**

- **Fear of being rejected, unloved, unaccepted or disapproved of**
- **Fear of public humiliation**
- **Fear of your mother being out of control**
- **Fear for your safety or survival**

Through my client work and case studies shared, there is a clear indication many children have been afraid of their mothers and still are, even as adults.

- **When you were frightened as a child what did you do?**
- **How did your fear manifest itself?** *(muscle tension, stomach ache, trembling, changes in body temperature, hyperventilation, crying, shaking, fainting)*
- **What is it you fear now as an adult in relation to your mother?**
- **When you are afraid of her what do you do, how does your behaviour change?**

Take some time to reflect on your fears and allow yourself to move beyond your fear- based thinking, apply this three step process:

1. **Thank your fear-based thoughts for being there and acknowledge you realise they are trying to keep you safe** *(i.e. I better not speak up, I will upset my mum and make her angry)*
2. **Remind yourself 'I am not my thoughts'** *(thoughts are only thoughts and not current evidence)*
3. **Replace the negative, fear-based thoughts by re-framing and creating positive empowering thoughts** *(every day in every way, I'm feeling more confident about voicing my thoughts and feelings)*

Acknowledging and understanding your fears, as well as exploring why they are present, is an important step forward. If you avoid transforming your fears, you live with a false sense of security with underlying pain and confusion.

Moving beyond fear exercise

Use a blank sheet of paper

On one side, write the titles 'Past – Present – Future'

On the other side of the page, list your fears which are based either in the past, present or future. On the other side of the page, identify your limiting beliefs related to these fears.

Many of the fears we keep hold of are irrational, outdated and untrue. Making time to explore outdated beliefs in relation to your fears sets you free from them.

<u>Two acronyms to remember for FEAR are:</u> Failure to <u>E</u>xperience <u>A</u>ctual <u>R</u>eality and <u>F</u>eeling <u>E</u>xcited <u>A</u>nd <u>R</u>eady. Fear and excitement create similar feelings in our gut area (solar plexus) so what we perceive as fear, may be another feeling entirely. With awareness, you are able to stop your fears escalating.

Susan Jeffers in her book *Feel the Fear and Do it Anyway* is a great resource if you wish to explore in greater depth how to turn your fear into confidence and action.

EFT as described later in this book and the Field Clearing Technique in Chapter Six can help you reduce and eliminate your unwanted fears.

GRIEF & LOSS

Grief is a normal and natural response to loss. It is originally an unlearned feeling process. Keeping grief inside increases your pain - Anne Grant

Grief and loss is something we will all go though as daughters, whether your mother leaves you through choice, personal circumstance or death. No matter how good or bad your relationship was with your mother, it will still have an impact on you when your mother is no longer there.

As well as grieving for the relationship you had or hoped for, you may also mourn for the loss of your personal history and positive memories that go with your mother. However small and insignificant those pockets of treasured moments may be, I am hopeful you can find a significant memory to treasure - or at least one positive strength, skill or attribute you have gained as a result of your relationship with your mother.

Without her mother, a daughter mourns not only what is lost, but also what she knows will never be.

Losing a parent through death, is like losing a part of yourself. You have lost the person who gave you life and you no longer have access to the person who had direct knowledge of your conception, birth and childhood. The things you may have wanted to know about yourself from your mother, will no longer be available to you. It is not until a mother dies that we realise there are so many unanswered questions. It is my hope that after reading Mothers and Daughters you are able to ask your mother questions, accept your differences, bridge the gap with your mother and re-build your relationship to one which is more meaningful for both of you.

Although your identity may change, as your relationship with your mother comes to a final end, you are able to you can also create new opportunities and new meanings for your future. You can reject the judgements made about you and the limiting beliefs placed upon you and start your life afresh and on your terms. You are set both free. You do not need to continue running old programmes and behaviours along your future time line; you have the ability to make a different life for yourself and for the lives of the daughters who come after you.

For some daughters there may be a sense of relief when a mother passes away. For others, the loss may feel vast, leaving a gaping hole which seems impossible to fill. Your grief will be unique to you and my advice is to let it out freely.

Although as children, many of us would have been told not to cry when we are hurting, delaying our grief will only come back tenfold if it remains.

Kate's Words of Wisdom

"When my mother died I was shocked at the emotions I felt in relation to her dying. One minute I felt sad, the next minute angry and everything else in between. All I can say is thank goodness for EFT; it's a wonder I haven't given myself a bruise I've been tapping so much."

If you are separated from someone and suffering from grief and loss, you may imagine you can see the person or hear their voice. You may experience disturbed sleep patterns, changeable appetite, disbelief, shock, numbness and the emotions of anger, guilt and, sadness. You may find it almost impossible to stop thinking about the person in question. A period of depression may be part of your grieving. You do need to give yourself time to go through the natural process of grieving, when your mother dies or your relationship with her ends. Welcoming the full range of emotions which will surface will serve you well.

Strategies to overcome your grief and loss are:

- **Expressing your emotions (sadness, anger, guilt, helplessness, anxiety) using EFT and the other processes shared throughout Chapters Five and Six**

- **Working towards accepting your loss and talking about it**
- **Living without the deceased or person you are estranged from and making decisions alone**

Grief and loss are far broader than physical death alone. Moving on from what is dead to us emotionally or what we hoped for, is the starting point on the journey towards recovery. Death might be the beginning of the separation process, if we as daughters, have remained attached to our mothers - or her to us, until this time.

Lisa Case Study

Lisa came to me for support to work through grief, loss and anger

Lisa acknowledged the ache weighing her down is the guilt of not wanting to grieve her mother, after all she stated 'why should she, her mother didn't deserve it.' Too many times her mother had abandoned her and run off with men, leaving her to fend for herself and her brother as a teenager. How she'd cried every time her mother left and came back again when it suited her, only to disappear again with a new 'uncle' or to find a new man moving in who would only ignore her and her brother.

After working through her feelings, Lisa realised she needed to let go of her anger towards her mother, before any true grieving could begin. We have begun our work and already Lisa is making progress in understanding that her mother had unfulfilled needs from her own childhood when her mother (Lisa's grandmother) behaved in exactly the same way, seeking love by the wrong means. She recognised her mother sought love in the arms of others, trying to escape her pain from her own loveless childhood. Lisa's mother had failed to notice she had the love of her children all along and did not recognise it.

Lisa is now able to see how her own unhealthy beliefs about finding love were just compounding the problem, for herself, her mother and grandmother. Since the early days of working together, Lisa is making many changes in her personal life. She is now planning to take a psychology and counselling degree and specifically wants to work as a counsellor with children and teenagers who have experienced family isolation, confusion and heartache. This is a classic example of someone using their past to work for them, not against them.

Every journey to healing, no matter how hard, will always be worth it. Grieving for the idealised mother, as well as mourning the loss of our mother in the physical sense, is exactly what we need to do in order to set ourselves free from the past.

The harsh reality of life is that our mothers get sick, suffer their own losses, disappointments and aren't necessarily happy with the role of domestic goddess, mother, chief cook and bottle washer and doing all the wife and mother duties. Many mothers have become exhausted caring for their own mothers, siblings, husbands and children.

Having the confidence to be a mother doesn't always come naturally. Your mother may be grieving her own losses which she may never discuss with anyone which leads her to internalise her emotions.

- **What significant losses did your mother experience in her life?**
- **What might your mother still be grieving for?**
- **How does your mother express her grief?** *(does she talk about it, hide from it, self-medicate, express herself through anger and rage, develop narcissistic behaviours etc)*

My mother did not have an easy life. I have found grieving for her losses, opened up a space of understanding, empathy and love within me. Your story may be completely different to mine, though I wonder if you were able to empathise with your mother's losses what this may in turn, release in yourself. How you deal with grief and loss will depend on what you have already learnt through our own experiences. Culturally there will also be different ways to grieve through various services, prayer, ritual and honouring the deceased.

Though far more can be written on the subject of grief and loss and the full range of human emotion this chapter is a short overview of some of the emotions experienced by daughters in relation to their mothers.

Jannine's Words of Wisdom

"It took me years to heal the wounds my mother inflicted on me. Parents are not always good for you. I love to see people being released from their own hell, to be able to take off the shackles and live a free life."

What is it you need to grieve?

- **Not knowing your birth mother?**
- **Not having secure attachments to any mother figure?**
- **Your mother dying in childbirth or when you were a child?**
- **Mourning the loss of your mother's absence for whatever reason?**
- **Grieving the loss of a strong supportive parent and stable family life?**

- **Coming to terms with not having the mother you hoped for?**
- **Mourning the loss of the relationship you hoped for?**
- **Childhood trauma?**
- **Grieving the loss of your childhood if you were an emotional or physical carer?**
- **Moving on from the break-up of your family as a unit?**
- **Grieving the loss of contact with family, friends and neighbours?**
- **Overcoming the loss of your family home and environment or country of origin?**
- **Letting go of the "ideal" relationship you would have liked with your mother?**
- **Grieving the loss of your mother through illness or death?**
- **Mourning the loss of not only your mother, but also your personal history and connection to the past?**

Some of the case studies and questionnaires reveal siblings who were stillborn, aborted, disabled, ill or who died in childhood. If this was part of your mother's reality too, it would certainly have had an impact on your mother. Hardship and circumstances beyond her control, may go some way in explaining why your mother was not able to be the mother you would have preferred.

It will be helpful for you and your mother to work through the following questions together (or independently) to gain further insights into her life and your relationship.

What might your mother still be grieving for?

What losses has she experienced?

How often have you talked about your personal disasters and how your mother isn't able to be there to support you?

What might your losses bring up for her, or remind her of?

Thinking about her losses, if she has not grieved them fully, she may be triggered by your losses, trapped inside her own pain, not being able to come to your aid because of her own memoires surfacing. This may be something you want to help her with or indeed she might also like to read this book in relation to her own mother and past experiences.

Emma's Words of Wisdom

"One of my greatest losses was being told 'no more pets' It might sound silly, but to me this was like being cut off from the only source of love I knew. As a kid I'd loved all kinds of furry friends - in particular, cats, mice, gerbils, hamsters and guinea pigs. We had to get rid of the guinea pigs because their squeaking irritated my mum. The mice, hamsters and gerbils I had, never seemed to have a huge life span and when my beloved friends died, I would cry my eyes out. My mum told me to stop snivelling and grow up. She banned me from having any more pets, because I used to get so upset when they died. I hated her for preventing me from having something to love and care for and to have the love, warmth and affection a pet gives you unconditionally."

Loss comes to us in many ways. Grieving the tangible things we miss and also the intangible things we hoped for.

GUILT

Anger has a twin sister and her name is guilt. When you feel guilty it is a voice inside of you saying "I feel I've been unfair

to someone"- Calvin D Banyan - The Secret Language of Feelings

It is possible to turn guilt into personal growth. Instead of guilty feelings limiting you, you can explore what made you do what you did. If, in hindsight, you wish you had done something differently, this is an opportunity to learn from the experience. Reflecting in this way, you know you could have made a different choice or taken a different action, though at the *time* of making your decision, you did not have the awareness or learning in place.

Guilt, like anger and grief can be worked through, healed and transformed. Going over and over an event and berating yourself for something you could have done but didn't - or did do but wish you hadn't, serves no purpose, and is wasted energy which helps no one. Forgiving yourself for your actions, behaviours and consequences, will aid you in moving beyond your current limitations.

When a mother has not been able to protect her daughter, she, may experience guilt. Mothers and daughters may think the mother has the power to make the daughter happy and that they are accountable for all events in a daughter's life though in reality, there is so much that is outside a mother's control. The constant loop of mother or daughter feeling guilty, helps neither of them move on from the pain of the past.

Daughters have shared with me how they have felt guilty for not intervening in cases of witnessing or hearing domestic violence in the home. Some daughters wish they had spoken up about abusive relationships that they or their mother have experienced. For other daughters, they realise in hindsight as they grow up, there is so much more they could have done for their mothers and vice versa.

- **How often do you feel you have failed your mother or felt responsible to make your mother well and have not been able to?**
- **How did she fail you?**

Guilt can be linked to the beliefs you have about the way things should or could have been. Guilt in my experience (and also working with others) is very much set in the past. We wish we had done something differently, made an alternative response, taken a different path etc. We learn about guilt in childhood and are conditioned to feel guilty about certain thoughts, actions and deeds. The things deemed 'bad' we are chastised for, not only by our mothers but reinforced by our family, teachers, religion, culture and society. We tend not repeat the behaviours which get us into trouble, though a sense of guilt may remain.

We are generally told as children not to be selfish and to put others first, which adds to the guilt when we do try and do something which is in fact about self-care. We are made to disapprove of our actions or behaviours based on prior conditioning, or we are disapproved of by someone who matters to us. The resulting guilt manipulates us into conforming, as the need for external approval and validation becomes the driving force and we do not want to repeat the behaviour. Overcoming your guilt means standing up for what you believe to be true and voicing your opinions, wants and needs.

Alison's Words of Wisdom

"Thinking back on my relationship with my mom, I feel guilty for having been frustrated with her. I resented her for not giving me the emotional support I needed as a child. But now I'm older, I remember the little things she did for me, the special gifts she bought me and the thoughtful things she said. I don't know why I couldn't see it at the time."

What is it you feel guilty about?

Think about some of the rules and conditions imposed upon you growing up. What was ok or not ok for you in relation to your mother? (Guilt is tied in with what we believe or are told to believe, is moral or immoral)

How many of these examples bring up guilt for you? Remember to use EFT (Chapter Six) if your emotions run high as you read through this section.

- **Things you've said or done in the past which have left you feeling guilty**
- **Making a decision which went against your mother's beliefs about what was right for you**
- **Believing you have caused your mother's suffering**
- **Being born when you've known your mother never wanted children**
- **Hating your mother**
- **Saying no to her**
- **Fighting with her**
- **Standing up for yourself**
- **Setting boundaries**
- **Lying about how you spend your time**
- **Not calling her every day**
- **Not wanting to visit**
- **Not liking or loving your mother**
- **Not wanting to be like her**
- **Being angry at your mother**
- **Having your own life**

- **Choosing to be estranged from her**
- **Feeling responsible for her and not wanting to be**
- **Disliking her neediness**
- **Resenting her illness, physical or mental condition**
- **Feeling repulsed by your mother**
- **Not wanting to be her carer or help with her personal care**
- **Wishing she would die**
- **Believing you caused her to die**
- **Not telling her you loved her before she died**
- **Not trying to repair the relationship before she died**

Your perception of your mother may change several times during your life. As your mother ages, the relationship dynamic may well change. Physical or mental illness could impact the way you experience her. Roles change and you may feel as if your mother is a patient or child as you find yourself in a mothering or caring role. Your mother may be demanding, needy and angry as her independence decreases and her reliance on you increases.

When what you do is never enough

Shame is the most powerful, master emotion. It's the fear that we're not good enough - Brene Brown

With a mentally or physically unwell mother, you may resent having to be the carer. Society expects a daughter to look after a mother, even when there may be male siblings or other family members who can help. Many daughters have shared with me how they've had no help or support from the family as a whole and the caring duties have fallen on them. As your mother ages, you might find that you resent giving up your time to take her to appointments and to help out with additional duties in the home.

Role reversal very much comes into play and your relationship with your mother can change as her needs and demands become even greater. You may feel at times as though you are mothering her and if your own needs haven't been met in childhood, you may either not know how to care for her, or simply resent the fact she is asking you for help when you feel you never received the same level of care in childhood. When you already have a busy life, fitting in caring for your mother can be overwhelming. If are working full-time, have a family, a home to run, your own health conditions, family problems and other balls you are juggling - the added pressure of an ageing and declining mother, impacts your emotional health.

Many daughters who have shared their stories, feel extreme guilt for not wanting the role of being parent to their mothers or to actively carry out the role of a carer. Some daughters have given up work to care for their mothers, others have been fortunate to have the support of family members and neighbours, though many daughters suffer in silence with no outside support.

If guilt is something you are still working through, recognise that holding onto guilt may be a way of punishing yourself or trying to control the outcome of the past, present or future. When you can forgive yourself and recognise you did all you could with the internal resources you had, your outlook becomes more balanced.

LOVE & HATE

Love and hate have a magical transforming power. They are great soul changers. We grow through their exercise into the likeness of what we contemplate - George William Russell

Every child needs love and your inner child is still very much a part of you. Now is the time to meet your needs by yourself and for yourself.

In the earlier chapters we discussed attachment and bonding with your mother. I go on to share here, the importance of having a mother who is loving, affectionate, sensitive and playful towards her children. It would be unrealistic to believe a mother can provide all of these things one hundred percent of the time, though having the ability to love, offer affectionate touch, being sensitive to a child's needs and playing together, leads the child to grow up in a healthy environment and in turn grow up to be healthier adults. The research and studies of Notre Dame Professor and Psychologist Darcia Narvaez, suggest these actions when given freely, willingly and in plentiful supply, show long-term benefits. Our children and adult children are less depressed, less anxious and have the ability to interact socially as a result. You can find out more about Narvaez's research in the appendix.

Included in the case studies shared throughout this book, you will gain awareness how your family is your first and most important community. As a child, your heart would have been wide open to receive love. However fragile the connection with your caregivers, the need for love may have been behind many of your actions as would be the need for acceptance and approval.

Author's Notes

''The first time I ever knew I was lovable was when a therapist told me, ''who you are is more than enough and who you are is so worth loving. There I was, thirty something, sitting opposite a woman I barely knew but in that moment it felt as though time stood still. The cogs inside my head slowed down as I processed what she said. I felt those words deep within a part

of me I never knew existed. I laughed and cried, then cried some more in-between smiling. I will never forget how I felt that day. It's as though my heart was opened for the first time. Walking out of the therapist's room, I felt like I'd grown three inches taller, a weight lifted from me and from that moment on, I never viewed myself in the same way as I did before."

Many daughters crave the physical affection of their mothers in terms of wanting her embrace and soothing touch. It became apparent in my work and what daughters have shared with me in their support sessions, that physical touch might mean no more than a face being wiped, air kissing at arm's length or a smack of the bottom. Many of the daughters who contributed to this book shared how they never felt anywhere near being mothered enough. Warmth, cuddles, caresses and tender touch were not on the menu. The deepest level of intimacy for some of you reading this, may have been the time spent in a mother's womb.

A person can only give as much love as they have found within themselves - Daniel Chidiac

The very issues you struggle with, your mother may have battled with too.

Begin to notice when you feel rejected, not only by your mother but with the people you share intimate relationships with. When we open ourselves to love if our perception is skewed and we believe the other person is withdrawing or withholding love, we react through our default behaviours, not because of the other person's action or inaction, but by the meanings we have placed on things and the limiting beliefs we have filtered through.

Perhaps you too have experienced loving your mother in one moment and hating her next?

How often do you have an internal conflict? One moment thinking about your mother as a *'good mother'* and the next verses a *'bad mother'*?

How often does your mother's mood change and how does yours change in relation to her?

Become aware of when your own mood changes towards her, one minute loving her and the next hating her and explore the contributing factors of what turns your love to hate

There may be acts of love our mothers offer us we are not even aware of. How we show love to another will be different for each of us, depending on who we have modelled love from.

We each show our love and affection to each other differently. Sometimes we may follow in our parent's footsteps, at other times we might be the total opposite.

Gary Chapman and Ross Campbell in their book *The Five Love Languages for Children* mention the following love languages, as a means of loving expression:

Giving gifts

Spending quality time together

Words of affirmation

Physical touch *(intimacy)*

Acts of service *(devotion)*

This list is not exhaustive, I personally learnt so much from reading Gary Chapman's books. They have enlightened me as to how my mother was showing her love and yet I had not realised this. His books include a full range of love languages for singles, couples, teenagers and men.

Gary shares how each person has a primary and secondary love language; he suggests we observe the ways in which others express their love. I share information about his teachings and recommend his books regularly in my client sessions discussing love languages. It's great to see people make a connection with how they are/were loved by their mothers, though the expression of love was different to what they might have recognised. I wonder what your predominant love language is?

Bryony's Words of Wisdom

"My mother communicated her love to us as a family when I was a child through acts of service (keeping a clean and tidy home, cooking, shopping for necessities as well as arranging doctor and dental appointments, school trips and writing letters of importance) The other love languages were not foremost for her. My predominant love language in my personal relationships is spending quality time together. I can see now why we disagreed so much. I wanted to be with her away from home creating happy memories and she wanted to stay at home and do the ironing. I couldn't have cared less if my clothes were ironed or not."

- **In what ways has your mother shown love to you when you explore the five love languages?**
- **What do you think is/was her predominant love language?**
- **What is your predominant love language?**
- **Having the awareness, perhaps you were more loved than you realised through an expression of a love different to your own, what changes for you?**
- **If you are able to communicate more fully by voicing and responding to each other's preferred love language, what might this be an opportunity for?**

Jenny's Words of Wisdom

"My mum didn't show me any physical closeness; she bottle fed me, disgusted at the thought of breast feeding I was brought up on formula. She left me when I cried using the 'cry-it-out method'. I can remember lying awake for what seemed like hours wailing at the top of my lungs and nobody came, there was no soothing touch, hugs, or words of affirmation. I think this is why I find it hard to cry now, it seems so pointless.

I never saw my mother kiss or embrace my father and the same with my grandparents; I did not witness any physical love or words of love between them or towards my mother. My mother's parenting style, on reflection, may have been related to how things were back in the day; my mother was born in 1943, my grandmother in 1915. Things were very different then compared to now. I've made it my mission not to be like her and to show as much love as I possibly can to my children."

REGRET

Never look back unless you are planning to go that way - Henry David Thoreau

Regrets, we all have them. Even Frank Sinatra in his song *'I Did It My Way'* sings about regret, but the ultimate message is how he did things his own way to live his life to the full and be all of who could be. We could each learn a lesson from Frank.

Regret is a natural part of life. With hindsight, we may have gone in a different direction armed with the knowledge, learning, wisdom and experience we have now. We make choices and decisions at points in our lives when those appear to be the only or most obvious options. There may have been nothing else we could have done differently at the time and we need to accept that we were doing the best we could with the knowledge, wisdom and experience we had in the moment. Self- forgiveness plays a part in moving on from regret and simply using the experience as a learning opportunity.

I like to think of regrets, as the *'If Only' syndrome.* If only I had done or said this or that. We can tear ourselves up with guilt, regret, shame and anger, if we spend too long playing the *'if only'* game.

Choosing from the list below and adding your own, what do you regret in terms of the relationship with your mother?

• **If only I had...**	• **If only I'd done...**
• **If only I hadn't**	• **If only I'd been...**
• **If only I did...**	• **If only I'd told her...**
• **If only I didn't...**	• **If only I knew...**
• **If only I'd asked...**	• **If only she...**
• **If only I'd said...**	• **If only we'd...**
• **If only I'd listened...**	• **If only I could...**
• **If only I was ...**	• **If only I'd learnt...**
• **If only I wasn't**	• **If only things were different I...**

It's natural to have regrets when we focus on what we could have done differently in the past. The problem is we judge ourselves harshly as to why we made certain choices. Guilt and regret go hand-in-hand, based on our disappointment about how things weren't or aren't different.

Guilt like any emotion can range in intensity. If we are not able to move beyond the past, accept ourselves and our faults we remain powerless, guilt becomes bigger than the event which caused the original feeling.

Zarina's Words of Wisdom

"I often wonder how things would have been different between us if my mother had been open to change. I'd been hanging onto the hope, however slim that we could improve our relationship as equals. It's my deepest regret she didn't want our relationship to change or even begin to understand and acknowledge I had other commitments. As I became more independent, knowledgeable, confident and successful, my mum turned on me, saying people didn't want what I had to offer and my business wouldn't be a success. I know now she didn't have a personal example of a happy, contented and successful life and possibly resented me having something she didn't. What I wanted from her more than anything was for her to say, "I'm proud of you". Just as well I wasn't holding my breath."

- **If your mother is still alive what would you like to tell her, now you've had an opportunity to reflect on your feelings of guilt and regret?**
- **What would you like to hear from her in response to your message?**
- **If your mother is deceased what do you wish you had said or done differently?**
- **Consider writing a letter to your mother if she is deceased or no longer in your life, in order to release the past and free yourself from any unresolved emotions**

In the same way I would recommend clearing and resolving the range of emotions using EFT. Working on forgiving yourself and your mother will play a key part in your recovery. Forgiveness means you are not only able to forgive the event and experiences which have shaped both of your lives, you are also able to forgive yourself and your mothers for your individual actions within those events. In the next chapter there are a series of forgiveness statements which can be worked through using EFT. Chapter Six offers you the full EFT process, if you want to jump ahead.

SADNESS

If you don't think your anxiety, depression, sadness and stress impact your physical health, think again. All these emotions trigger chemical reactions in your body, which can lead to inflammation and a weakened immune system. Learn how to cope, sweet friend. There will always be dark days - Kris Carr

Sadness often lies hidden beneath anger and love. In order to avoid feeling sad, we bury the emotion of sadness in the same way we might also bury our anger and the love for our mothers. We may be sad about our childhood, sad to have left different family homes, sad not to have quality time with our mother and sad for the parent who has left us through circumstance or death. If we have been taught not to show our feelings and find ourselves unable to communicate, express opinion or concern - the sadness stays inside us just waiting to be triggered.

We may feel sad when a parent dies at whatever age we are and wonder *'who will look after me'* now. Whether we are speaking metaphorically or factually, knowing a parent is there in whatever capacity gives us a sense of security, when it's taken from us we can feel unsafe and adrift in the world. Some mothers and daughters have shared how much they have taken each other for granted and it's only when a relationship ends they realise how much their mothers or daughters gave them.

It is worth reflecting on why you may previously have hidden your sadness and the meaning you place on being able to express your sorrow. Sadness as well as anger can be deemed as a negative emotion and one society says we should not display.

In truth, healthy expression of anger and sadness would serve us all far better than keeping it inside.

Author's Notes

"I can remember aged seventeen laying in my bed banging my head against the wall over and over; I just wanted to stop what I was hearing. I had no knowledge of how to move beyond the confused feelings in my mind. I hated living with my mum and step-dad listening to their fights, tears and then apologies. I felt sad for my mum because I didn't know how to stop what was happening and she was afraid of leaving him. If I had to describe that time I'd have to say it was like living in my worst nightmare, I just wanted to wake up from it all and find I'd been dreaming."

Owning up to and acknowledging your sadness is one of the most difficult human experiences you may ever face. If you have been taught not to express your feelings, the grief you experience deep within may never be processed - leaving you with a sense of melancholy and despondency, as you go through life. It may be difficult to trust or form long-lasting relationships with others, if you have a deep, ingrained, fear and the belief that to love eventually means to lose.

Many daughters I have spoken with, regret that they never knew their birth mothers. Some share there is an overwhelming disappointment and that the relationship with their mother is beyond repair. For other daughters' - sadness is present every day, as they have not yet been able to separate from their mothers and truly live their lives on their own terms.

Children do not always know how to process and release the emotion of sadness, we learn from our parents and caregivers. By addressing our emotions as adults and acknowledging what made us sad in childhood and later years, we are able to heal old hurts. With this awareness we can move on from feeling resentful and holding onto memories which are painful and keep us feeling small. Now, as adult daughters because we recognise the childhood patterns of seeking the love, approval and acceptance from our mothers, we no longer have to try to mould and shape ourselves into being perfect to be loved.

If your mother had problems of her own and was not able to give to you what you needed, healthy expression of sadness will provide a catharsis and opportunity to heal at a deeper level. Mourning the loss of your ideal mother gives you freedom from the heartache you feel inside. It is time to acknowledge the part of you at the age when you first experienced sadness, for not being honoured as who you are. Further on in Chapters Five and Six, we explore the opportunity for inner work which will give relief to the hurt part of your younger self, the part of you which you may have never allowed the freedom to express her sadness.

Alison's Words of Wisdom

"I'm sad I never had the opportunity to have a happier relationship with my mum before she died. She continued to treat me as a subservient child and fearing upsetting her, I continued to respond in the way she moulded me. She remained the needy and narcissistic parent right to the end of her life and I continued to be the needy child seeking her love, approval and acceptance. I never knew my mum as a friend or a person in her own right, I only knew her as my mother and this makes me very sad."

- **What do you feel most sad about?**
- **What unmet childhood needs bring up sadness for you?**

- **What did you learn about the emotion of sadness growing up?**
- **How often have you been soothed by your mother when you were sad?**
- **When you cried or showed emotion for whatever reason, how did your mother respond to you?**
- **How often was it acceptable for you to show sadness in front of your mother?**
- **How did/does your mother express her own sadness?**
- **When do you deny your own sadness?**
- **When others show sadness through crying and communicating how they feel, how do you respond?**

What influences may have shaped your mother's ability to express her sadness?

Mental illness?

Physical illness?

Personal traumas?

Disassociation from her emotions?

Inability to be emotionally or physically available when you needed emotional support?

Not having the opportunity to show sadness as she believed it to be wrong?

Your sadness bringing up unhealed or denied parts of herself?

Dealing with sadness is a natural part of grief work. Even if your mother is still alive, there may be aspects of the relationship you had (or indeed wish you'd experienced) which need to be mourned.

STRATEGIES TO DEAL WITH EMOTIONAL RELEASE

Expose yourself to your deepest fear, after that, fear has no power and the fear of freedom shrinks and vanishes. You are free - Jim Rohn

Remember having the thoughts, feelings and emotions mentioned in this chapter are a completely normal part of life. Humans are naturally emotive creatures and express what they experience. Emotion (E-Motion) is energy in motion. Emotions come and go in the same way our energy changes at any given moment.

There may be times when something or someone, triggers off one of the feelings or emotions mentioned in this chapter and it may require you to do some self-work around them. If you are concerned about the strength of your feelings, I recommend you work with a trained therapist, to help you release the build-up of emotion.

The Eight Step Process of Identifying a Feeling

1) **Identify the feeling by naming it** *i.e. anger, sadness, guilt, frustration etc*
2) **Identify the root cause of the feeling** *i.e. what is your earliest memory of feeling this way?*
3) **Identify a different response and meaning** *i.e. for example, with guilt if what you said/did was unfair, what can you do to resolve the situation now? Can you choose to forgive yourself for what happened, what was said, not said and the actions and behaviours connected with this?*

4) **Apply EFT (Chapter Six) to any remaining emotions, until they are reduced or cleared** *(be aware some of your emotion, thoughts and feelings are a motivator and may also have a secondary gain attached to them, so it's worth questioning the following)*
5) **What are the negative aspects of no longer having this problem?**
6) **What would you lose if you didn't have this problem?**
7) **What are the positive aspects of you not having this problem?**
8) **What needs to happen to end this problem?**

When you are able to review and re-frame the meaning you place on things, you are able to recognise when your judgement may have been deleting, distorting or generalising information. Becoming more objective and re-evaluating your thoughts, feelings and emotions, is a great way to place new meaning on your experience.

Re-setting your focus

Between stimulus and response there is a space. In that space is our power to choose our response. In our response lies our growth and our freedom - Victor E. Frankl

- **Write down a list of the negative feelings you experience the most in relation to your mother**
- **In a column alongside these feelings, you might like to look for counter evidence and record the positive feelings you have towards her (i.e. appreciation, love, connection, gratitude for your life etc)**
- **Completing this exercise will help you to reframe your focus and get in touch with the more positive aspects of your mother's personality and behaviours**

- **Keep going with this, until the positive list is longer than the negative**

THOUGHT PATTERNS

Become aware of your automatic negative thought patterns, stopping yourself when you go into:

- **Mind reading** - you assume you know what your mother is thinking without having any evidence
- **Fortune telling** - you predict the future of your relationship with your mother negatively
- **Catastrophising** - you believe what has happened or will happen with your mother will be so awful and unbearable you won't be able to stand it
- **Labelling** - you give negative traits to yourself and your mother, ignoring the positives
- **Negative filtering** - you focus on the negative aspect of your relationship and do not notice the positives
- **Over generalising** - you see a global pattern of negatives based on a single incident with your mother
- ***'Shoulds'***- you see events in terms of how things 'should' be, rather than simply focusing on what is
- **Personalising** - you assume an unreasonable amount of blame for negative events
- **Blaming** - you focus on your mother as the source of your negative feelings
- **Unfair comparisons** - you interpret events in terms of standards that are unrealistic when you compare your mother to other mothers

- **Regret orientation** - you focus on ways you could have done better in the past, rather than on what you can do better now
- **Emotional reasoning** - you let your past feelings guide your interpretation of reality
- **Inability to disconfirm** - you reject any evidence or arguments which might contradict your negative thoughts
- **Judgement focus** - you view yourself, your mother and past events with your mother, in terms of good-bad or superior-inferior, rather than simply describing, accepting or understanding things to be the way they are. You are focused on the judgement of your mother, as well as on your judgements of yourself

EMOTIONAL AND SEASONAL TRIGGERS

There can be many emotional triggers when you think of your mother. Perhaps you have felt unwell and needed her love and care or seen a film which might trigger your grief in relation to her. Seeing other mothers and daughters laughing and hugging might make you feel pleased for those in a loving relationship or, it can make you ache to the core, as you experience the loss of love in your life. Certain smells: perfume, flowers, home baked goods; cigarettes etc may remind you of your mother. Music too, can be emotive and the lyrics of a song could touch you in the most unexpected way. It is my belief, our emotions help us to feel, to experience being alive and being real. It is how we deal with those emotions which either lifts us up or keeps us down.

Seasonal triggers such as Mother's Day, Christmas, birthdays, anniversaries, family celebrations can all add to the emotional turmoil. It is natural at specific times of the year, to remember your mother with love or distaste. I know many daughters who want to acknowledge Mother's Day, but do not agree with the loving sentiments expressed in a typical Mother's Day card. If they haven't felt truly loved by their mothers, it can feel I a lie to buy a wordy card declaring a wonderful relationship. For others, this particular time of year brings up much sadness as they grieve again after the loss of their mothers or for the relationship they hoped for.

Allow yourself to experience the range of emotions which come up to the surface. Sometimes, when you think you have released all you can, please know that any further triggers are an opportunity for healing. When you are able to express and release the full range of emotions, it frees up a space for love.

Negative emotions like loneliness, envy, and guilt have an immortal role to play in a happy life: they're big, flashing signs something needs to change - Gretchen Rubin

Remember to check out the audio downloads which go with this chapter at www.mothersanddaughters.solutions

Chapter 4

Mining for Gold

MINING FOR GOLD

Peace is not in the absence of conflict, it is the ability to handle conflict by peaceful means - Ronald Regan

Mining for Gold is an opportunity to dig deeper and genuinely begin to understand your mother as a woman, not just as your mother.

It is fair to say that no one enjoys a life completely free from problems or unexpected setbacks. Your mother will have gone through personal traumas with her own doubts, insecurities and fears. She may have unresolved issues from the past, personal regrets and disappointments. It's possible she has unanswered questions about her childhood and her own unmet needs connected with her mother (your grandmother).

Your mother may have experienced struggles she has never told you about, either because she wanted to protect you or, because, she may be in denial of hurtful past events.

Once you become aware of your mother's personal history, you will have a better idea of the battles she has overcome or may still be working through. Making the time to find out about your mother's past, will help you to understand how her experiences have shaped her character, behaviours and ability to be a mother.

If you and your mother are both open to the idea, you might decide to work through this book together. This will give you both an opportunity to discuss your experiences in a loving way in order to connect at a deeper level. If, however, you feel that at this point, your mother would not be willing to share her experiences with you, you might like to give her a copy of this book and when she is ready to read it will help her to understand and resolve her own mother-daughter issues.

It is all too easy as daughters to judge our mothers when we have limited information about her life experiences. Gathering facts together about her personal history may help you ease some pain from the past not just for your own personal transformation and healing but for your mother's too. Understanding why your mother acted in certain ways means you no longer reject yourself for her actions or inaction. You simply become more comfortable with accepting your experience of her behaviour. None of us know what the future holds, though with understanding we are able to let go of the past and be present in the moment, learning along the way.

YOUR ROADMAP TO UNDERSTANDING YOUR MOTHER

But there's a story behind everything. How a picture got on a wall. How a scar got on your face. Sometimes the stories are simple, and sometimes they are hard and heartbreaking. But behind all your story is always your mother's story, because hers is where yours began - Mitch Alborn

In this chapter, we will explore how to move beyond the notion that your mother has to be perfect. There may come a time when you go on to have your own daughter, or find yourself in another mothering and nurturing role. Taking time to read and utilise what's shared within these pages, will aid you in understanding and transforming the relationship you have with yourself and your mother. Even if she is no longer in your life, you can still transform your perceptions and memories of her.

I am not asking you to wear rose tinted spectacles, or minimise experiences which have been painful for you, but I invite you to explore where you may have been distorting or generalising aspects of the relationship and even deleting some of the positive experiences with your mother. What you choose to focus on, will grow and become the dominant perspective of the relationship. The good news is that when you are able to reflect on the attitude you have towards your mother and work out the limiting beliefs you have made about her, you will begin to understand yourself and your beliefs.

We all misconstrue, eliminate and theorise information depending on our beliefs and the meanings we place on things. Mining for gold is an opportunity to gather together the positive aspects of your relationship with your mother and in turn, will create more balanced ways of thinking.

Working with both mothers and daughters, I am always curious about a mother's life before her daughter came into the world. Who was she before you began?

Know thy mother, know thyself...

Jess's Words of Wisdom

"When my mother retired she spent much of her time researching her family tree and sending away for birth, death and marriage certificates. My mother was an only child and said at times she felt very much alone. She seemed to find comfort in researching her distant past and finding out who she was related to. It filled her time writing up records and telling me what she'd found. I saw my mother differently during this time; she was like an excited child every time she made a new find. I'm pleased she found connection to people in her blood line and had a sense of belonging through exploring her ancestry. She found a distant cousin in Hong Kong who became an email pen friend and made many new online friends who were also searching for relatives. Doing the searches cheered up her disposition massively. I'm happy she found something which made her happy and gave her a sense of purpose."

GOLDEN NUGGETS

To become optimally healthy and happy each of us must get clear about the ways in which our mothers' history both influenced and continues to inform our state of health, our beliefs and how we live our lives - Christine Northrup M.D

What do you know of your mother's life before you came into being? Perhaps she experienced her own childhood challenges and personal traumas. She may have suffered loss, grief, fear, abandonment or isolation. Our mothers hide much from us, either to protect us or simply because they may not want to share parts of their past which they would rather forget or have not yet come to terms with.

Before and after you were born, it's possible your mother experienced illness, financial hardship, death of a loved one, divorce or separation, verbal or physical violence, domestic or sexual abuse, depression, stress or emotional problems. Your mother may have lost her home, emigrated, been made redundant or ostracised from her community. Just how much do you know of your mother's past?

None of the experiences mentioned would have been easy to get through. Bringing children up at the same time means for many mothers, life has been a constant juggling act with no guarantee that all the balls will stay in the air.

Motherhood may not have been fulfilling for your mother. Physical or emotional discomfort during conception, pregnancy or after the birth is not something a daughter generally asks about, though this may have impacted her ability to bond with you.

After childbirth your mother's life will change dramatically, as well as getting used to being a mother there are frequent sleepless nights, feeds on demand and later on the school run, duties of homemaker and caretaker of the family, the responsibility is huge and often overwhelming for mothers. The role of the mother has no ending and no beginning with other family members having the expectation that 'mum will do it'. Many mothers I have spoken with are frazzled, emotionally overwhelmed, exhausted and just about holding it together while at the same time trying to be the 'Perfect Mother', wife or partner and daughter.

It takes emotional intelligence to be a mother and if your mother was no more than a teenager herself when she gave birth to you, she may not have had the knowledge or maturity to care for you fully. Not having enough emotional or physical support to raise you, would have also taken its toll on her as well as you. If your grandmother, other mother figures or other caregivers were unable to guide your mother in raising you, she would have more or less been making it up as she went along, following the trial and error approach that many mothers do, until they find a pattern of parenting which works for them.

Whether you felt loved, unloved, over protected or under protected, you have the opportunity to learn a little more about your mother, by reflecting on the following questions.

What do you know about the parenting and guidance your mother received?

- **Did she feel loved, approved of and accepted by her mother or caregivers?**
- **What were the highs and lows of her childhood?**
- **How well did she get on with her mother and grandmother?**
- **What are her memories of significant special moments with her mother?**
- **What are her childhood regrets?**
- **How old was your mother when she gave birth to you?**

- **What support did she have in raising you through your childhood and teenage years?**
- **What practical knowledge and experience of mothering did she have before you were born?**
- **Did she match up to your idea of a mother in childhood and later years?**
- **Where did she learn how to be a mother? How many of your mother's personal and professional goals did she sacrifice to put you and your family first?**
- **What resentments or regrets may remain for your mother, if she did not fulfil her dreams and aspirations?**
- **Would you have preferred your mother to have followed her dreams instead of making the choices she did?**
- **What have you learnt from your mother about being a woman, a daughter and a mother?**

Author's Notes

"I wonder what would have happened to me, had my mother taken her own life when I was a child; she was so close to it. She told me when I was in my thirties, "as much as I wanted to end it all, I wondered what it would do to you and your brother." She made a choice to stay in this world and despite wanting to end her pain she never went through with ending her life. I will always be grateful to her for her consideration of us, although she talked about not wanting to stay in this world, my mother never committed suicide. I don't know how I would have coped if she had made that choice."

Using the following framework of questions, imagine how your mother may have behaved differently towards you if she had been able to work through and resolve her own problems. I wonder, did she ever feel loved and supported and connected with her family of origin? How have her experiences shaped her life and yours as a result of her childhood and younger days?

- **What difficulties has your mother lived through, which may have shaped her character, behaviours, beliefs and parenting style?**
- **What was her experience as a daughter under her mother (your grandmother's) parenting role?**
- **If your mother was not raised by a maternal mother or grandmother, what was her experience of being raised by her caregivers?**
- **How *'deserving'* did your mother believe she was?** *(Taking into account if she believed she was worthy of love, affection, attention, approval)*
- **How similar are you to your mother in this aspect?**
- **Who did your mother talk to when she was afraid, upset, uncertain etc?**
- **Thinking about what you have learnt about your mother's past challenges, her fears and failures – how does your judgement and opinion of her change?**
- **What new opportunities do you have, in the light of this new knowledge about your mother?**
- **Coming from your heart instead of your head, what would love do here?**
- **What do you need to start doing, stop doing or do differently, to improve your relationship with your mother or carry more positive memories of her? Mother and daughter relationships can be fraught, with each person trying to get their needs met.**

The mother-daughter battle can continue right through until adulthood unless changes are made in the relationship dynamic to create a win-win situation. Things improve when mother and daughter (as adults) are independently meeting their own needs or are giving to each other willingly, their time, attention, love and care. Having a deeper insight into your mother's past and understanding what she went through, takes away some of the negative emotions you might feel towards her.

COMPASSION FOR YOUR MOTHER

No one saves us but ourselves. No one can and no one may. We ourselves must walk the path - Gautama Buddha

When in conflict with your mother, consider her responses. She may not be reacting to you personally, but speaking from a hurt place within herself. You are able to move beyond getting hooked into reacting and behaving towards her in a way which distances you both. It takes just one person to change a behaviour loop and by making this change, you create an opportunity for new communication styles between you. Whatever we choose to pay attention to grows. Making sure that we notice the good things, creates a healthy balance in life and relationships.

Understanding your mother and learning to accept her for who she is, sets you free from trying to make her into something she isn't. Acknowledging her imperfections, lowering your expectations and opening your heart to your mother, will bring transformation at the deepest level. Holding on to anything other than this, means you continue to hold onto your own suffering. My wish is that from now on, you allow more happiness, joy and love to flow into your life.

Learning about your mother's past, will give you insights into what has shaped her behaviour and who she has become. Without this awareness the mother-daughter struggle continues, with each operating from the position of the wounded child. Healing personal traumas must come, before we can know, love and accept ourselves. In healing ourselves, we transform the relationship with our mothers.

Peace cannot be kept by force; it can only be achieved by understanding - Albert Einstein

Our mothers are individuals in their own right with their own needs. It is an impossible task for any mother to give one hundred percent all of the time and it's our job to recognise the times when she has been there for us in whatever capacity.

Take a moment to ponder the following questions. If you find yourself drawing blanks on the answers, you might like to explore how you can gather the missing information. Whether it is speaking directly to your mother, contacting other family members or researching the era your mother grew up in. To be forewarned is to be forearmed. The more information you have, the greater your capacity to understand your mother.

- **How might your own mother's identity be shaped through her upbringing and societal expectations?**
- **What were your mother's dreams and goals in life before she gave birth to you?**
- **How might the era your mother grew up in shape her parenting style?**
- **What religious conditions may have influenced your mother's parenting role and the rules and conditions passed down to you?**
- **What, in your opinion, has stopped your mother from providing you with what you needed most in childhood and now as an adult?**
- **What limiting beliefs did your mother have about herself and as a mother, a parent and as a woman generally?**
- **Reflecting back on your life experience with your mother, what do you appreciate the most?**

Many mothers shared with me how they feared losing their baby in pregnancy or their child being harmed or unwell in later life. Others were frightened of giving birth and anxious about how they would cope afterwards. Some mothers have also shared how hard it is to be a wife and mother along with all the traditional womanly duties. It will be worth asking your mother what fears she had in relation to you being born into the world and even prior to your conception. If your mother is no longer alive, think back to your birth, the era your mother grew up in and the support she had to raise you. What fears may have been present for her during this time?

Katie Case Study

Katie came to work with me to gain some insights into how to set boundaries and to be more assertive in her relationship with her mother. Mother and daughter also attended individual and joint sessions so I could mediate between them, helping them to understand each other at a deeper level.

Katie shared with me, she was a sickly child and would cry almost nonstop as did her sister once Katie became restless. The relentless crying from two children under the age of four drove her mother Pauline to distraction, despite what she tried to do to calm her children's' crying, it wouldn't cease. Her mother had spent a small fortune on parenting books, classes and seeing various specialists trying to get things right, she spent hours comparing herself to other mothers who had babies who slept through the night. In truth, Pauline never felt good enough as a mother and became an anxious and hyper vigilant parent.

Katie now understands as an adult, her mother's need to check up on her. Although the attention was overwhelming and unwanted, Pauline still felt responsible for Katie's well-being even as an adult. Working with both mother and daughter each were able to make some headway in understanding their relationship dynamics and how, as an adult, Katie no longer needed her mother to be so attentive.

Katie told her mother how much she loved her and explained her need to set new boundaries. Her mother received some separate support with me to reduce anxiety and to come to terms with past events which had been distressing for her. Katie made contact with me recently to say they were enjoying spending time together and the relationship had moved from strength to strength. The mother-daughter bond remains but has changed in a way which is far healthier, allowing both mother and daughter to gain the all important separation process while still having a positive equal relationship.

Without a game plan of how to improve things, it is possible your mother was stressed, had sleepless nights and judged herself on her abilities to be a *'good enough'* mother, on top of all the usual pressures and demands of life. Making time to ask her or find out from her peers, what her challenges as a mother were, will aid a deeper understanding of her hopes and fears. It is not until we are mothers ourselves or have the responsibility of looking after young children can we understand what a demanding task it is to care for someone 24 hours a day.

KNOWLEDGE IS POWER

Those who have hurt you in the past cannot continue to hurt you now unless you hold onto the pain through resentment - Rick Warren

Our mothers live within each of us. We are part of her and she is part of us. But how well do we actually know our mothers? Through finding out more about your mother and her mother before takes away some of the 'mother blame' and you can begin to recognise your mother was never going to be perfect.

You can take her down from the pedestal you may have put her on and accept her for who she is, warts and all. By doing so, she is more likely to accept you and your behaviours, creating a more harmonious relationship between you.

Linda's Words of Wisdom

"I know in the past, I've had many negative beliefs about my mother. It was difficult at first to move beyond my hatred of her. I have been guilty of only focusing on lack, magnifying the things I haven't liked about her, playing over old scenarios where her words wounded me. The last thing on my mind was forgiving her. She had hurt me so much over the years with her comments, coldness and put-downs; I just didn't know where to begin. Now, on reflection and after doing the inner work, I'm aware it was me, hurting me, by constantly reminding myself of my mother's absence of nurturing. Taking time to learn more about my mother's past, I now empathise and understand why she wasn't more loving. I no longer blame her, I just feel very sad for her. What I've discovered is compassion of sorts and this gives me huge sense of relief. I finally feel free from having to search for my mother's love, in its place I have found my own kind of peace with the past."

IN SEARCH OF GOLD

Love is the only gold - Alfred Lord Tennyson

For most of us, our relationship with our mothers is a mixture of negative and positive, happy and sad, good and bad experiences. If we focus on the negative, sad and bad then it leaves little room for the positive aspects of our relationships to flourish.

An honest examination of your relationship with your mother can be completed at any time. However, the sooner you expand your beliefs and knowledge about your mother, the better you will feel. This exercise will help you to mine for gold and focus on the positive aspects of your experiences with your mother – even if you feel these are few and far between.

- **Divide a sheet of paper into two columns, label the right hand side 'Positive' and the left 'Negative'**
- **Write down the positive and negative aspects of your relationship with your mother**
- **Include such occasions as her caring for you if you were unwell, making your favourite meal, coming to your school plays, encouraging you to try new things etc** *(this will go in the positive column)*
- **Record times when your mother was being punishing, judgemental, critical, ignoring you or playing you off against your siblings etc** *(this will be for the negative column)*
- **Take your time with this exercise and keep adding to the list for up to a week**
- **The list is not to cast blame, but to create an awareness of both negative and positive behaviours**
- **When you have completed the list take time to reflect and compare the negatives and positives. Do the negatives outweigh the positives or, is it the other way round?**
- **Writing this list should be cathartic, an opportunity to release negative feelings and help you to remember the happy times and treasured moments with your mother, no matter how few and far between**
- **Allowing yourself to feel the range of emotions connected to both the positives and negatives, will**

further aid your awareness of what needs to be healed and transformed

- **Use of EFT, journaling or art work will support you in letting go of your mother wounds and will take you to a place of healing (see Chapter Six for more detail)**

Author's Notes

Please do make time to complete all the exercises in this book. If you find yourself skipping some sections, make a note of the page number and come back to the exercise. Be aware, that the thought of doing something is nearly always worse than actually doing it. The more inner work you complete, the more you will improve your relationships in general.

ACCEPTANCE

Before you can live a part of you has to die. You have to let go of what could have been, how you could have acted and what you wish you could have said differently. You have to accept you can't change past experiences, opinions of others at that moment in time, or the outcomes from their choices or yours. When you finally recognise the truth then you will understand the true meaning of forgiveness of yourself and others. From this point you will finally be free - Shannon L. Alder

Allowing your mother to be human, you permit yourself to be perfectly imperfect. The pressure is off both of you, as you work towards accepting you are both learning about life and dealing with its many challenges. As you discover events which go towards explaining why your mother may not have been able to love you in the way you wanted, healing can begin.

Every daughter will have something to say on the topic of her mother. Some daughters roll their eyes, vent a barrage of abuse and criticise - while others feel pity, even despair for their mothers. Growth comes when you are able to change what you can and accept what you can't. Releasing any blame you might feel towards your mother frees you from being a victim of your own suffering. Having the wisdom your mother is who she is, purely from her own life experience helps towards knowing your life could not have been different, because she has been living her life and raising you based on her own learning.

Our underlying need for love, validation, acceptance and approval, becomes the driving force in our lives and can cause much destruction in all our personal relationships. Some of us may project these needs into our adult relationships and partnerships, setting up another chain of unrealistic demands when we expect our husbands and partners to parent us. It will be impossible for another person to give us a mother's love. Working through your relationship problems with your mother, will improve significant other relationships too. We cannot change our mothers but we can change the meaning we place on our experiences with her.

It is impractical for us to expect our mothers to parent us in the way we need for the whole of our lives. Admitting we may never receive what we want from her is part of the process of letting go of an unrewarding quest. Instead we become our own inner mothers and are able to love, validate, accept and approve of ourselves independently. Breaking the cycle and letting go of the idealised mother, we are able to begin embracing who she really is and in turn take responsibility for ourselves.

Within each of us there is a spark which can understand, forgive and accept we are not our pasts. Being aware of the past is helpful, living there isn't. Always remember, you are so much more than what has happened to you.

Growing yourself back up

I think every girl needs to love herself, regardless of anything. Like if you're having a bad day, if you don't like your hair, if you don't have the best family situation, whatever, you have to love yourself and you can't do anything until you love yourself first - Julianne Hough

There is much sadness, anger and grief which goes with the realisation the child within is no longer a child and therefore those childhood needs can never be met in the traditional sense. Having this understanding aids us in nurturing ourselves, taking us further into healing.

Eleanor Case Study

Eleanor came to see me to improve confidence and self-esteem

Ever since her mother died when Eleanor was 19, she found herself searching for the validation she never received from her mother looking to lovers, friends and colleagues instead. With awareness of what was happening at a deeper level, Eleanor was able to deal with her unexpressed anger, sadness and grief, not just in terms of mourning her mother but also, in the sense of saying goodbye to the mother she hoped for. Working through her feelings of guilt (for arguing with her mother, blaming herself for her mother's ill health and eventual death) and seeing the relationship with more clarity, Eleanor realised many teenagers fought with their parents and that she wasn't personally to blame for her mother's decline.

By talking to her father more openly, Eleanor learned that her mother had a long-term health condition which her parents had not wanted to discuss this with her. As you can imagine, although her parents were trying to protect her Eleanor felt angry because she would have related to her mother in a different way had she known about the illness.

Eleanor and I worked together using EFT to release her anger and to find a way to forgive herself and her mother and accept her parent's choices. In doing so, she formed a healthier bond with her father and has the loving support of other female family members, as she continues to process her loss.

Coming to terms with the past and your life circumstances, also includes the self-acceptance that as a child you did the best you could with the knowledge and wisdom you had at the time. Acknowledging there may have been times when you struggled to live up to your mother's ideals, removes the excess baggage of blaming yourself. Self-judgment is removed and you simply "let go" of what was an impossible task.

EMPATHY

I do not ask the wounded person how he feels, I myself become the wounded person - Walt Whitman

Every woman on the planet is another woman's daughter. Our experiences are unique and varied. Not all daughters are able to show empathy, for if empathy has not been taught to us by our caregivers, we may not have any model to refer to - although it is a skill which can be learned.

Empathy is the ability to step into another person's shoes in order to understand their actions, feelings and perspectives so we can respond accordingly. Empathy is different to sympathy, kindness or pity. Developmental Psychologist Carolyn Zahn-Waxler reveals we are primed for empathy in the first two years of our lives if we have strong attachment in our relationships. Empathy can also be developed throughout our life, long after early childhood experiences. Listening and having empathy with what is being shared, gives us the ability to transform our relationships with others and with ourselves.

Empathy skills can be learned by a number of means, including reading books, looking at photographs or watching films. Perhaps a start would be to watch various television programmes and imaginatively step into the shoes of the characters for a portion of time, identify with them and begin to think like them. Acting 'as if' and imagining what it is like to *be* a certain character, reacting, responding and behaving in the way they do, flexes the empathy muscle. The more we are able to show empathy and imagine what it's like to enter another's world, the easier it is to re-frame our personal experiences.

You may face new challenges with your mother as you both age and change. The case studies shared throughout may or may not relate to your own personal circumstances, though by having an empathetic slant on what other mothers and daughters have been through enables women to heal collectively.

As adults we have far greater expectations of how our mothers 'should be' than we do when we are children. Rather than empathising with our mother as she ages and taking into account that she may no longer be able to look after herself so well, many daughters resent the new level of neediness and the reversal parenting roles. Several daughters have shared with me how they have not wanted to care for or even spend time with their mothers as they didn't feel their mothers had cared properly for them. Resentment lingers and it can be hard to forgive past actions which complicate the relationship if left unresolved. It becomes a battle of *"why should I look after her if she didn't look after me"* as Liz explains in her words of wisdom coming up next.

When roles reverse and we become the parent of our mothers, where there has been past conflict, a residue of anger and unfairness colours the relationship in the present, making the situation worse than it needs to be. Empathy is an all important skill to learn, in order to navigate the terrain of your relationship which will change as your mother ages.

Liz's Words of Wisdom

"I personally found this phase of my relationship with my mother difficult. As she aged and her health deteriorated, her depression worsened as did her angry outbursts and callous comments. Her tantrums reminded me of my childhood where she would fly into rages, throw things, slam doors, kick things, smack me and shout at the top of her voice. Even as an adult I was sensitive to her mood, I felt vulnerable around her and at the same time responsible for her well-being and happiness.

My mother was not able to find anything to be grateful for and seemed to blame everyone and everything for her plight. Choosing to be housebound with no desire to mix with the outside world or to allow the outside world to come to her, I became my mother's crutch, she expected me and only me to do for her what she could not do for herself. It was difficult for me to escape from what felt like the darkness of her self-imposed confinement, feeling like she would swallow me into the pit of her own despair. To be with her was exhausting. I felt drained and empty while with her - as well as long after any visit.

My mother wanted me to live with her and care for her when her health declined, her fear of hospitals far outweighing listening to medical professionals and what kind of care she needed. This was an impossible ask and one I did not want or was able to fulfil. She was not open to any form of holistic intervention or counselling support stating "they didn't have it in the war and you just had to get on with it." I did consider how I could care for her but her controlling opinions of what was right for me as an adult would have meant I could not live my life in the way I wanted to while living with her.

It feels like I have given up much of my life for her already and as I became closer to self-actualising and finding the things in my life which made me happy, her demands on me increased as did the put-downs. I found it hard to speak up as the fully grown woman I was, any time I tried to voice my thoughts I would be cut back down with harsh words and reprimands. The guilt experienced from saying 'no' to her has been huge, as in the past I had always made her needs a priority and as far as possible gave everything to her within the realms of my capability. Saying no to her meant saying yes to me, I was on un-familiar territory, I felt selfish for not doing as she wished and have suffered huge guilt in the process.

I can admit to not fully empathising with my mother and her various medical conditions including COPD. Instead of empathising and trying to understand why she felt the need to chain-smoke (she said she used it as a form of stress relief and to ease boredom) I was angry she wouldn't stop smoking. It seemed she had little respect for her health, her body or even taking responsibility to get well. Her smoking habits and related complications contributed to her eventual death. I realise now I could have been more supportive in listening to her complaints even if I couldn't change them for her. I could have acknowledged her reasons and why she believed her habits were helping her. No one knows when their mother's life will come to an end or how you will feel when it does. I hate to say it, but in many ways I believe it was a relief for both of us."

Empathy can never be underestimated; it's a powerful catalyst for change when it comes to your relationship with your mother. Listening to what your mother has to share (whether or not you agree with it) will take you a long way towards understanding her and transforming your relationship.

I love this poem by Jessie Swick. I came across it many years ago while searching for something on the internet. The poem is frequently shared across social media and in blog posts because I think it resonates for so many women. I am just grateful to have discovered it by chance, its essence goes way beyond the written word.

PLEASE JUST LISTEN

When I ask you to listen to me

And you start to give advice,

You have not done what I asked.

When I ask you to listen to me

And you begin to tell me 'why' I shouldn't feel that way,

You are trampling on my feelings.

When I ask you to listen to me

And you feel you have to do something to

Solve my problems,

You have failed me, strange as that may seem.

Listen! All I ask is that you listen,

Not talk, nor do - just hear me.

And I can do for myself - I'm not helpless

I may be discouraged and faltering, but not helpless.

When you do something for me, that I can

And need to do for myself,

You contribute to my fear and weakness,

But when you accept as a simple fact that I do feel what I feel,

No matter how rational

Then I quit trying to convince you

And can get into the business of understanding

What's behind this rational feeling?

When that's clear,

The answers are obvious and I don't need advice.

Irrational feelings makes sense when we

Understand what's behind them.

So please listen, and just hear me, and if you

Want to talk,

Wait a minute for your turn,

And I'll listen to you.

FORGIVENESS

Forgiveness releases you from the past that no longer defines you. Allow yourself to move on - Cheryl Richardson

Within each of us there is a child longing for its mother. For whatever reason your mother wasn't able to love you in the way you wanted, when you are able to forgive her you draw a line between childhood and adulthood. Separating yourself from the past and becoming fully present in the here and now, you are able to move on from the hurt place inside yourself.

For as long as you hold onto your pain, you are not completely whole. Part of you remains split off in the past and at the mercy of your emotions, thoughts and feelings. In the absence of forgiveness it is you who suffers. The best way to resolve conflicts you've had with your mother is through forgiveness. By forgiving, you are able to release emotional baggage from the past and you will feel lighter, freer and more joyous about life.

In the romantic comedy film *'Because I Said So',* Diane Keaton plays the role of an overbearing mother with three daughters. You can hear her plaintive cry *"motherhood is the most impossible task, I was only trying to protect you from being me."* There may be times when your mother means well, but if she is interfering in this way, her attention becomes pressurising, embarrassing and unwanted. However, when you are able to explore in order to see beyond those things which annoy you there is often a loving meaning behind her actions and behaviours.

The price we pay for not forgiving

Not forgiving, means we remain connected to a person, event or situation. We keep the story alive, as if it were happening in this very moment. We are hurting ourselves by not forgiving. Our hearts and minds become hardened. We operate from a victim mode and the energy of feeling we are being victimised, spills over into all areas of our lives. We stay inside the pain, focused on injustice, trapped within the prison of hurt, attached to despair, locked into the past and frozen in time. In this space, there is no room for personal growth or relationships to improve.

Forgiving means you care about yourself enough to unlock yourself from the confinement of limiting thoughts, feelings and emotions. Forgiving puts you in control, it releases the pain and sets you free, free to live the life you dream of and deserve.

Forgiveness is giving up the hope that the past could be any different - Oprah Winfrey

Perhaps you may also need to forgive yourself for past actions, words and deeds in relation to your mother. This is an opportunity to work through your own forgiveness process using these questions to gain insight into your underlying emotions.

- **What does forgiveness mean to you?**
- **How has forgiving another person benefitted you in the past?**
- **How has someone forgiving you been an asset to you?**
- **What grudges do you have towards your mother that would benefit from forgiveness?**
- **What do you need to forgive yourself for?**
- **What is the cost of not forgiving yourself or your mother?**
- **What emotions do you hold onto when you choose not to forgive?** *(anger, fear, hate etc)*
- **How do these emotions limit you?**
- **What would you need to stop doing in order to forgive?**
- **What would you need to start doing in order to forgive?**
- **How will forgiving your mother in particular benefit you personally in the short and long-term?**

I have worked with many daughters over the years, who have held onto anger, grudges, hatred, frustration, spite, injustice, jealousy and fear because of something that happened in their past. It has been they who have kept the story alive and in doing so, the emotions and physical feelings related to the problem. Our bodies bear the burden of holding on to the past, often manifesting as ill-health and *dis-ease.*

The thought of forgiving your mother may evoke many strong emotions for you. It does not mean you agree after all with what she said, did or didn't do - this is not the case. Forgiveness gives you the opportunity to choose your thoughts, reactions and outcomes, based on what you want, not on what you don't want. Forgiveness gives you the wings to fly free and enables you to let go of the hurt, the pain and bitterness you have been holding onto.

Forgiveness is the greatest gift you can give to yourself. Forgiveness gets you past the past, so you live your life in the now.

Forgiveness could relate to something your mother did, didn't do, something she said or didn't say, or how she has behaved towards you. If this exercise is difficult for you, start by forgiving yourself for not wanting to forgive using EFT, until the emotional intensity decreases. (See Chapter Six for the EFT process)

What is it you need to forgive?

- **Past hurts from childhood**
- **Disappointing relationships growing up**
- **Times of emotional challenge with your mother in adulthood**

Use EFT to tap through all of your points, speaking out loud to include the name of the person you want to work towards forgiving, or use the title 'my mother', 'my mum' etc. You may simply prefer to copy out the statements adding endings which apply to your own circumstances.

I forgive myself for not wanting to forgive *'my mum, my mother or name of person/people here'.....*

- **Even though it's hard to forgive** *'my mum, my mother, name of person/people here'* **I'm working towards forgiving her to set myself free**
- **I might be able to forgive my mum.....**
- **I could probably forgive my mum.....**

- **I could someday forgive my mum.....**
- **I could consider forgiving my mum.....**
- **There is a possibility I could forgive my mum.....**
- **I might be able to forgive** *'my mum, my mother or name of person/people here'* **someday.......**
- **Maybe I could let go of not forgiving mum.....**
- **Maybe '***my mum, my mother or name of person/people here'* **was just doing the best she could and I forgive her**
- **Maybe I could forgive** *'my mum, my mother or name of person/people here'*
- **Maybe I could forgive myself for.....** *(e.g. my choices, my own mistakes, my actions, my behaviours)*
- **Maybe I didn't know any better and I forgive myself for.....**
- **I'm not agreeing with what** *'my mum, my mother or name of person/people here'* **said or did - though I choose to forgive her, so I can be free from hurting myself with this memory**
- **I no longer want to be a prisoner in this memory and I choose forgiveness now.....**
- **Forgiveness means letting go of the past and I choose this for myself right now.....**
- **I choose to forgive.....**
- **I am willing to forgive.....**
- **I forgive** *'my mum, my mother or name of person/people here'* **right now...**

If you have been holding on to anger, resentment, hatred and pain or any other intense and limiting emotion which has stopped you from forgiving, applying EFT will support you in reducing the emotional intensity and working through the unresolved emotion.

As well as improving relationships, the benefits gained from forgiving include: a reduction in anxiety and stress, a stronger immune system, healthier heart, reduction in physical and emotional pain, lowering of blood pressure, fewer symptoms of depression, greater spiritual and psychological well-being and higher self-esteem. The *Journal of Behavioural Medicine* offers further insights into the benefits of forgiveness. As you let go of grudges, you no longer determine your life by how you've been hurt.

GIFTS FROM YOUR MOTHER

The greatest gift my mother ever gave me is life - Wendy Fry

You might be surprised to learn just how many gifts your mother has passed on to you - whether it is something physical as in amazing health, being a fast runner or an excellent swimmer, or speaking a language fluently. Perhaps it is having the ability to think on your feet and be efficient etc. These gifts may also present themselves as practical skills, maybe you share a love of baking, gardening, animals, nature, singing, or homemaking. There are so many gifts your mother will have passed down to you whether you are aware of them or not.

In *Remembering Mother, Finding Myself,* Patricia Commins, shares insights from clinical psychologist Dr Patricia Garrity, who calls these connections with our mothers *"cherishable memories."* As daughters, we are able to remember the nurturing presence of our mothers and bring this influence into our every day experience if we choose to. Remember too, that life doesn't always have to be serious. You can laugh at the fact that you share negative traits with your mother – like being a perfectionist, too quick to over react, or a control freak etc.

I know that my mother's nurturing skills were demonstrated by providing a hot meal each day, having our clothes washed and ironed and in keeping a clean and tidy home. Following in her footsteps, my home is clean and organised, I get things done, I can multi-task and have great attention to detail. I only wish my lemon meringue pie was as good as hers, but I thank her for all these gifts as it was her way of showing she cared.

If you don't remember much about your mother, you may be able to ask her friends or other family members, about the pleasures and passions she enjoyed. Not only does asking others to share the things your mother enjoyed doing keep her memory alive but the insights discovered are gifts by way of learning about her life and how you remain connected through shared interests and pastimes. You can re-connect in love by doing the very things she used to enjoy. What brought her joy may also bring you comfort.

It's possible you have kept hold of cards and gifts your mother gave you, heirlooms which have been passed down, or special keepsakes which you hold dear. Some of us may not be fortunate enough to have these things depending on circumstances. Finding ways to connect with your mother and recognising the gifts shared will not always be physical but rather having a connection energetically. If there are photographs and family mementos which you have not yet had an opportunity to look through you might find some hidden treasures you were unaware of and gain awareness into your mother's life which you never knew about. In learning more about your mother, you learn more about yourself.

Lorna Case Study

Lorna came to work with me for support in overcoming stress and depression

Lorna had a wonderful relationship with her mother. It was the kind of relationship where mother and daughter were friends but they had healthy boundaries. Mary, Lorna's mother, was an encourager. Mary supported Lorna to live life to the full and to experiment with being all she could be. While Mary was alive, Lorna found herself excelling at school, she was sporty, well liked by her peers and was confident. She achieved much and went on to be a teacher like her mother. She later married and had two daughters. Lorna felt 'she had it all'. She was in a stable job she loved, had a supportive husband, happy kids and good friends. But then, her mother died suddenly. Lorna came to me stressed, depressed and feeling as though life wasn't worth living without her mother. Grief work can be delicate and so working slowly with Lorna, we uncovered different ways to keep memories of her mother alive whilst at the same time, finding closure around her mother's sudden death. Lorna had not been able to say goodbye in the physical sense and she needed to find new ways to fully separate from her mother and understand that she could stand on her own two feet and carry on living a happy life.

Lorna had always been a creative soul; she spoke fondly of her treasured photo albums, things her mother had made for her to wear and recipes passed down through the generations, as well as mementos she had from her grandmother (her mother's mother). We discussed different ways of working through her pain. As Lorna was artistic and had a great eye for colour, detail and collage work, she decided to make some artwork which she called 'Mother's Love. Lorna found this project was a really enjoyable way to record happy memories and it also gave her the emotional release she needed.

Lorna spent many happy afternoons making a collage of her memories. She was able to scan and print photos, use pieces of fabric and include snippets of information from her mother's and grandmother's past. She kept her mother's memory alive through her creative pursuits and by asking family members to talk about her mother and to share their own happy memories of her. Her artwork allowed her to feel and express the buried emotions she had kept inside after her mother's death.

Although Mary was no longer physically there to support Lorna, she came to realise she had everything inside of her she needed to continue to build on the positive life and love which had been handed down. She learnt how to nurture herself in times of stress, she grew more confident in herself and her abilities without her mother's support and acknowledgement. Lorna made it her mission to show the same love and care towards her daughters as Mary had shown her.

There are so many different ways to heal. Lorna's way was through artistic expression. For you, it might be journaling, writing poetry, carrying on the family traditions through baking, gardening, singing etc. It's never too late to have a happy childhood and if your own upbringing wasn't as happy as Lorna's, I want you to know it's never too late to make positive change.

FINDING PEACE

It isn't enough to talk about peace. One must believe in it. And it isn't enough to believe in it. One must work at it - Eleanor Roosevelt

Peace comes from within; it is not something someone else can give to you. Completing the inner work and exercises shared throughout *Mothers and Daughters* will aid in healing your mother wound and finding inner peace. We do not have to be what we have always believed ourselves to be. We can begin to change the patterns in our behaviours and responses in relation to our mothers.

Through sharing our experiences woman to woman and adult to adult, there is so much to gain. Communicating with the intention of understanding and transforming our relationships with our mothers, we can move beyond the pain of birth, childhood and adulthood. We allow ourselves a sense of peace in being able to openly express all of who we are and allow our mothers to do the same.

Whether you are still striving for your mother's approval, acceptance or love, even though she's gone or are working through remaining anger around past arguments or guilt, allow these emotions to surface. This will help you to deal with any controversy concerning your mother and her death. By re-parenting yourself and becoming your very own inner-mother, you will become gentler and more accepting of yourself, free to nurture and love yourself for who you are in your own right. Acceptance and forgiveness of yourself and your mother pave the path to peace.

"My life's work has crystallized into one single overarching idea. It is the idea of three invisible connectors: the space, the bridge and the encounter. When people make these three invisible connectors visible in their lives, and embrace them fully, the "miracle" of connection happens. The space is the relational space "between" people. In order to honour that space, one must cross the bridge, and bring one's full and authentic presence to the world of the "other". And in doing so, the perfect conditions are established to create a true "meeting", an encounter of the souls. Once the space has been honoured, and the bridge has been crossed, a genuine nourishing and fulfilling relationship is established." - Hedy Schleifer *(for those of you interested in Hedy's work, she has many insightful talks available on YouTube)*

THE AGING OR UNWELL MOTHER

It's being here now that's important. There is no past and there's no future. Time is a very misleading thing. All there is ever, is the now. We can gain experience from the past,

but we can't relive it; and we can hope for the future, but we don't know if there is one - George Harrison

The emotional and physical health of your mother may fluctuate as you both go through life. Recognising this as inevitable and being prepared for these changes as she ages, will serve you at least in being able to set boundaries or to become more flexible with those already set. You may be able to work out a routine for making contact and supporting her which suits you both.

If your mother is still in your life, this will be an opportunity for you to discuss openly and honestly what you can realistically provide for each other. There may be circumstances beyond your control which do not allow for this conversation to take place, if this is the case it's about stepping back and doing the best you can and finding out what other sources of help are available to you and your mother if you wish to be involved in her well-being. Chapter Five offers you 10 steps to set healthy personal boundaries, which will offer you the opportunity to speak assertively with your mother and let her know the limitations of what you can and can't provide for her.

Your mother will have her own unmet childhood needs and she may voice these for the first time when she finds herself immobile, helpless and afraid. Physical and mental health usually decline as a natural part of the aging process. As a result, your mother's demands upon you may well increase. Your mother might gradually lose the ability to care for herself. Doing basic things such as washing and dressing, preparing meals and even walking if she becomes infirm or disabled, are things to take into account. These changes will influence your mother's outlook on life.

As your mother ages, her clarity and speed of thought may not be so sharp or quick and she may find her life changing rapidly as she loses her independence. She may require more help from you such as shopping, lifts to medical appointments and help around the home. How much you can do or are willing to do, will depend on your free time and how much you actually want to do things for her. Setting boundaries at such a time might be difficult, though if you aren't clear about how much you can or can't do, you may find your own life slipping by as you care for your mother.

I have known daughters who have cared for their mothers for more than forty years. They have been the dutiful daughter for so long that they have no other sense of identity or life of their own.

Stacey Case Study

Stacey came to me for support to manage stress and ill-health

Stacey's mother Ann had never been a well woman, she'd had several health complaints since childhood. As a single parent, Ann relied heavily on Stacey to be her carer. From an early age, Stacey would help her mother to cook, clean their home, run errands and also attend her mother's medical appointments as there was no additional family support in place to help Ann with her needs. It seemed natural to Stacey to care for her mother; it's all she ever knew. She didn't complain and simply accepted her duty without questioning it.

Ann's biggest fear was dying; Stacey too would worry about her mother's health and longevity. With no one to talk to about her mother's predicament, Stacey carried on with her silent role of carer - passive, loyal, giving, and feeling her mother's distress as if it were her own.

Stacey came to me in her 40's, suffering from stress and ill-health. Working full-time on top of caring for her mother, she was depressed, overweight, suffered anxiety and panic attacks and generally felt as though she was losing the plot. Stacey very much wanted to have a relationship but it felt wrong for her to leave her mother and begin building a life for herself. Stacey had never had a boyfriend or even left her home for a holiday or weekend break. She was running on empty and desperately needed some help.

After discussing Stacey's upbringing and how it was that she felt totally responsible for her mother, including her health, well-being and living circumstances, Stacey knew something had to change. I taught Stacey EFT to manage her emotions, panic attacks and emotional overwhelm, as well as encouraging her to seek outside support in caring for her mother. This was not something Stacey had ever considered. We worked on guilt, fear and uncertainty using EFT and I also helped her to compose a letter to her mother in order to set some new boundaries.

Through finding out what care and support was available in the community, a care package was arranged for Ann. Stacey was not only able to enjoy time to herself, her mother formed new friends amongst her care team and joined local groups being picked up from her home by the various charities and returned again. Stacey and her mother also had a holiday as well as individual breaks organised by a carer's charity. Their relationship has become healthier as they had new experiences to share. If you find yourself in a similar situation to Stacey or Ann, please do consider what external support beyond the family unit is available.

After joining a walking group, swimming regularly and using EFT, Stacey's low mood improved and she now enjoys rather than resents the time spent with her mother. Checking in recently, Stacey and Ann are both doing well, Stacey is now dating for the first time in her life and mother and daughter are happier as a result of making some changes and seeking the help and support of others.

If your mother is not able to meet her own needs, it is unlikely that she will be able to meet yours. It is unfair to expect her to do so if her health and emotional stability are in decline. This in itself may bring up unresolved anger from the past of those other times when your mother hasn't been there for you. Inner work is important and if your mother can't be there for you in the way you wish her to be, you can learn how to parent yourself and find love from other sources while giving your mother as much love as you can willingly give in her in her later years.

Holding each other accountable to meet each other's needs, has to stop at some point, as it isn't always healthy to place demands on each other which can never be met. Clear communication needs to take place to clarify what each of you can give to the other. Whether it be financial support, housing, your physical energy, time or care, setting clear boundaries with each other leaves no room for vagueness or trying to read each other's minds. Making time to check out local services, care provision, outside agencies and applying for funding for care (such as attendance allowance) are considerations which you may wish to discuss with your mother.

Grieving the loss of your mother's youth and vibrancy, as well as acknowledging she may no longer have the ability to care for you as much as she did is also something to be aware of. She may well still be alive, but if you feel she is gradually slipping away, your hopes of what you wanted her to be also need to be mourned.

Many daughters whose mothers have lost the ability to communicate have shared with me how difficult this is. They have lost communication with their mothers and they are in limbo, having a mother physically present in body but with her mind somewhere else. Sometimes it's hard to know what to do when you see your mother changing before your very eyes. Roles are reversed; care giving roles are exchanged. There is a sense of despair in knowing you can never claw back the relationship you had or find the one you hoped for.

Where possible, before it gets to this point, having open communication and asking your mother what she needs and letting her know what you can provide or organise, will make choices easier to make later on. Looking at your mother through new eyes, crossing the bridge to meet her where she is at this stage of her life, contributes to your own healing as well as hers. Holding grudges doesn't serve any positive purpose and simply gets in the way of closing the distance between you.

It is possible that your mother has not come to terms with losing her independence. You may find her getting very frustrated. Having empathy rather than anger towards her as she grapples with her changing situation is far better than arguing or making demands which she cannot fulfil. I have known daughters spend some beautiful quality time with their ageing or un-well mothers, while seeking additional support from family, friends, extended family and care agencies. If this has been discussed during the earlier stages of deterioration, mothers and daughters say it has been easier to plan ahead and embrace changes as they come. By being flexible and embracing change, you will find a deep inner strength and a level of compassion you never knew you had.

Your mother may well want to make peace with you at this stage. For the sake of both of you moving on from past pain, if she offers you the olive branch, please do consider taking it and making your peace with her. You are not condoning her past behaviour, you are simply recognising that as her health declines and her life comes to an end, it is time for the resentment you feel towards her to end too. By choosing to let go of the past, your relationship can flourish in new ways and you will be able to remember your mother with a touch of love.

If you have been a carer as a child, or you lost your mother at an early age, *Motherless Daughters: The Legacy of Loss* by Hope Edelman is a wonderful read which will support you as you work through your emotional pain.

SAYING GOODBYE TO YOUR MOTHER

We can never obtain peace in the outer world until we make peace with ourselves - Dali Lama

The importance of the grieving process can never be overestimated. Not to grieve, prolongs the agony and left unresolved, spills over into other areas of your life. Allowing yourself to feel the full range of emotions in relation to your mother will aid you in your grieving process. Whether it is grieving the happy times shared now she has gone, or your anger, sadness, regret, guilt or shame, grief work can begin, even when your mother is still alive. Being honest with yourself and giving yourself permission to release what needs to come out, prepares you for your mother's physical decline and death.

Although your mother may have been doing the best she could in raising you, unless you grieve the loss of the mother you hoped for, unhealed emotions will remain in your current relationship with your mother, or linger even after she has gone from this world. One of my favourite quotes is by Sir Walter Scott *'oh what a tangled web we weave'.* It seems to sum up the complicated and tangled bonds we form with our mothers.

In retrospect and seeing the bigger picture of what your mother experienced in her lifetime, what do you notice about your feelings towards her?

- **How have you judged your mother in terms of her parenting?**
- **What unfair demands might you have made on her?**

- **What criticisms do you have of your mother's actions, behaviours and parenting style?**
- **How do you suffer when you hold on to negative emotions towards your mother?**
- **Knowing what you now know about your mother, what were your previous limiting beliefs about your relationship with her?**
- **What new beliefs will be more beneficial to you when you are able to accept she didn't live up to your expectations?**
- **What would you say to your mother right now, if you gave yourself the freedom and permission to say anything?**
- **What is the most positive impact your mother has had on you?**
- **What golden moments have you shared?**
- **What is your best memory?**
- **What are you grateful to your mother for?**
- **How can you use your experience with your mother to change your life or other people's lives for the better?**
- **If your mother is no longer part of your life, what would you say to her right now?**
- **What were the missing events you needed in childhood?**
- **If you make it your responsibility to heal your past and give yourself love, time, nurturance and care, what would change?**
- **How can you best meet your needs now as an adult?**
- **How will making this change benefit you?**

There are various ways to say goodbye to our mother's physical body when she dies and also to incorporate saying goodbye to the mother we hoped for.

I will share with you some strategies to release the past, acknowledge your mother and the relationship you had with her and also some techniques to help you heal. More tools and resources can be found in Chapters Five and Six as you read through.

Writing a Letter to Your Mother

More than kisses, letters mingle souls - John Donne

Whether your mother is no longer with you through bereavement, because you are estranged or because circumstances keep you apart, you might wish to write her a letter. Please consider if you actually want to send this letter or whether you simply write it as a means of personal closure.

If you are bereaved, you will obviously not be able to send the letter, however, writing it will offer you a sense of release.

1. **Begin your letter with a friendly form of address (Dear Mum/Mother...)**
2. **Keep the tone of your letter positive and good-natured**
3. **Refer to any positive memories you have of her (if there have been few then thank your mother for giving you the gift of life)**
4. **Voice your enjoyment of any positive experiences shared**
5. **Express your sense of loss communicating honestly how you feel**
6. **If your letter is in response to a difficult moment in the relationship, avoid making negative comments, keeping the tone light and as positive as possible**

7. **Offer your mother your good wishes for the future (even if you are bereaved, sending your mother your positive intentions and good wishes aids to sooth you). If you are estranged and do not wish to open communication channels, this is also a way of saying 'goodbye' perhaps more positively than if you had done it face to face. There are lots of different versions of letters which you can write (sent or not) for the purpose of healing. Practice the craft of writing and journaling to express your thoughts and feelings. However, if you intend to send the letter, then leave it alone for a week and review it afresh before you send it.**

Poetry as a Form of Expression

It is beautiful to express love and even more beautiful to feel it – Dejan Stojanović

Writing poetry is another way to express how you feel. Whether it is writing poetry you send to your mother or writing as a means of releasing pent-up emotions, poetry can take many shapes and forms. Whatever you write, it isn't about rhyming or perfect prose, it's about allowing yourself to be who you really are and expressing your truth in whatever way you want to.

If you write something you think you would like to share with your mother, follow the letter writing guidelines above in order to keep your words positive. By all means have a separate rant on paper but consider if it will solve anything by sending something attacking, blaming or judgemental. If negative emotions do surface as you write, acknowledge them, allow them to be there and use EFT (Chapter Six) to clear them.

Candle Ceremony

There are two ways of spreading light: to be the candle or the mirror which reflects it - Buddha

Burning a pink candle is said to aid emotional healing. Pink represents love in its purest form. It is the colour of universal love. Burning a pink candle can be used for self-healing to ease anxiety and reduce depression. Pink candles also carry the associations of self-love, joy, friendship and harmony. I love pink because it is the colour of femininity and spiritual healing.

Of course, it will be a personal choice if and when you decide to burn a pink candle. This may be something you do once, on special occasions in remembrance of your mother, when you feel you need to, or as part of a specific ceremony to honour your mother's life or to say goodbye to her. There are no set rules here. Personally, I like to create a clean space in an area of my choice inside my home. I place fresh flowers in a vase (my mother's). I sometimes have photographs close by which capture memories of when we were together and looked happy and relaxed in each other's company. Sometimes, I just burn the candle and send love and light to my mother.

You don't need to follow a religion or belief to perform this ceremony. I share it here as a self-healing opportunity as a way to say goodbye to your mother or the mother you hoped for. I have found this to be an important part of grief work and an opportunity for self-reflection and a way of remembering my mother and some of our golden moments.

GOLDEN NUGGETS FOR SELF-HEALING

I must choose between despair and Energy - I choose the latter - John Keats

EFT (Emotional Freedom Technique) is an energy-based technique aiding you to release emotional build-up. Many female celebrities such as actress, Whoopi Goldberg, Soprano Rachel Cobb, Bond Girl Naomi Harris, actress Nicole Kidman and singer-songwriters Madonna and Lily Allen are all using EFT to provide emotional release or to overcome a variety of problems. The Guild of Energists (GoE) provides some wonderful research and studies in this area. See Chapter Six for full details relating to the GoE and EFT. As you work though *Mothers and Daughters* addressing past hurts, fears, disappointments and regrets in relation to your mother, you will find a deep sense of relief when you finally let go of the past. EFT is one of the best energy-based techniques I know; it's easy to learn and it is there at your finger tips whenever you need it.

My first book Find YOU, Find LOVE: Get to the heart of love and relationships using EFT, offers an array of information, tools and techniques to help you find love within yourself. You can download some free resources related to the book at www.wendyfry.com see appendix for further details on self-help resources.

Talking it Through

The best way out is always through - Robert Frost

Talking about your thoughts, feelings and emotions will always aid the healing process. Finding a non-judgemental friend who will listen and offer support, or working with a qualified therapist to help you ease the pain from the past, will be one of the best investments you ever make.

Writing all your thoughts down in a journal is another way of speaking, if you feel you are not ready to work with a therapist.

Journaling

Journal writing is the voyage to the interior – Christina Baldwin

There are so many benefits to journaling. It clears your mind and gives you a new perspective. It is a means of stress reduction, improving personal growth, healing, enhancing intuition and creativity and offers an opportunity for you to capture your life story.

The things you may fear saying to your mother or others, can be voiced freely in your journal. This is your private diary to write in, read back and reflect on whenever you feel like it. Alternatively, you can simply let it all out and then destroy the entries as you go along.

How to Journal

1. **Make a commitment to write every day (for up to 20 minutes on two sides of A4 paper). Pick a quieter time of day or include it as part of your self-care routine**
2. **Make it easy, keep a notebook or pen and paper close to hand to write down your thoughts as they come to you**
3. **You might wish to name your journal, 'My Memories', 'My Reflections' or 'My Self-care Journal'. There is no need to name it if you do not want to, as it may include a combination of all these things, once you begin the writing process**
4. **Pick a theme to write about each day (for instance, writing about happy times spent with your mother, or about the things you've learnt from her which have been helpful to you)**
5. **You could create a timeline in your journal and make a record of your childhood years right up to adulthood, including in the account, areas of your past which have caused you pain and which can be worked on through EFT**
6. **Write uncensored and record whatever feels right for you. Let the words flow freely without worrying about grammar, punctuation or spelling. Handwriting too, can be freestyle; you may even like to write with your non-dominant hand (i.e. if you are right-handed, try it with your left).** *The Creative Journal* by Lucia Capacchione

details use of your dominant and non-dominant hand to further communicate and express emotion

7. **Use your journal as you wish. It can be used alongside this book or separately, as you see fit**
8. **Through use of journaling, you are taking care of yourself, helping your own healing and expressing all of who you are**

If you want to read more on the benefits of journaling, I recommend Kathleen Adams, *Journal to the Self: Twenty-two Paths to Personal Growth.*

Please do consider these forms of self-expression and those shared in Chapter Six if you need further closure.

To conclude Mining for Gold, it is my sincerest wish you find some buried gold and memories to treasure. You never know what riches you will find when you take the time to understand your mother and honour the life she gave you.

Chapter 5

Living With Purpose

THE BEGINNING OF YOU

Despite our entrance into the world, or even because of it, we become the magical people we are. Each and every one of us has a story to tell about birth, life and death. Now is the time to tell and transform our stories - Sharon King, Heal Your Birth, Heal Your Life

I want you to know, *you* matter! Whether or not your mother has shown you love, I know there is a place within you that wants to believe you are lovable, worthy and whole. Repeat after me, *'I matter'*, say it again and again. Let the tears flow if they need to, by doing so you are setting yourself free from the past and beginning anew.

If your mother is deceased you may think you do not have an opportunity to change the past. The truth is you change your past by changing your future. When you explore what has shaped you, accept your experiences and then commit to making the rest of your life the best of your life, so much will change. Now is the time to let go of the past, take the lessons you've learned and turn them into stepping stones which will lead you to an amazing future.

Every ending is a new beginning, the beginning of you.

EMERGENCE AS AN ADULT

Human beings are not born once and for all on the day their mothers give birth to them, but...life obliges them over and over again to give birth to themselves - Gabriel Garcia

Being aware of the differences in your relationship with your mother, recognising why they have been there and learning how to transform them is the beginning of adulthood. If you've found yourself searching for love and meaning, this chapter will aid in further healing. However, you must deal with the past in order to create an inspiring future.

Your mother is still a part of you, within you and perhaps beside you on this journey. How you decide to use your past experiences, will either make or break you. It may take strength and courage to emerge from the wounded child into an adult who no longer needs her mother's love. Staying in the mindset of a needy child will limit you in many ways. When you are able to *'grow yourself back up'* and personally nurture the child within you, you transform not only your past but your future too.

In Chapter Two, I shared details of the ACE study which considered the Risk Factors of Adverse Childhood Experiences. You may wish to take the ACE Test as detailed in the appendix yourself for greater insights.

The study also looks at Family Protective Factors, which I will share here. The protective factors in our lives are what shape us into healthy functioning adults. Our own parents of course may not have had "ideal" circumstances in which to raise us and this list describes the ideal.

Family and Community Protective Factors

These are the ideal factors according to The ACE Study.

Protective factors when present contribute to the health and well-being of children and families. Research has found that focusing on positive factors, is more productive than focusing on risk factors alone. (See appendix for information on the study)

- **Supportive family environment and social networks**
- **Nurturing and attachment**
- **Parental resilience**
- **Knowledge of parenting and child development**

- **Household rules and child monitoring**
- **Parental employment**
- **Adequate housing**
- **Access to health care and social services**
- **Caring adults outside of the family who can serve as role models or mentors**
- **Communities that support parents and take responsibility for preventing abuse**

Your experience as a child may have contained some - or none - of the above. If you were lacking in any area, it is still possible to “re-parent” yourself as an adult and provide for yourself by meeting your own needs. Having an awareness of these protective factors also offers insights into healthy parenting if you decide to be a parent. These might be aspects of your life and environment to strive towards, bearing in mind that these factors are said to be crucial for both parent and child to fare well.

Here are some examples of celebrities who have prospered, despite not having an ideal childhood. I find their stories about overcoming hardship, insightful and motivational. It goes to prove our potential power to overcome those limiting beliefs learnt in childhood. Oprah Winfrey, Lucille Ball, Jeanne Moreau, Marilyn Monroe and J.K Rowling - to name but a few - of the female daughters who have survived personal struggle and hardship and gone on not only to change their lives, but also to make a difference through their presence in the world. We would all benefit from using these women to inspire us, recognising that despite personal trauma and tough childhoods, it is still possible to rise above those setbacks and enjoy success.

UNDERSTANDING YOURSELF AND FULFILLING YOUR OWN NEEDS

Don't be afraid. Change is such a beautiful thing, said the butterfly - Sabrina Newby

When we forgive our mothers, we grow individually and collectively as daughters. Owning and accepting past experiences and unleashing ourselves from the pain our mothers have caused us (directly or indirectly) will mean we take back our personal power, aiding further separation from our mothers whatever our age. We no longer spend our time and energy being a victim of circumstance; we grow beyond the pain of our past and focus on where we are now and what we want for the future.

By getting to know our mothers, we begin to understand even more about ourselves and how to meet our own needs independent of her. There is such strength in taking personal responsibility and mothering ourselves truly and completely.

Understand who you are as a person

The greatest barrier to self-understanding is our fear of knowing the truth within ourselves, but when we do understand ourselves, we greatly enhance what we are capable of - Carla H Krueger

Identifying who you are as a person regardless of your mother's opinion or judgement, will serve you as you develop beyond the status of a daughter.

Children are told things about themselves which are often said thoughtlessly in the heat of the moment. Such comments impact the child's self-identity. They may go on to form limiting beliefs about themselves which they carry through to adulthood. Exploring the section on limiting beliefs and how to change them (Chapter Six) will further support you.

You might like to use the following exercise to further explore who you are as an individual in your own right

- **Who am I?**
- **Who am I beyond my name?**
- **Who am I beyond my role as daughter, sister, mother, aunt etc**
- **What are my character traits? (i.e. empathic, loyal, patient, understanding, humorous etc)**
- **What persona do I portray to the outside world: friends, strangers, partners or your mother?**
- **If I were to be all of who I am, unashamedly, what would I reveal to others which I have up until now, kept hidden?**
- **By being more of who I am and less of who I'm not, how will this benefit me? (i.e. full self-expression, confidence, self-acceptance , pride in self etc)**
- **What actions can I take today and every day which allow me to show the world who I am?**

When you are being true to yourself, you are able to express all of who you are, holding nothing back. This indicates a deep level of self-acceptance and knowing you have the confidence to be yourself, regardless of other people's responses or opinions. The following sections will guide you in understanding your core values, likes and dislikes, hopes and dreams as well as your emotions. Every day, take an action which will stretch you out of your comfort zone and into the zone of being more true to yourself. The more you do it. The easier it becomes to show up as your amazing self!

Uncover your core values

Basically discipline, effort, patience and courage are hugely important core values for kids to grow up embracing - Karen Salmansohn

We all have core values whether we are aware of them or not. Core values are the moral codes or principles we live by in our daily life. Defining your core values helps you to find out what's truly important to you.

My core values in a relationship are love, unity, nurturing, empathy, kindness, appreciation, connection and affection. You may find yours are entirely different based on your own experiences.

To work out your core values

1. **Identify the times when you have been happiest and most proud**
2. **What are the themes which have run through your life when you have felt satisfied**
3. **Determine your top values based on your experience of happiness, pride and fulfilment**
4. **Write all your values down in no particular order (it's helpful to write each one down separately on post-it notes for the next part of the exercise)**
5. **Compare each value with the next and ask yourself 'If I could satisfy just one of these values, which would I choose?' Keep working through the notes, until you have an order of preferences.**
6. **Check your values order. When making decisions about your relationships or life in general, be sure to be taking actions and making choices which meet your values**

Uncovering your core values means you can decide what's best for you. Living your core values daily, puts you on track to living your best possible life. The closer you live in accordance with your ideals, the nearer you are to having happy and harmonious relationships. Understanding your core values opens up an opportunity for discussion about whether or not those you have relationships with, accept your core values and that you accept theirs. *Dr Gary Chapman's The 5 Love Languages for Children,* shares greater insights into how we communicate our preferences in relationships, when he discusses the five love languages in depth. In my opinion, these love languages portray your core values.

Get to know your likes and dislikes

When attachments increase too much, dislike will arise - Dada Bhagwan

Likes and dislikes are similar to core values. Our mothers may think we like a certain thing – but maybe we do not. If you mentioned once that you really enjoyed her bread pudding your mother may make a special effort to offer you more of the same when you visit. However, maybe you no longer want the pudding, because you are trying to reduce in weight or have developed a food intolerance. You try to explain, but feel your mother isn't listening – whilst she feels "unloved" because you are turning down her pudding. This is where clear, ongoing, communication is needed. Voicing your likes, dislikes, preferred options and talking about the things which make you happy, all contribute to having a healthy relationship.

The positive "feedback sandwich" when expressing likes and dislikes to your mother, might go something like this. *"Mum I love that you make something special for pudding when I visit, Your bread pudding and cream is delicious but I've recently become intolerant to wheat unfortunately. Would it be possible to have one of your lovely fruit salads instead?"*

Or, *"Mum I love catching up with you each week, but talking every day is a real stretch on my time, what with work and the kids. I'd love it if we could make Sunday afternoons between 4pm and 6pm our time to catch up and I promise, you will have my undivided attention, thank you".*

If we don't communicate our likes and dislikes, we end up doing things resentfully. If we do not voice thoughts and feelings, we cannot strengthen our relationships. It will serve you well to voice what you would like in your relationship and also ask your mother if there is anything about you and your behaviour which annoys her. Honesty (not unkindness) will go a long way to improve the relationship.

Follow your hopes and dreams

Go confidently in the direction of your dreams. Live the life you have imagined - Henry David Thoreau

It's never too late to dream a new dream – or, for that matter, take action to realise an old one. Children never stop daydreaming, fantasising and creating stories about how they want their lives to be. When we mature and grow into adulthood, real life takes over and we forget to invest in our fancies. We believe we have to put up with what we've got and play small.

Perhaps you are at a point in your life when you are approaching a certain age and re-evaluating your life. How far you've come, where you are now and where you want to be? If, as a teenager, you wanted to study art and never got round to it, now might be the time to find out more.

I have known many adult daughters who start new careers as teachers, midwives, communications experts, chefs, interior designers etc. When a woman no longer has to be a dutiful daughter she can devote all her energies in other directions and will very likely find new and exciting opportunities.

What is it you really want?

1. **State your goal in the positive** *(i.e. "what I want to achieve is…."*
2. **Write it down**
3. **Be precise** *(separate what is important from what is irrelevant or a distraction)*
4. **Set priorities** *(and motivate yourself by breaking the priorities down into individual tasks)*
5. **Keep actions small, realistic and achievable**
6. **When you've achieved your goal, take time to celebrate** *(build your confidence and set a new goal)*

Having short and long-term goals gives you something to strive for and celebrating your successes along the way, builds confidence and resilience to achieve those things which are important to you. If you feel blocked from achieving your goals in any way, work out what's stopping you from reaching your desired outcome. EFT can be used to clear any resistances - including self-sabotage, fear and confusion.

Listen to your body and emotions

Take care of your body. It's the only place you have to live - Jim Rohn

Your mind and body has been a shelter to you for many years. Like a filing cabinet your mind and body has stored everything you've ever been through. Whether you remember those things consciously or not, subconsciously your experiences are stored within. Getting to know your body in terms of aches and pains, physical discomfort, *dis-ease* and where you hold your emotions (energetically) will aid you well on the road to health and well-being.

During my work as a therapist and energist, when daughters complain of anger, sadness, shame, fear etc, I ask them 'where in your body do you feel this the most?' It's interesting to note sometimes the area of the body where the emotions are stored, also suffers a physical symptom or complaint.

Body as witness

Reflect on the following questions, making a note in your journal if you wish to.

- **What is your current state of emotional and physical health?**
- **What negative beliefs, thoughts and feelings do you have about your body?**
- **What negative beliefs, thoughts and feelings do you have about becoming emotionally or physically healthy?** *(i.e. "if I get well I will not have the attention or support from others I'm getting now" or "if I get well my mother will make more demands on me and that scares me")*
- **Who or what triggers these beliefs, thoughts and feelings the most?** *(this could be thinking about a memory, a person you know, a social situation, fears for the future or a place where this happens most frequently)*
- **What have been the top three most traumatic events that have impacted your body and your physical and/ or emotional well-being?**
- **Who from your past are you carrying any anger, hatred or resentment towards?**
- **Where do you feel these emotions in your body most strongly?**
- **What are the positive aspects and gains from keeping any current physical or emotional health challenges?**

- **What fears do you have about being well again?**
- **Is anyone else benefitting from you being unwell?**
- **When you think of your symptoms what emotion comes to mind?**
- **If your symptoms went away tomorrow what would you have to do that you might not like doing?**
- **Who or what is holding you back from having a healthy mind and body?**
- **What is preventing you from taking action to improve the way you experience your health and well-being?**
- **How have your beliefs about your mind and body limited you?**
- **What positive and empowering beliefs would you like to have about yourself instead of the above?**

Our bodies have an amazing capacity to store information and emotions. In *"Molecules of Emotion: The Science Behind Mind-Body Medicine"*, Candice Pert writes, *"by simply acknowledging emotions, they are expressed. In being expressed, emotions can be released, even old emotions stored in the body memory. Allowing my emotions to surface into awareness and to be able to name my emotions, is the beginning of emotional exploration. I am moving forward, trying to find my position within the family, within the community and in life."*

Louise L Hay's book *'You Can Heal Your Life'* is also a wonderful reference book if you're ready to learn more about healing your body and healing your life.

REALITY CHECK - MAKING THE BEST OF A BAD SITUATION

When the Japanese mend broken pots they aggrandize the damage filling the cracks with gold. They believe when something has suffered damage and has a history it becomes more beautiful - Barbara Bloom

It takes maturity to understand your mother and who she has become as a result of her own reality. You do not need to follow in her footsteps and can choose how you use your experiences of the mother-daughter relationship.

If your mother was unavailable due to depression, poor health, addiction, overwork or, because of her own grief or unmet needs, it is still possible for you to move past the physical or emotional neglect you have experienced. This does not condone her behaviour, it simply means you are able to move beyond your experiences with your mother and begin to heal. You are no longer being a victim of your past but instead, you are using your past to make you ever stronger.

Will you choose rage or resolution?

When we hold the belief that we are un-loved, we may have attachment and trust issues as well as feeling unsafe in the world. Left unaddressed, this spills over into all our relationships.

Although our past may be considered undesirable, we are able to learn discernment and consider our choices. We can as adults learn to protect ourselves from the unwanted behaviours of others and learn how to create boundaries, so that our choices are in line with our core values and self-worth. Our adverse childhood experiences need not create a negative future.

WHO AM I - WHAT DO I WANT?

When you are balanced and when you listen and attend to the needs of your body, mind and spirit, your natural beauty comes out - Christy Turlington

If we yearn for more love and connection with our mother than she is able to give then, rather like rowing upstream against the tide we will become frustrated and exhausted in our quest. It would serve us better to go with the flow and accept what is. By doing so, we end the inner struggle of wanting more than is available to us. By choosing to end the struggle, we will gain a sense of freedom and inner peace.

Consider what you want for your future using the 'do want', 'don't want' exercise which follows:

Turning your 'don't wants to do wants'

Take some time to reflect on what you are choosing for yourself, not just in this moment but for the future. When you choose these things for yourself from your heart, you open up a fountain of endless love and self-fulfilment. Turn your don't wants into do wants and you will change your energy vibration. The more focussed you are on what you want, the more likely it is you will get it.

Use the exercise below adding your own Do Wants and Don't Wants in the spaces provided

Don't Wants	**Do Wants**
I don't want to feel unloved	I want to love and honour who I am taking full responsibility to meet my needs as an adult
I don't want to continue arguing with my mother	I want to communicate assertively in a calm and clear manner when speaking with my mother

I don't want my mother to keep calling me and dropping round unexpectedly	I want to arrange definite times to see my mother and be able to enjoy her company
I don't want to feel sad and lonely as a result of my mother abandoning me	I want to come to terms with what's happened in my past and to know I'm worth loving regardless of her actions
I don't want to suffer from the past	I want to move on from the past and focus on getting my life back on track

If you find it difficult to state precisely what you want in relation to your mother, please do consider working with a qualified therapist, ideally one who specialises in relationship work who can support you in making lasting positive changes.

EFFECTIVE COMMUNICATION

Words are singularly the most powerful tool available to humanity. We can choose to use this force constructively with words of encouragement, or destructively using words of despair. Words have energy and power with the ability to help, to heal, to hinder, to harm, to humiliate and to humble - Yehuda Berg

All too often in relationships, we say one thing and the other person hears something else. Conflicts and misunderstandings arise if we fail to communicate effectively. Effective communication is more about listening and less about talking. It is about focussing on what you want to say. Understanding the emotions of the speaker through listening to tone of voice, considering the words spoken and concentrating for subtle intonations reveals much about the communicator's message. When a person feels heard and understood, you are able to build more positive relationships.

Learning how to convey or receive a message with positive intention, enables you to communicate or take in difficult messages without creating conflict. As giver and receiver of communication, work towards being clear on what it is you want to communicate, the intention of the message you want to share and the outcome you are hoping for.

Improving communication skills combines assertive expression, understanding your emotions and the emotions of the person you are speaking with, engaged listening, managing your personal stressors in the moment and nonverbal communication (body language, facial expression, body movement, posture, tone of voice, eye movement, breathing and muscle tension).

Managing your own communications when things become heated by staying calm and relaxed helps you to balance your feelings and in turn your behavioural, verbal responses and physical actions.

While effective communication can be learnt, it's more valid when it's spontaneous. The more effort you put in to saying what you mean and meaning what you say builds a solid foundation from which to communicate from. Effective communication is not about forcing your opinions on your mother or winning arguments against her, but the basis of communication should be to consider what it is you want to communicate, the end goal of the communication, while also reflecting on her responses to further understand her.

Being empathic in your conversations whilst still valuing yourself and your personal opinions, staying true to your needs and wants while considering your mother's, allows you an opportunity to feedback positively, expressing your thoughts in an assertive but caring way.

You might find it interesting to notice the different communication styles when you are watching TV, shopping in a supermarket, watching parents interact with their children and also in your workplace. You can learn much from watching others and seeing what does and doesn't work when it comes to effective communication.

SETTING BOUNDARIES

All I can tell you really is if you get to the point where someone is telling you you're not great enough or not good enough, just follow your heart and don't let anyone crush your dream - Patti LaBelle

What is it you want to change?

May I remind you with a nudge, followed by a gentle hug, making changes and setting new boundaries with your mother begins with you. It might mean you have to step out of your comfort zone, feel uncomfortable for a while and face your fears but without making the change to make new choices, nothing will change. You can jump back to Chapter Two if you wish to use the advice on how to speak more assertively.

Reflect on these questions first before reading The 10 Steps to Setting Healthy Personal Boundaries

- **What do you want your mother to stop doing?**

- **What would you like her to start doing?**
- **What do you want her to do differently?**
- **What are you willing to stop doing?**
- **What are you able to start doing?**
- **What can you do differently to improve your relationship?**

In relationships, until we can speak up and communicate our needs clearly, assertively and respectfully, the problems, challenges and the behaviours of those we are in the relationship with, remain the same. When we change the way we communicate consistently, there is every possibility those around us will be influenced by the change and mirror back to us the positive communication.

10 Steps to Setting Healthy Personal Boundaries

1. **Speak from the 'I'.** *("I would like you to listen to what I'm about to say. I intend to make some positive changes in our relationship. I feel we would benefit from putting the past behind us. It would mean so much to me if you are able to hear what I've communicated and consider my requests, thank you for considering this") Saying thank you at the end of a statement like this voices the assumption that the other person will listen and acknowledge your proposal.*
2. **Keep communications in the positive and future tense** *("What I would like is for us to spend some quality time together on our own at least, once a month. I'd like to get to know you better as a person as well as my mother, I believe we would both benefit from this change")*
3. **Clearly identify your boundary. Spend time figuring out what you want before you voice your limits** *(Do you need your mother to stop turning up unannounced or calling you when you're in the middle of preparing an*

evening meal. Would you prefer her to call at a specific time when you are both free?)

4. **Understand why you need a boundary.** What's your motivation and reason for setting this boundary? *(If it's not convenient for your mother to turn up or call without notice, let her know you will have undivided time for her if you can call her at 8pm for 30 minutes once the children are in bed)*

5. **Make your communications clear. Be direct and assertive in your conversation** *(If you fear conflict or confrontation you may not say exactly what you mean, which leaves room for confusion or doubt). It might spare your mother's feelings if you aren't direct and to the point but how will you feel? What is the cost if you do nothing to make this change, who suffers?)*

6. **Don't give long explanations or apologise** *(Setting boundaries isn't something you need to say sorry for and it doesn't have to be a long drawn out process. Short, sharp and clear communications works best. e.g. ("I would like weekends to myself, I need more time to study, thank you for understanding this. I look forward to meeting you on Wednesday afternoons to catch up")*

7. **Remain calm and polite** *(Boundaries are best set outside of an argument, getting into dialogue about making change in the heat of the moment when both of you are angry, neither person can really hear the other. Keep your anger in check and leave all sarcasm and condescending tone out of your communications)*

8. **Start with firm boundaries** *(It's easier to loosen a tight boundary after it's been set rather than trying to tighten a weak boundary, e.g., "I'd prefer it if you don't come into my home when I'm not there. I want the way I've left my home to stay the same, I like it how it is." It's easier at a later date to invite your mother to take a mini-break in*

your home while you are away, on the condition she leaves things as they are, or to pop round an hour before you get home if she wants to watch something not available on her own TV package). Don't overextend yourself or try and 'people please' or agree to commitments you will later have to cancel or do begrudgingly. Get clear from the start.

9. **Address any breaking of boundaries early on.** As soon as a boundary is broken, reset it. Remind your mother of your boundary. *("You may have forgotten mum, I need the weekends to study, I can see you on Wednesday afternoons instead")*

10. **Don't make it personal.** Rather than tell your mother everything you think about her being inconsiderate of your time, your appointments and plans it is far easier to be direct. *("I'm happy to pick you up and take you to Maggie's, but you will need to be ready at 10 a.m")*

It's possible your mother won't welcome these changes though in order for your relationship to improve, it's important to end the struggles you each have within your relationship and find new solutions to old problems.

What's your experience of your mother? Has she been overbearing, bossy, controlling and narcissistic? Or, has she been emotionally distant and physically withdrawn? Getting clear about what you want and communicating this (instead of what you don't want) will serve you well every time.

Daughters and mothers are both guilty of not being able to meet each other's needs at different times throughout their lives. This chapter is about being as realistic as possible about how much you can do for each other. Having clear guidelines of what you want from your relationship with your mother and also considering what your mother may want from you, is the basis for a discussion. You can discuss what is possible and what is not in order to reach a healthy compromise.

Honest and open communication clears up misunderstandings and creates hope for your relationship to improve and flourish. When each of you is able to express your needs and you begin to explore and negotiate with mutual respect things will become much easier.

When you set new boundaries and your mother agrees, then it is about trusting her enough to make the changes you have asked for. Dredging up the past isn't helpful, along with berating, complaining or yelling. To put the past behind you and start afresh with your mother is one of the most healing opportunities you will ever have. You can even agree to disagree on various views and opinions whilst both working towards the common goal of improving your relationship.

Your mother's circumstances could change unexpectedly but it's never too late to set new boundaries over and above agreements already made or indeed, to discuss your relationship anew.

THE CHOICE TO BE ESTRANGED

Do not expect too much from your child and she will grow in your love...But if you push her too much, you will push her away. A child is not yours to own but to raise. She may not be what you want her to be, but she will be what she has to be. Remember what they say, that 'wood may remain twenty years in the water, but it is still not a fish' - Jane Yolen

There may come a time in your life when you do not want to be part of your mother's life. The separation (short or longer term) will allow space for each of you to reflect on the past and find new ways to move beyond conflict and disagreement. It's possible to make the split without hostility, when you are able to communicate effectively why you have chosen to make this decision. You cannot be responsible for your mother's reaction, only your communication.

Many daughters have shared with me that they feel unworthy, second-best, unloved, unheard and disrespected in their relationships with their mothers. They have stated there is nothing there for them, physically or emotionally, which validates them as a daughter. No bond, connection or love. Others declare the stress of having a relationship when there is narcissism, antagonism, conditional love and aggressive communications in the mix and they would rather not have a relationship at all. Family difficulties occur between those who are unable to communicate effectively, often finding tension exists in nearly every interaction. Although rifts can develop over long periods of time, for some mothers and daughters it might be an unexpected change which leads to the decision to leave the relationship.

Estrangement may take place for different reasons. Poor communication, ongoing feuds, differing values and beliefs, disappointments, major life events, lifestyle choices, lack of empathy, negative behavioural patterns, parental alienation, and arguments over money, sexuality, religion and parenting. Disagreements over weddings, death of a family member, Christmas, Mother's Day and other significant events can also trigger a decision to step right away from the conflict zone.

Divorce and separation of parents may also mean you make a choice who to see more of. If parents re-marry this could change how you feel about your birth mother and family of origin. Although it may be painful to find yourself in the position of considering estrangement, sometimes you have to make a choice to break away, make time for self-healing and fill the void with our own self-love.

I have also known mothers choose to be estranged from their daughters as the relationship is toxic and unhealthy for both parties. The choice to be estranged can in fact be one of the best options for both the mother and daughter's well-being.

If you decide to write a letter to your mother (there is a sample letter in Chapter Four) or meet with her to talk through why you are considering or have made a decision to a step back from your relationship; be prepared, you may not get a response at all, or you may get a response which is hurtful. Nobody likes to feel dismissed, left out, unwelcome or rejected and setting boundaries with our mothers is likely to bring up old wounds which your mother is yet to heal. Her response or lack of response will be more about her and less about you.

Being clear as to why you want to make this change and being able to communicate effectively by setting boundaries, is sometimes the best way for a relationship to run its course. Nothing is set in stone or cast in steel and sometimes the choice to be estranged for however long this pans out, makes for the healthiest of relationships. If you choose to be estranged, be sure to look after your own needs as different emotions may surface for you once the estrangement is in place. EFT is one of the best techniques I know of to support you through adjusting to estrangement and the roller coaster of emotions you may find yourself going through.

RECONCILIATION

The present changes the past. Looking back you do not find what you left behind - Kiran Desai

Failure to heal the first relationship in our lives leaves many daughters with a gnawing ache long after their mothers have passed away. This filters through into all relationships, most of all, the relationship with the self. It takes two to make a relationship work. Commitment and consideration is needed from both parties, striving at all times to speak and act from a place of love. When we focus on what's the best that can happen, it's possible to transform a relationship into one which brings new meaning and one where we can eventually allow the love in our hearts to flow.

If you are going to reconcile with your mother, make sure it is wholly your decision and not based on other people's opinions, expectations or judgements. If you are receiving pressure from other family members or your mother's friends, simply explain you have personal reasons for your decision to remain estranged. Whatever your reasons for estrangement, you are not to blame for how your mother or other relatives respond. Choices are made based on the facts we have at the time of making a decision and the knowledge, learning and wisdom within.

Time apart can help the dynamics of your relationship and it is possible to reconcile, if your thoughts and feelings towards your mother change after having some personal space. To reconcile, effort must be made by both mother and daughter to restore the relationship by stating their respective needs clearly. Putting the past behind you and beginning again, is the healthiest way to reconcile. It may mean agreeing to disagree, though also making a condition between the two of you to let bygones be bygones. Knowing you have at least tried to build your relationship while your mother is alive, will give you a sense of peace when she is no longer in this world.

Why do we demand our mother's love when we are guilty at times of withholding love from her?

Conditional love creates a divide. When both mother and daughter are stating the conditions and neither one will budge, it may as well be a stake-out at The O.K. Corral - though it doesn't have to be this way. It only takes one person to change their behaviour and responses. One of you must begin to be the adult in the relationship. Making this change and operating from a new mindset, breaks the behaviour loop. You can put the guns down and let the dust settle forever.

Peace is a daily, a weekly, a monthly process, gradually changing opinions, slowly eroding old barriers, quietly building new structures - John F. Kennedy

The intention behind doing the inner and outer work is to build bridges with your mother, close the distance between you, understand your differences and put the past to rest. Letting go of old habits in the way you respond to her, will not only help with your own stress reduction, but your life as a whole will improve and so will your relationships generally.

- **Thinking about past conflicts, what are you or your mother still holding onto which causes stress in your lives?**
- **How does emotional stress manifest for you physically?** *(i.e. headaches, backaches, anxiety, tension, sleeplessness)*
- **Taking the above two statements into account, when you are able to forgive each other, how will this change your relationship for the better and what physical ailments would you both gladly be free from?**
- **What workable solutions can be created between you both in order to move forwards?**

Steps to reconciliation

1. **Accept the past is the past. You cannot change the past, though you can change the beliefs and meanings you have placed on previous experiences**
2. **Start afresh and be willing to move forward, working towards improving your relationship with your mother**

3. **Educate yourself about your mother's past, the events, situations and experiences she has been through which may have shaped her behaviours, responses and ability to parent effectively. Her behaviour is only part of her, not all of who she is**

4. **Find a place inside yourself where there is empathy, compassion or at least the beginning of an understanding towards your mother and what has shaped her into who she is**

5. **Realise your mother is not fully to blame for your current problems. Situations from her past experiences led her to behave in the way she did**

6. **Work towards forgiving your mother's actions and behaviours** *(It is not about condoning what happened, forgiveness sets you free from the past dictating your future)*

7. **Revise your expectations of your mother and make them realistic**

8. **Renegotiate your relationship with your mother using assertive communication**

9. **State what you want (not what you don't want) in your interactions with her**

10. **Make your goals and ideals realistic and achievable**

11. **Convey your hopes for the future (positively framed)**

12. **Set clear boundaries of what is ok and not ok for you**

13. **Take care of yourself (self-nurturance) as the adult you are. This is about meeting your needs independent of your mother**

14. **Accept responsibility for making positive change and be willing to work towards this**

15. Remember, forgiveness works towards setting you free from the past and aids in finding a space for reconciliation, inner peace and love

For reconciliation to take place, it is possible you and your mother can agree a time to meet and talk without the need for a mediator. If so, make a time to meet for a specific duration (about an hour to two hours). Just like a business meeting, create an agenda containing positive hopes for the future. Stick to the agenda without blaming, focussing on the desired outcome you want. If you need to, use an egg timer to give each other equal time to make a point. Or, you can use a soft toy, pebble, or small item which you can hold in your hands to pass to the other person, when you have finished speaking.

This way of communicating allows for each person to speak while the other agrees only to listen while the item is being held, or timer is being used. Holding onto the item isn't about being overbearing and controlling the conversation, it is used as a 'talk stone' and helps to alternate fairly between 'talker' and 'listener'.

It's important to set clear boundaries before you consider reconciliation. This will be helpful if you are to build a positive relationship. Reconciliation isn't about conditional love though it is about changing the relationship dynamics which may not have worked up to now. In the next chapter I will offer suggestions for therapies and processes which are effective tools for healing.

A TIME FOR HEALING

The walls we build around us to keep sadness out also keeps out the joy - Jim Rohn

Some of the greatest healers on this earth are un-mothered children. Emotional shifts in our lives can be gained by expressing our emotions.

Each new day is an opportunity to heal. It is your personal responsibility now as an adult to nurture and sooth yourself. When you are able to do this, you are no longer dependent on another as a source of love.

Make a list of what makes you feel good. Create time to select from the list the things which nurture your heart and make you feel alive and do them often.

Here are some ideas:

- **Cook yourself a delicious meal**
- **Have an early night with clean sheets and bed wear**
- **Relax in a comfortable setting where the space around you is peaceful**
- **Play with or care for a pet**
- **Paint or create something**
- **Go for a walk**
- **Buy yourself some flowers**
- **Take a run**
- **Write in a journal to express your feelings**
- **Take a relaxing bubble bath**
- **Have a massage**
- **Meditate**
- **Keep a gratitude journal**
- **Garden or invest in an allotment**
- **Listen to your favourite music**
- **Light a scented candle**
- **Go for a swim**

- **Self-heal using Reiki, EFT or your preferred healing modality**
- **Create a clean and safe space within your home or garden where you can relax, read, listen to music**
- **Explore your environment and get outside**
- **Spend time in nature**

Author's Notes

"Even though my mother wasn't able to express love in the way I needed, I know this was because of her own experience of being mothered, she simply acted in the same way my grandmother did towards her. I am grateful I've learned from my experiences and in doing so, have found inside of me an endless fountain of nurturing love. My past has enabled me to help others love themselves through sharing my learning and using the same tools and techniques which have got me through the highs and lows of the mother-daughter relationship."

INNER CHILD WORK

When we practice self-compassion, we look after ourselves just as though we are nurturing a small child. In fact a major part of grieving our original pain work (so that we can heal and be emotionally liberated) is to re-parent ourselves and reconnect with our inner child - Christopher Dines

Your Inner Child is the most important person in the world. Our truth and our answers are within us all. When you commit to making some time for your personal growth, change can happen. Trusting the process and doing the inner work will not only serve your inner child, but the woman you are today and the person you are becoming.

Dominant vs. Non-dominant Handwriting

Your dominant hand is the hand you write with (this side represents your adult/responsible side). For this exercise, I invite you to write the questions you would like answers to with your dominant hand and then answer all questions with the non-dominant hand. Responses from the non-dominant side can come from various aspects of your child self (the toddler, teenager as well as the emotions of the inner child i.e. angry, happy, sad etc)

Children only need a few words to express themselves. How your inner child communicates back with you may vary, either saying little or saying a lot depending on the questions asked.

You can begin as follows:

- **Ask your inner child's name**
- **How do they feel today? (Do they feel good, sad, happy, mad etc?)**
- **Let them know you love them**
- **Ask if they would like to play today**
- **How old is that part of you which is emotionally stuck in the search for your mother's love?**
- **Ask them what it is they don't like about their mother, their childhood etc?**
- **Ask them what they need right now**
- **What did they need back then**
- **How can you meet your inner child's needs as an adult now?**
- **Make time to acknowledge them, listen to them and help them to heal the hurt places of themselves**

Writing a series of questions like this will become easier the more you work with your inner child. The answers you write in response to the questions may surprise, upset or enlighten you. Accept all the answers without judgement.

As adults we can react in many different ways to our inner child. We might be the critical parent, teacher, caregiver or coach. Getting into the habit of speaking to your inner child in a soothing, lovingly supportive, encouraging and caring way supports the inner child. The inner child will then feel more visible which will help them to speak up and let feelings out. If needs be, allow the inner child to tell the critical parent voice how she feels, as the parent may not be aware.

It is important in this kind of work to keep communications open between you and your younger self. Be sure to make special plans after any kind of self-development work to reward your inner child by doing something fun.

Whatever your experiences of your life, you must accept yourself and the child within. Please know, you have already come such a long way on your journey and will continue to build on the progress you have made so far.

What were the missing events and unmet needs in your life as a child?

Using the chart below, record what you feel was missing from your life and be sure to make up for lost time by giving your inner child now, what she needed back then.

• Acceptance	• Laughter
• Acknowledgement	• Listening
• Affection	• Love
• Approval	• Patience
• Attention	• Play
• Caring	• Physical touch
• Compassion	• Praise
• Devotion	• Recognition
• Empathy	• Respect
• Encouragement	• Support
• Fun	• Time
• Honesty	• Trust
• Kindness	

What your mother never gave you when you were growing up, you can now give to yourself. Add your own needs to the list and be sure to give to yourself and your inner child, the time, love and attention you were missing in childhood.

FILLING THE VOID

Never make your home in a place. Make a home for yourself inside your own head. You'll find what you need to furnish it - memory, friends you can trust, love of learning, and other such things. That way it will go with you whenever you journey - Tad Williams

It is only you who knows how to love yourself completely. The deep inner work offers introspection and you learn the fundamentals of making yourself feel whole. Working through abandonment, trust issues, anger, grief, guilt and the whole range of human emotions in relation to your mother, offers the opportunity to let go of the emotional overwhelm and create space for something new.

Re-parenting ourselves and becoming our own inner mothers fills the void with love, self-care, awareness, reflection, wisdom and most of all, possibility. When roles reverse, instead of looking outside ourselves for love we are able to parent ourselves and find new ways to satisfy our needs by doing the things we enjoy and also making the time to care for ourselves.

Mia's words of wisdom

"There were times as a child and even now as a woman when I would have loved nothing more than my mom's arms around me and to hear the words 'everything's going to be alright'. I know now I can't change the past, what's gone is gone. I've learnt how to deal with my emotions when they come up. I now nurture myself and choose to spend time doing things which make me feel happy, loved and cared for."

LOVE FROM OTHER SOURCES

It sounds corny, but I've promised my inner child that never again will I abandon myself for anything or anyone else again - Wynonna Judd

Each of us still has a desire to be mothered. Just because we might lose our mother through death, estrangement or abandonment, the need to be loved and nurtured remains.

Other people who have shown you 'mother love' in the past, could include other family members, friends of your mother or mothers of your friends. Perhaps you had a nanny or hired help to raise you and so were supported and shown tender loving care from another woman. Many women I have worked with told me it was their family pet who gave them unconditional love – the animal noticing when they were sad and comforting them. Love might well come from other sources too such as meeting with groups of like-minded friends. Social media also does a wonderful job of helping people feel less alone and there are groups for just about everything which connect people together (see meetup.com). In the UK too, we have many women's groups where females meet, support and encourage each other. Whatever country you are in, a simple internet search will reveal what's on in your local area as well as telling you about international and national groups you can join. Some of the meetings are for business networking though many are simply groups of women from different areas meeting up for a coffee and chat and they can go on to form meaningful friendships. Why not find out what's going on in your town, city and country and get exploring or perhaps consider setting up your own group or women's circle.

Children are rarely taught 'self-love' but as adults we can learn how to best care for ourselves. It's unrealistic as an adult daughter to place all our needs on our mothers. When we begin to learn how love can be found from other sources (and indeed within ourselves) we can take the pressure off our mothers and simply enjoy being with her on new terms, accepting what she can offer and expecting nothing more.

Betty's Words of Wisdom

"I guess I'm kind of old school; I really wanted my mother to devote herself to me and make me the centre of her world. I've always had an expectation she would protect me against life's hardships, the frustrations, the losses and despair. We both had the same needs; she wanted the love of a mother who wasn't there for her, as did I. The reality when I bring myself up to date is I couldn't be her mother and she couldn't be mine.

Working through my mother stuff has actually been easier than I thought it would be. Now I know about my mother's past, how her mother treated her and how for most of her life she never moved beyond the need for a mother's love, I actually get her, I understand her need. All I can say is, I'm so very blessed to have my wonderful female friends who I know I can call in the middle of the night if need be, they have been my rocks in times of need. My mother had no one to help her through the mess of understanding her mother or finding love within herself or from others. Every day I count my blessings and I'm grateful for my friends who I love and I know who love me. I also know if my friends aren't available I still have little old me to fall back on. In fact there's nothing I like better than pleasing myself and doing what I want when I want to do it. There is so much freedom in parenting yourself. If I feel like a day off from it I'm lazy, but most of the time I treat myself like a princess!"

INNER MOTHER AND OTHER MOTHER FIGURES

She held herself until the sobs of the child inside subsided entirely. I love you, she told herself. It will all be okay - H. Raven Rose

Although it may not always be easy to find, there is a gift in every situation. The gift, however painful your past may have been, is often the gift which will go on and change not only your life, but the lives of others in a very positive way.

Perhaps because of your own unique experiences, you have indirectly been able to parent yourself and are strong, confident, assertive, and forward thinking, empathic, caring and understanding. Much of your past and the lessons learnt may have made you more self-aware, nurturing, considerate, welcoming, compassionate, loving, independent, supportive or wise. Take some time to reflect on your character traits, attributes and abilities not only as a daughter but as the wonderful woman you are. What nurturance skills have you found yourself developing which have helped you get through your most difficult times?

Thinking about some of the missing events in your childhood, what do you wish your mother had said to you to make you feel better? You may never have heard these words from anyone, though I offer to you a range of statements which will aid you in becoming your very own 'inner mother.' You can add to the list of suggestions, the words you need to hear which will help you through the hard times. It will be helpful for you to get into the habit of self-soothing and talking to yourself in this way.

- **I'm here for you**
- **What's wrong?**
- **How can I help you?**
- **What do you need right now?**
- **I love you**
- **I will never let you go**
- **I'm right beside you**
- **I will support you**
- **You matter to me**
- **I care for you**

Whatever you feel in any given moment no matter how hurtful, is an opportunity for further healing. When you feel grief, despair, sadness, regret, anger or frustration, it's often connected with the child part of you who didn't have her needs met for whatever reason. Now, as an adult, you can re-parent yourself by becoming your very own inner-mother who listens, comforts, supports, encourages and nurtures you.

If it's a hug you need, wrap your own loving arms around yourself. If it's warmth you need, take a luxury bath or enclose yourself in soft blankets. If it's anger you need to express use EFT, go for a run, jump on a mini trampoline, journal or do some expressive art work. If it's love you need, what can you do for yourself to show yourself more love? Will it be to give yourself the time, love and attention, to get well? A massage, a swim, a walk in nature to clear your head, or writing a letter to yourself in recognition of your strengths, gifts and attributes. You can choose whatever you need, moment by moment and as your needs change you can make new choices.

There are so many ways we can nurture ourselves as adults, no longer do we need to look for love outside of ourselves. If love is offered, it adds to our lives and if it's taken away we are still ok because we have our own love 24 hours a day.

Mutual mothering is an option

Many daughters have amazing friends who take on the mother role naturally without being asked. It's the female friends we make along the way who support us and care for us through friendship and we feel held, supported, nurtured and loved by their presence.

Think about the female friends you have in your life.

- **How long have you known your female friends?**
- **Where did you meet?**
- **What connected you together?**
- **How has the friendship served each of you?**
- **What do you value the most about your friendship?**
- **When you are in the presence of your closest friends how you do feel?**
- **What qualities do your friends have that you would have liked your mother to have?**
- **How has having these friendships benefitted you long-term?**

- **What do you believe about yourself in relation to your friends? *I.e. I'm loved, cherished, supported, held dear etc***

Love does come from other sources and we may not realise how valued we are in our female friendships or how much love and care we offer to our friends. If you wish to connect with other women on the same path as yourself, you might like to find a local women's support group close to you, or consider setting one up so you can support each other.

ADOPTIVE MOTHERS, STEPMOTHERS AND FOSTER MOTHERS

You don't need to be a primary care giver of your children to be of primary influence in their lives. What you do for them behind the scenes in your own unique way is what makes the true difference in the long run - Miya Yamanouchi

Mothers come in many shapes and sizes; it's not a case of one size fits all. If your mother was not able to parent you in the way you would have liked, perhaps there have been significant women in your life who have offered you unconditional love and who have helped to raise you. It's possible those women were other members of your family such as grandmothers, aunts, sisters and cousins etc though I also wanted to acknowledge the role of other mothers who take a hand in raising daughters.

Many of the case studies shared have been blessed with having a foster mother, adoptive mother or stepmother who have taken on the role of birth mother and who have done a marvellous job of nurturing someone else's daughter as their own. Children need love and whether this love comes from a blood relative or not, solid and meaningful relationships can be formed. I've known many daughters who take on the mother role never having had children of their own, but who offer nurturance, care and love to another person's child.

It's true to say some daughters do not have great relationships with those who raised them. I hope that some of what is shared in this book touches on similar experiences of your own and will be helpful to you in understanding the women in your life, their past and their own mother's parenting.

If you have been blessed with the love of another mother, you have been fortunate.

STAYING STRONG

Forgiving does not erase the bitter past. A healed memory is not a deleted memory. Instead, forgiving what we cannot forget creates a new way to remember. We change the memory of our past into a hope for our future - Lewis B. Smedes

When you realise your mother's love is not something you can take for granted and which will continue throughout your life, the reality of this can be a very bitter pill to swallow. You may need to remind yourself your mother could not meet your needs as a child, because of her own experience. Staying strong and taking responsibility to care for yourself as an adult means you give up chasing a dream, you cannot go back and physically change the past though you can explore what limiting beliefs you may have formed about yourself, your mother and the world around you and then you can re-frame your experiences placing new meaning on what happened to you.

Mothers and daughters cannot always shield each other from pain; pain is a natural part of life. It is the challenges we go through which make us stronger. When you are able to reach beyond the difficulties in your mother-daughter relationship and actively parent yourself by providing your own needs, true healing begins.

You are far stronger than you may realise. Inside of you there is a light which will never go out. Allow your inner light to keep you safe in times of struggle, direct your light towards the thoughts which lift you up, use your light to explore unexamined parts of yourself and to guide you home, back home to you, the place where love resides. The Spotlight Process in Chapter Six, will aid you in staying strong and moving beyond the pain of the wounded child.

Create your own affirmation or mission statement

Let today be the day you learn the grace of letting go and the power of moving on - Steve Maraboli

The past gives us courage for the future. The obstacles already overcome are the foundations we build upon to create a more positive future.

Over the years, many people have asked me, 'what got you through, how did you overcome your own self-doubts, insecurities, lack of self-belief etc?' The answer is I turned up my positive voice and decreased the negative one. Sure, I've done plenty of EFT, talked to friends and therapists etc though fundamentally, I had to take responsibility to change the voice inside my head to one which was more encouraging, no one else could do that for me, so I made it my mission and took total responsibility to change my life. I simply started nurturing my inner-child and speaking to myself more positively. Since those dark days, I have continued in doing so every day of my life.

Here are some ideas of the affirmations I used to support me to overcome challenges and limitations. Some may resonate with you or, you can invent some of your own.

- **I am safe right now**
- **I will get through this**
- **All is well**

- **I am alive**
- **I can do this**
- **I'm going to be ok**
- **I am strong**
- **This too will pass**
- **I embrace my inner-child**
- **I choose to let go of my past**

Repetition of affirmations and mantras of this kind, help you overcome the difficult times. According to Bert Herna, author of the wonderful little E-book *Affirmations and Self-Talk,* without repetition - after 24 hours, 25% any new learning or idea is forgotten, 48 hours 50%, four days 85% and after 16 days a massive 98% of new learning and new ideas are forgotten. Repeating affirmations indicates they are more likely to have long lasting benefits.

My favourite affirmation is 'this too will pass'. I have it engraved inside a bracelet and I never take it off to remind me everything is transient. It is my hope that the more you speak your own words of affirmation you too, will experience the joy and freedom of letting go of the past.

How can you affirm yourself today and every day?

THE MISSING PIECE OF THE PUZZLE

A daughter is a gift of love - author unknown

No matter how imperfect your relationship with your mother is or how flawed, your mother gave you the gift of life. It's down to you to achieve your dreams and fulfil your life's purpose independent of her. Whether you have experienced rejection, being ignored, intimidated, isolated, corrupted, exploited or felt unloved, your past need not influence your future. Put your focus in the now, plan for your future, take action, be open to new experiences, look ahead as to what else is possible. Shape your life into what you want it to be. You are the creator of your destiny.

You, yes you, are the missing piece of the puzzle. Whatever your unmet childhood needs, you have the capacity as an adult daughter to meet the needs of your younger self. If you felt rejected, look for the situations in your life now where you are accepted. If you were ignored, be sure to give to yourself your undivided attention to meet your needs. If you were intimidated, notice how resilient you are now in terms of having got this far. If you felt isolated, stretch yourself and get involved with projects where you connect with like-minded people. If you were exploited, how can you learn from and use your experience to improve your future and the future of others?

Reflect on the following questions and make changes where necessary to add more joy to your life

- **What do I want?**
- **What is working well in my life right now?**
- **What do I want more of?**
- **How do I want my life to be in six months time, a year from now, in five years and ten years time?**
- **What actions can I start taking now which will bring me closer to my goals?**
- **What can I do daily, weekly, monthly which brings more joy and love to my life?**
- **To experience more balance in my life, what do I need to start doing, stop doing and do differently?**
- **To experience more love in my life, what limiting beliefs do I need to let go of?**

- **In order to be my best self what's the one thing I can begin with today?**
- **In recognition of my 'inner child' how can I show her the time, love and encouragement she deserves as the adult version of herself?**
- **What would I say to the younger version of me right now?**
- **By continuing to give to myself my own love, how will this benefit me in the future?**
- **What behaviours, beliefs and actions do I hold myself accountable for to make my future the best it can be?**
- **Knowing I am changing my future by changing my thoughts followed by actions, how can I best serve myself today?**

As with any puzzle there are many pieces which make a picture complete. It could be after working through Mothers and Daughters you and your mother are able to become friends, in which case you can review your mutual puzzles and decide what you want to create for the future. Relationships do not always need to go back to the same shape; we can change them at any time. When the puzzle is complete there is always a sense of satisfaction. For further help and support go to www.mothersanddaughters.solutions to check out the range of free resources and support programmes.

PERSONAL LIFE-LONG TRANSFORMATION

How does one become a butterfly she asked pensively. You must want to fly so much that you are willing to give up being a caterpillar - Trina Paulus

Your mother is the link to the legacy you leave behind. How you choose to use your experience of your relationship with your mother can add new meaning to your life as you reflect on what you are able to change and what you can't.

Personal life-long transformation is like a muscle, the more you use it the stronger you get. Making a commitment to yourself to make your past work for you rather than against you, is the greatest gift you could ever give yourself. For your internal 'inner mother' to flourish, you must be willing to respect yourself and to know it's ok to treat yourself with tender loving care and in doing so, accept your own love and positive regard.

It is said we suffer growing pains in our teenage years when our physical bodies change, emotionally we must grow too. Now is the time. Changing from chrysalis to butterfly is no easy feat, though the butterfly knows that in order to fly free from its containment, inner and outer transformation must occur.

Chapter 6

Recovery & Beyond

RECOVERY AND BEYOND

The most beautiful people I have ever met are the ones who always see life in full colour. They are the ones who have been through hell and back and still stop to savour the parts of life that many seldom pay attention to. They will always use their past experiences as a guiding light to bring forth a more authentic way of life. These are the people I admire most because no matter how much they have suffered, they will always find a reason to make the best of this imperfect world - Karen A. Baquiran

Healing the wounds of your inner child may have felt like a lifelong journey up until now. However hard it's been, you made it, you got through! Take a bow. I honour and respect you for having come this far and I believe in you. You have so many wonderful inner resources and qualities you may not even be aware of. I wish to acknowledge all that you are and all who you are becoming. Now is the time to step into your personal power and claim back what was once lost, you are the decider of your destiny. It is up to you to make the rest of your life the best of your life and I know you will, I have faith in you.

Your past need not influence your future and the beautiful thing about doing the inner work is not only do you move on from the past, heal old hurts and overcome limiting beliefs, you also create for yourself the kind of life you want to live. This section offers you the tools and techniques to get you back in control of your life, living it with passion and purpose.

Come join me, together we will continue forward in the direction of your dreams.

UNCONDITIONAL SELF-LOVE

Imagine knowing what it feels like to have an endless source of love, one you can rely on, one that is available to you unconditionally and without judgment....

We all have an 'inner mother ', who can, through self-awareness, respond to our every need. In the same way we might nurture and attend to a two-year-old, show affection to a pet, love to friends, and connection with our tribes, the inner resources you already have can be built upon. With the help of this book you will be the most amazing inner mother and your inner daughter will benefit from all the love you have to give her. Make a commitment to yourself, from this day onwards, to be your own 'inner mother' and give to yourself your own love!

This chapter offers you a range of empowering techniques to put you back in control of your life. Utilising the processes offered, reflecting on the open ended questions previously shared and applying the energy based strategies and tools for emotional release, you will find yourself not only becoming stronger but also more resilient. You will feel lighter and freer by doing so.

YOUR COMMITMENT TO YOU

Beautify your inner dialogue. Beautify your inner world with love, light and compassion. Life will be beautiful - Amit Ray

Lasting change begins with you. Making time to work through the relationship difficulties you have, or have had with your mother, means things will never go back to the same shape again. Whether you are able to repair your relationship fully, set new boundaries or come to terms with the fact your mother wasn't the mother you would have liked her to be, you are able to meet your own needs as an adult - independent of her.

Change begins by taking small actions to understand and transform the relationship with your mother. As you grow in confidence and make adjustments in your reactions and responses to her, you will feel proud of yourself for changing your behaviours and you will benefit on so many levels. When you are happier generally, you will notice improvement in health and well-being, career, family, friendships and personal growth. All aspects of your life benefit from making those changes. You may even find yourself having more fun and discovering things about yourself you never even knew.

SHAPING YOUR LIFE INTO WHAT YOU WANT IT TO BE

You've always had the power My Dear. You just had to learn it for yourself - Glinda, the Good Witch, Wizard of Oz

Just like Dorothy in The Wizard of Oz, you too have the power to create a magnificent life for yourself. Your life and how you live it is your choice, no one else's. Dorothy had to move beyond her belief that she couldn't find her way back home to Kansas and you, too, may need to understand and identify your limiting beliefs, before you find yourself heading in the right direction. All journeys shape us for the greater good and if you meet a lion, a tin man, a straw man or a wizard along the way, all the more interesting. Whether the colour of your yellow brick road is indeed yellow, blue, purple or gold, set the goal in your mind of what you want to achieve and take the steps along the path to reach your ultimate destination - singing and dancing along the way is optional.

SELF-CARE USING EFT (Emotional Freedom Technique)

Caring for your inner child has a powerful and surprisingly quick result: Do it and the child heals - Martha Beck

EFT may seriously improve your emotional wellbeing and in turn your relationship with your mother. The technique is easy to learn and requires no tools or expertise. I am hopeful that once you have learnt and applied EFT to the areas of your life you wish to work on, using it will become as regular as brushing your teeth. EFT has the potential to change your beliefs and in turn, transform your life. When you free yourself from past hurts and fears, clearing emotional baggage easily and quickly, you break old patterns and behaviours and open up for yourself a world full of love and opportunity.

The History of EFT

Gary Craig, founder of The Emotional Freedom Technique (EFT), is a very wise man. Gary suggests with EFT to "try it on everything", I couldn't agree more. Gary understood "the cause of all negative emotions is a disruption in the body's energy system." He's used it with thousands of people to improve their physical and emotional health. What a legacy to leave behind, to be able to change lives for the better, using this simple technique.

What is EFT and how can I use it?

EFT is classed as an Energy Psychology. Energy Psychology focuses on the connected relationship of energy, emotions, behaviours and health. EFT works by shifting the brain's electrochemistry and works by stimulating energy points on the surface of the skin. EFT combines the principles of Chinese Medicine with modern psychology. Our emotional and physical health depends upon the smooth flow of energy through our body's energy meridians. Emotions affect our energy systems and when we are tuned into a negative thought, emotion, situation or event our energy system disrupts and literally responds to the thought.

Improving energy flow

By clearing and releasing emotional conflicts through EFT tapping, our energy system is stimulated and balances out any energy disruptions. Our energy flow is improved, in turn our physical health and emotional wellbeing is also improved. EFT works in a similar way to acupuncture though without the use of needles to stimulate energy flow. With EFT, we use our fingertips to tap gently on some of our energy meridian points/ energy pathways to stimulate energy flow, transforming and releasing emotions as we go.

Once EFT has been learnt (it's so easy to pick up) it can be used anywhere in any circumstance, it's portable and easy to master and can often reduce an emotional intensity in as little as five to ten minutes of tapping. For some longer standing problems, several sessions and rounds of tapping may be required to reduce the emotional intensity. Persist with using EFT regularly and you will reap the benefits tenfold.

EFT can be used to clear past traumas, release fears, anxieties, past events, current challenges, upsets, disagreements, physical ailments and emotional problems. It is my wish for you, EFT transforms your life in the way it has transformed mine and the lives of the people I have shared this valuable technique with.

What the people at the top are saying about EFT

Many self-help authors, gurus and teachers endorse EFT; the world is waking up to the positive changes EFT brings.

Louise L Hay author of You Can Heal Your Life said *"When I first heard about using tapping or EFT (Emotional Freedom Technique), I thought it was delightful that something this simple and easy could really work".*

Dr Wayne Dyer recently said *"put away your scepticism, this really works...I've had great results with tapping in my own life."*

Jack Canfield, Co-creator of Chicken Soup for the Soul, calls it *"the most powerful new transformational technology to come along in years."*

Further information about EFT can be found in the appendix.

Measuring energy flow using the SUD Scale

EFT uses a scoring system to measure the depth and intensity of a problem and this scale is called SUD (Subjective Unit of Distress). The System measures on a scale of 0 - 10. 0 equates to feeling neutral and 10 equates to feeling high emotional distress. It's helpful as you work through various problems to measure before and after tapping, the level of distress you begin and end with. This scale was introduced in 1969 by Joseph Wolpe. Using this scale helps you to identify how much the problem may be affecting your physical and emotional wellbeing.

SUD Scale Subjective Unit of Distress										
0	**1**	**2**	**3**	**4**	**5**	**6**	**7**	**8**	**9**	**10**
Neutral Emotional Charge Low intensity of emotions		Intensity of emotion builds Emotions often manageable but not ideal			Intense emotions escalate Emotions often overwhelming				Maximum emotional charge High intensity of emotions	

EFT Tapping Points

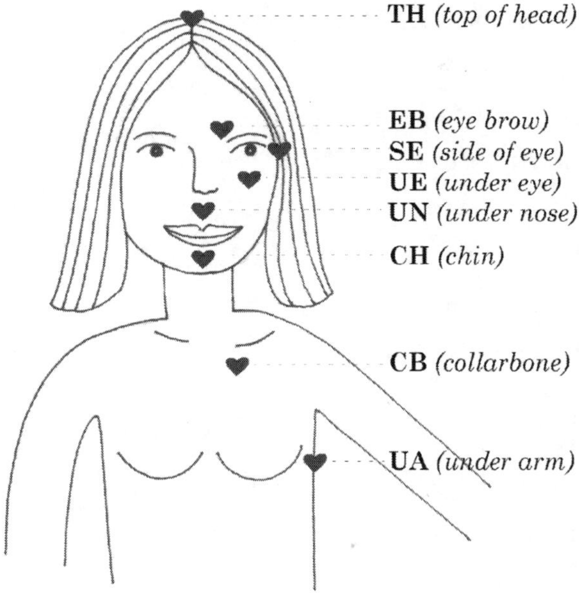

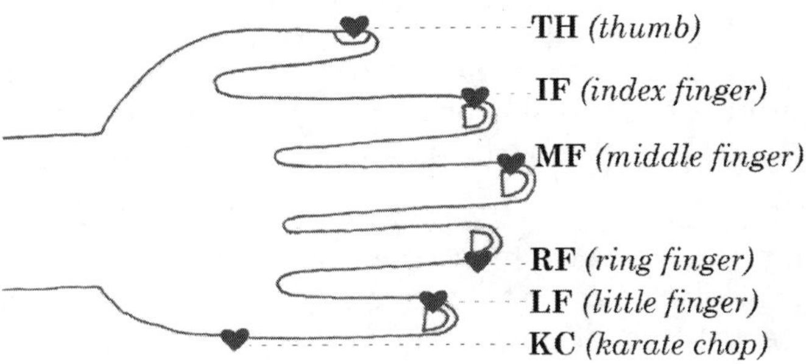

The EFT Process:

Tap in this order

- karate chop point KC
- Top of the head TH
- Eyebrow EB
- Side of the eye SE
- Under the eye UE
- Under the nose UN
- Under lower lip CH
- Collar bone CB
- Under the arm UA
- Thumb
- Index finger
- Middle finger
- Ring finger
- Little finger

STEP 1 Recall a specific past or current problem/event you wish to work through. Be as clear as possible what the feeling, issue or problem is you want to work on. Is the problem thought-based, behaviour-based, physical or emotional? I.e. "I wish my mother would praise me more often", "I would prefer to see my mother once a week", "I don't think my mother and I understand each other we are too different" etc

STEP 2 Determine the level of distress on the SUD scale (0 not being a problem and 10 being intense). You may wish to write this down, to compare the before and after scores and measure the reduction in distress going down in between each tapping round.

Gather the various aspects of the problem. Where in your body do you feel the emotional issue most strongly? Does it have a colour, a shape? What does it feel like? What is its weight? Does it have a smell, a sound, a taste? We store information through our senses – visual (seeing), auditory (hearing), kinaesthetic (feeling), gustatory (taste), olfactory (smell) and the way we store a memory/emotion often relates to one or more dominant sense.

STEP 3 "SET UP": The set up is where we begin the actual EFT tapping process. While tapping with our finger tips on the karate chop point, on the side of either hand in line with the little finger, we use a 'set up statement' repeating it three times.

The traditional EFT set up statement is, "Even though I have this *name the problem or issue here,* I deeply and completely love and accept myself." Repeat this statement or variations of this statement on this point three times before moving on to the additional sequential tapping points. If this statement is uncomfortable for you, you may prefer to select an alternative set up statement from the choices offered further on or, make one up of your own which feels comfortable for you.

STEP 4 Follow the full tapping sequence after you have started, with the karate chop point. You can tap on either side of your body with either hand. Tap round all the tapping points lightly with the finger pads in sequence, about five to seven times on each point, while repeating the reminder phrase (this is a shorter version of the problem) i.e. the issue, symptom you are working on (this stress, this anger, this disappointment, this lack of self-belief)

STEP 5 Repeat several rounds of tapping in this manner until you feel the problem starting to reduce in emotional intensity (SUD reduces)

STEP 6 Reassess the emotional intensity of the problem using the scale 0-10

STEP 7 Continue tapping round all points with further rounds, until the emotional intensity reduces to a 0

STEP 8 Now, think about the original problem and see if any emotional intensity remains

STEP 9 If any part of the problem you started with remains, work through the various aspects of the problem and persist with tapping through the tapping sequence, until the problem subsides. "Even though I have some remaining (state the problem), I deeply and completely love and accept myself". Sometimes when we're tapping on a problem, it can change. It may feel as if the energy of the problem has shifted and moved around the body, some aspects of the problem, including the emotions which surface may have changed too. If necessary, to re-evaluate the problem and the aspects of it, start the procedure again from Step 1 and work through the aspects of the problem which come up or have changed as a result of tapping.

EFT set-up statements

There is a choice of EFT set-up statements you can use to transform your emotions. Decide from the following statements which statement feels right for you. Each set- up statement is repeated three times, either using the same statement or a variation of the problem before moving on with the additional sequential tapping points.

You will repeat the ending statement while tapping on the karate chop point on the side of the hand in line with the little finger i.e.:

"Even though I have this *name the problem or issue here,* I deeply and completely love and accept myself''

"Even though I have this *name the problem or issue here,* I accept who I am and how I feel".

"Even though I have this *name the problem or issue here* I allow myself to move through this".

Alternative EFT set-up statements

If the traditional EFT set-up statement feels uncomfortable in any way i.e. "I deeply and completely love and accept myself" select an alternative end statement below which resonates with you more.

Even though I have this *name the problem or issue here*

- **I'm learning to love and accept myself**
- **I am willing to love and accept myself anyway**
- **I accept myself just the way I am**
- **I accept who I am and how I feel**
- **I am special, unique and valuable**
- **I accept myself without the need for my mother's approval**
- **I choose to be ok with this**
- **I'm open to accepting myself just the way I am**
- **I've decided to be more open and accepting of how I feel**
- **I allow myself to move through this**
- **I'm in the process of loving and accepting myself**
- **I honour myself**
- **I am learning to love, accept and appreciate all parts of me**
- **I'm a good person**
- **I accept all of me and the feelings I have**
- **I accept I'm doing the best I can**
- **I am beginning to feel it's ok for me to let this go**

- **I allow myself to move through this**
- **I've decided to take it one day at a time**
- **I choose to find new ways to work this out**

Be persistent. EFT can be used as a standalone form of support for a short period of time, to work through one specific issue or, on a regular basis, to work through a range of problems. EFT will help to reduce the emotional intensity of many issues, past, present and future.

Alternative ways to tap

21 Day Field Clearing Technique (Apply EFT for 5-10 minutes daily for 21 consecutive days)

You might like to use the EFT tapping script below for 21 consecutive days or more and notice what changes for you. The 21 Day Field Clearing Technique works well on longer standing issues.

This exercise has been adapted from 'Matrix Reimprinting using EFT' by Karl Dawson and Sasha Allenby.

Karate chop: Even though I haven't always felt loved, I'm working on resolving this (repeat three times)

Top of the head: I haven't always felt loved

Inner eyebrow: I want to always feel loved

Side of the eye: I choose to always be loved

Under the eye: I love to always be loved because...then list all the reasons why you want to be loved, either in your own mind or out loud

Under the nose: I am open to receiving love

Chin: As you tap, ask yourself what you would hear inside your own mind if you were more loving towards yourself?

Collar bone: As you tap, ask yourself what you would need to do on a regular basis to be more loving towards yourself, or receive the love offered by others. Either speak the things out loud, or simply bring them to mind as you tap through the points

Under the arm: Ask yourself how you would feel if you regularly acted in a way which was more loving towards yourself. Get into the feeling of being more lovable and open to love. If you have difficulty in getting into this place of feeling, simply remember a time and place where you were kind and loving to yourself or, when another person showed kindness and love towards you

Thumb: As you tap, choose an image or symbol you associate with love and take this image into your mind

Index finger: As you tap on your index finger with the image in your mind, think about and see, sense, or imagine all the neural pathways in your brain connecting with this image and make this picture and experience your reality

Middle finger: As you tap, send a signal to every cell in your body, love is your new reality

Ring finger: As you tap on your ring finger, take the image or symbol of love into your heart, making the image bright and clear and really feel what it feels like to experience the energy of love flowing through you

Little finger: As you tap, send the image out from your heart (spend a couple of minutes doing this), and enjoy sending the love through you into the outside world

If you are finding your main issue with your mother is connected with not being able to forgive her, remember, using EFT on forgiveness sets you free from holding onto the past, reacting and responding from the hurt part of yourself. Chapter Four offers more insights into the benefits of forgiveness.

EFT Forgiveness Statements

Use the full EFT process and tapping points as you read these statements aloud - choosing the statements that mean the most to you. In addition to these statements, you might like to write your own and tap them through.

- **Even though my mother never loved me in the way I wanted, I accept myself and who I am**
- **Even though my mother rejected/abandoned/didn't want me/gave me away/left me, I love who I am just the same**
- **Even though my childhood was hard, I got through it and have found an inner strength I never knew I had**
- **Even though my mother was unkind to me I understand she was suffering and didn't know a better way to express herself**
- **Even though I'm angry with my mother I know holding on to this anger is hurting me**
- **Even though I have these unresolved emotions in relation to my mother, I'm willing to work through them using EFT**

You may find it helpful if you wish to understand your thoughts, feelings, emotions and limiting beliefs in more depth, to read my first book Find YOU, Find LOVE: Get to the heart of love and relationships using EFT. For free resources and audio downloads related to Find YOU, Find LOVE go to www.wendyfry.com/book/resources

The capacity to create loving relationships comes from loving yourself first. Your outer world will reflect back to you your inner world. What you believe about yourself, both the positive and the negative, you may well attract back towards you. When you are more tender and loving towards yourself, you will attract boundless opportunities for love.

You have an opportunity right now to learn from the past and to work towards treating yourself differently, learning to respect, love and honour yourself completely. It's time to start appreciating and acknowledging yourself for who you are. Any time you lose sight of your greatness and your lovability, gently forgive yourself and go back to treating yourself with love, respect and care. When you slip back into old behaviours of self-criticism, self-judgement and harshness, think about what it was that made you act in an un-loving way towards yourself and be aware of any thoughts, words and actions you expressed about yourself which were hard-hearted and insensitive. When you learn to be more loving and considerate to yourself first and foremost, your inner mirror reflects to the outside world that you are happy, content and already filled with love and this is what will show up for you then?...yes, even more love!

Positive EFT

Silvia Hartmann developed Positive EFT and the SUE scale (Subjective Unit of Experience) in 2009.

Positive EFT is used to measure energy flow through the body from a minus ten to a plus ten. **SUE Scale (Subjective Unit of Experience)** Hartmann 2009

Use positive EFT when you feel you have cleared enough negative emotional energy around your relationship issues with

EFT. It's best to clear first to reduce emotional intensity and then work up the positive scale to a +10.

For Positive EFT, it is usually best to stand up and move around as you work through the process. It is a wonderful technique and energy can move quite quickly up and through your body. You may feel with this technique like laughing, giggling, smiling and moving about. My first experience of Positive EFT, made me feel like running around as the energy shift was so huge.

Positive EFT – The Process

- Imagine the emotion, thought, feeling and positive energy you want more of. Think about what having more of this positive energy would mean to you and how much you want it. Let's for example assume you want more love?
- Score yourself as to how much love you feel you already have using the SUE Scale so you can measure progress. If you are on a low plus or a minus we basically want to move you all the way up to a +10, why would you want anything less?
- Start by placing both hands over your heart centre (the centre of the chest where you might point to yourself when you say 'I am' - your name or 'me'). It doesn't matter which hand is on the top.
- Take in three deep breaths in and out stating the positive you would like i.e. "I want more love" and say it like you mean it, allow your voice and tone to increase, say it with conviction and pride "I WANT MORE LOVE".
- Tap lightly on each meridian point according to the EFT Tapping Chart with your index and or middle finger, making light contact with the area you are tapping on. Take a deep breath in and out at each point before moving to the next.

- Repeat your chosen positive word e.g. 'love' at each point. It is best to work on one positive at a time and not several choices at the same time and work towards getting a +10 for all choices.
- Keep calm and relaxed throughout and move your body if it feels like moving, as the positive energy starts flowing.
- Take a moment, at the end of each round of tapping, to place both hands back on the heart position and reflect on what you are feeling, where you are feeling the positive energy of love and what you have learned.
- At the end of each round of tapping, you might like to reflect how far up the positive love scale you have reached.
- Keep tapping in a new round, repeating your positive word. Allow yourself to really want more love (or whatever it is you have chosen). The aim is always to get you to a +10. Why stop at anything less!
- If you are meeting your mother, have an important date or something in the future connected with your relationships, love or anything else for that matter you might like to use the words "sending myself more love", or "sending love to the future me", or "sending more love to my future self" or "sending *'your name here'* more love". This helps by giving you more of the positive energy wanted in the future.

I hope you enjoy using this technique to bring more balance into your thinking and more balance into your body's energy.

Turning negative to positive

Love wins back what was never lost - Byron Katie

When we are able to think and act from the place of 'what else is possible?' so many things become possible. Change work and tapping in the positives after clearing the negatives, works beautifully together. You might like to work through a series of memories and emotions and turn those experiences to positives. This can be achieved by following the order below:

1. **Identify your subconscious fear/s about your mother, love and relationships (this equates to a belief) i.e. I'm not worthy of love**
2. **Measure how strong your fear is for each emotion on a scale of 1-10, 10 being the most intense (SUDS/ Subjective Unit of Distress)**
3. **Re-phrase the subconscious fear (i.e. "Even though I have this fear of not being worthy of love, I deeply and completely accept myself and how I feel")**
4. **Tap round the meridian points until the fear starts to move down the SUD scale to a 0**
5. **Once you have a achieved a neutral, zero score, convert the subconscious fear into a positive statement (i.e. "I am worthy of love, I am lovable, I attract loving relationships into my life")**
6. **Keep tapping round the positive statement you choose i.e. I want more love, until you go up the positive scale from a 0 up to a +10**
7. **As you work through resolving any negative emotions, as long as the negative emotion is reduced down to a 0 (neutral), you can tap in any number of positives. Working in this way is wonderful and you may notice huge energy shifts as you literally transform your beliefs**

When was the last time you said 'I love you' to yourself? If it was a long time ago or never, now is the perfect time to start.

THE SPOTLIGHT PROCESS

The Spotlight Process - bringing balance to your thinking

When you have come to the edge of all the light that you know and are about to drop off into the darkness of the unknown, faith is knowing one of two things will happen: There will be something solid to stand on or you will be taught to fly - Patrick Overton

Having worked therapeutically with many mothers and daughters over the years, I have observed how they limited themselves and stopped the relationship from flourishing because of negative thinking. They were either spending too much time thinking about the past, focusing entirely on current problems, or projecting catastrophic and disabling fears into the future. Often there would be a combination of the three mixed together, with little focus on what had been working well in their relationship.

I developed The Spotlight Process to help you acknowledge where you may have been spending most of your thinking time and to guide you to achieving a better balance.

Where have you been shining your spotlight?

- **How often do you find yourself stuck in the past thinking about the arguments and conflicts you've had with your mother?**
- **How much time do you spend thinking about your current problems, feeling there's no way out, overwhelmed, bogged down, fed up and tired of life?**
- **When do you find yourself evaluating, judging and filtering for all the things which could go wrong in the future in relation to your mother?**
- **When do you find yourself too scared to take a risk because you believe that what has happened in the past will happen again?**
- **How often do you find it hard to trust, to be vulnerable and to be open to receiving love?**

Now is the perfect time to apply The Spotlight Process simply by examining your thoughts.

- **Wherever you are at this moment, I invite you to think about a spotlight and the light which shines from it. Whether you see it, sense it or imagine it, think about that spotlight right now. This ray of light could be a light in the form of a torch, a lighthouse, a stage spotlight. Whatever spotlight comes to mind is perfect for you.**
- **Think of this ray of light as a ray of your thoughts, feelings and emotions. This light can shine back into your past, ahead to your future or into this very moment.**
- **This is your spotlight. You are in control of shining the light. You are the director of where you narrow your beam and what you choose to illuminate and**

think about. Whatever you shine your light on, you will experience.

- **Using The Spotlight Process, consider where you have been spending most of your thought time?**
- **In the past, present or future?**
- **Examine your thoughts and feelings about the past. Are they positive or negative in terms of the relationship you have with your mother?**
- **How do you feel about your current relationship with her in the present?**
- **Consider what concerns and fears you have about the future of your relationship with her?**

Using this process you will gain insights into what has been holding you back from having happier relations with your mother and relationships generally.

The Spotlight Process - Key Questions:

I suggest you copy out these questions and carry them around with you until the questions become part of your natural thought process.

1.	**Where is my thinking right now? (Past, Present or Future?)**
2.	**What proportion of my thinking is negative?**
3.	**How does it affect me when I focus on the negative?**
4.	**Where is the evidence that what I think will happen will happen?**
5.	**What do I want instead of thinking or feeling this way?**
6.	**Coming from my heart instead of my head, what would love do here?**

- **Reflect on your learning from The Spotlight Process**
- **Where have your thoughts been most of the time?**
- **Past, Present, Future?**
- **What do you want to move on from?**
- **Establish what kind of relationship you want with your mother in the future. Consider the actions you need to take now:**
- **What do you need to stop doing?**
- **What do you need to start doing?**
- **What do you need to do differently?**

When you are clear about where you have been spending your thought time and how this may be limiting you, the path ahead is brighter and more achievable, using this process will support you as you bring your thoughts into balance and decide what you need to do to change them.

Past – Present – Future - Where are you shining your light?

- **Past**: If your light is always in the past, you cannot see the future.
- **Present**: If you're bogged down with current problems and that's all you're thinking about and focusing on, it's impossible to move on in the direction of your dreams and create the future you would like.
- **Future**: If you're worrying about the future and you don't take any action to achieve the things you'd like, you stay stuck where you are. When you shine your light in only one direction and your thoughts are negative and limiting, it's impossible to see the light in other areas of your life.

Using The Spotlight Process on the stories in your mind

From this moment on, when you get caught up in a story running through your mind, please take a moment to reflect:

- **Which part of your story is a replay of what happened in the past?**
- **How often do you tell this story?**
- **When you tell this story, how do you feel?**
- **Is your story one you are creating about the future with a negative expectation based on the past?**
- **How is thinking in this way limiting you?**
- **What are the consequences of thinking this way?**
- **What do you want instead?**

When your story is a replay from the past or is a negative projection into the future, your body responds as if you are actually experiencing the event from the past all over again simply because you are thinking about it. The memory itself is abstract, but your mind and body think it is reality and project worst case scenario thinking. Our unconscious mind will do everything it can to keep us safe, even when there is no actual risk. It's a self-protection mechanism.

Janice - Case Study

Using The Spotlight Process and EFT to overcome limiting beliefs

Janice was a classic example of letting the past limit her up until the point we met. She had a constant gremlin babbling away inside her mind telling her she was foolish, useless and mustn't speak up or think well of herself in any way.

After working with Janice on a day's support programme and following up with some after-care sessions, we uncovered some of her childhood memories of growing up at home and school where she was often told to keep quiet, to be seen and not heard and quite clearly not to think too much of herself as it was deemed selfish and egotistical. She was frowned upon by her mother and teachers if she showed any emotions such as anger, sadness or frustration. It felt unsafe for her to express herself for fear of reprimand or criticism, so she closed down. She acted like a 'good girl' at all times and went to bed sobbing most nights, feeling desperately lonely, unheard and believing she wasn't loved. Janice stopped showing what she felt (it felt unsafe for her to be 'real' both at home and school). She felt insignificant and invisible for much of her life and this had carried on into adulthood until she came to work with me.

At the age of forty-five, Janice was still listening to the internalised voice of her mother and teachers reprimanding her as a child, she was acting and responding from her younger self. There is no blame here, Janice's mother was communicating in a way learnt through her own upbringing and experiences, she was simply telling Janice what her parents had told her, to be seen but not heard. Janice was in conflict with who she intrinsically believed herself to be as an individual - and who she was told she could be, based on what her mother and teachers told her and the limiting beliefs she formed as a consequence.

Running with the belief she was invisible, unloved and mustn't speak up, meant Janice was incredibly shy and self-restrained. She had little self-belief, put herself last in her family and constantly put other people's needs before her own. Janice didn't speak up when she felt she was being taken advantage of, she found it hard to say no to others and never gave her honest opinion in important matters, all of which lead to intense anger, desperation and a sense of emotional overwhelm. Janice really did believe love was conditional and meant looking after others, believing you could only be loved if you didn't show your emotions or give an opinion.

Janice had spent most of her life feeling powerless and inadequate; she was unhappy in her relationship with her mother, her marriage was in tatters and her health suffered with intense periods of stress and anxiety. Janice came to me in a state of grief and despair, not trusting she was capable of making the right choices for herself or her family, doubting she was able to make the simplest of decisions without seeking clarification from her mother or husband and their approval it was ok to do so.

Using The Spotlight Process, Janice came to a realisation she spent much of her life reacting to situations from the perspective of her childhood beliefs which she had formed about herself. She had formed many limiting beliefs about how she thought she 'should be' rather than who she was.

Janice was able to understand how the beliefs formed in childhood were no longer the best way of running her life as an adult. Having her mother's or teacher's approval was no longer necessary now she was a fully grown woman. She discovered it was ok to set personal boundaries with her mother and husband and speak up about the things which were important to her.

We used EFT to clear the frustration, anger, disappointment and sadness she had been carrying around since her childhood days. She transformed the belief she was unloved by her mother and released the sense of being powerless and inadequate, replacing it with feeling in control of her life and her future.

After some additional time working with Janice to improve communication and assertiveness she is now taking action. She speaks up clearly with her mother and husband without feeling the need to explain her opinion; she is making time for herself and prioritising her own needs. Janice is also learning to love herself and to give herself the time, love and care she didn't feel she had growing up. She is blossoming into a confident woman with a happy future ahead of her. As a mother to two children, Janice is also teaching her son and daughter it's ok to say no to others and to voice an opinion. The changes she has made in her actions and behaviours have benefitted not just her, but her family too. There is now much more consideration for others in the mix and I'm delighted for Janice that making some small changes has indeed reaped great rewards.

Practical Exercise using The Spotlight Process

Periodically throughout the day and at the end of each day, use The Spotlight Process to take stock of where you have spent most of your thought time (past, present or future) and answer the following questions which complement the process beautifully.

- **What have I been focusing on?**
- **Where have my thoughts been (past, present, future?)**
- **How have I been talking to myself for the last hour or two?**
- **Have I been talking to myself in a kindly way or a critical way?**
- **What images, stories, thoughts or feelings have I experienced today which have caused me distress?**
- **Which emotions and feelings have I experienced the most today?**
- **Have I been thinking about the future negatively or positively?**
- **What advice can I give myself to make tomorrow a better day?**
- **What choices can I make which will take me closer to my love and relationship goals?**

When you use the past to work for you rather than against you, you are able to filter your perceptions from the adult you. Responding from the grown-up part aids not only your personal development, but also encourages you to take action and to achieve things you desire. The child and adult you, will blossom when you treat yourself with love and kindness and this is exactly what Janice did.

You don't have to stay trapped in your thoughts just because you think them - Doug Dillon

Past – Present – Future

It's time to think about where you have been shining your light.

If you have been directing your light beam towards the pain and disappointments from the past, this is what you will see. If you have been shining your light on failed relationships and lack of love, this is what you may attract in the future. If you have been pointing the light on being alone, feeling lonely and on loneliness this only magnifies the feelings associated with being alone. Whatever you shine the light on, multiplies and grows, so shine it wisely.

When you are ready to direct your beam to a positive future, your focus will bring to mind all that is possible, all that is achievable and all that is attainable. Your sunbeam of light will bring hope, create joy and illuminate the potential in your relationships.

Shining the light on your past

If the light is within your heart, you will find your way home - Rumi

In this chapter, you will be creating a life inventory based on your negative past experiences with your mother to date. By completing this exercise, you will gain an awareness of how your relationship experiences have affected you. Within the inventory (a timeline of events in your relationship) please also record your emotions, thoughts, feelings and beliefs that were present at the time of each experience. Think about a specific memory of an event and record the feelings and emotions that remain connected to the event itself and/or towards your mother i.e. anger, hate, fear, grief. This Life Inventory can be used many times over across a range of personal experiences, you might want to work through.

The Life Inventory

The life inventory exercise can be used time and time again to work through any unresolved emotions from the past. If you find the following Life Inventory exercise a little upsetting, apply EFT as you go along, in the knowledge that any journey of transformation begins, by taking those first few steps. By getting over the first few hurdles, you will make positive change. If you prefer to work through this with guidance, please do make contact via my website: www.mothersanddaughters.solutions

Spend just 10-15 minutes working through the inventory, listening intuitively to whatever answers come to you as you read through. Use the life inventory for each memory you wish to transform.

Memory/Event/Title of the memory
(i.e. mum leaving me, mum threatening to kill herself, mum dying etc)

How old were you at the time of this experience?

What were your thoughts, feelings and emotions at the time? i.e. fear, anger, frustration, loneliness

Level of Distress

0 Neutral – 10 Intense

Who were you with in this memory?

↓

What happened in this memory?

↓

What belief did you form in this memory, about yourself and/or your mother?

↓

Is this belief currently benefitting you in any way right now? How may have this belief benefited you in the past?

↓

Tap through all the EFT tapping points until the level of distress has reduced to a 0

Where in your body do you experience this memory/emotion? (i.e. sensations in stomach, throat, chest, head etc)

↓

What does it feel like? Is there a colour, texture, sound, smell or taste connected to this experience?

↓

How has this belief presented itself in your life to date?

↓

What do you want instead of having this belief? (What was the missing event which didn't happen?)

↓

Check back to the original memory and notice what's changed

You will be working through emotions and limiting beliefs connected with each event and applying EFT to the specific tensions within your relationship with your mother. EFT stimulates and improves energy flow and releases the blocks which have become stagnant in the energy meridian system. Regular EFT tapping is encouraged to keep one's energy system in balance.

The past is over

All relationships, negative and positive, have an impact on you. It's up to you what you choose to focus on - Wendy Fry

The past is over. It's gone. It's history. Only your thoughts and energy of these negative experiences keep the past alive. It is your thinking and the energy connected to this experience which remains, not the actual experience itself.

Ponder these questions in terms of moving on from the past

- **What would it be like for you to move on from the past?**
- **How would your life change?**
- **What opportunities might come your way?**
- **What about love?**
- **What about relationships?**
- **How might your relationships be different if you choose right now to put the past behind you?**

You have the power to change your thoughts and your relationships. You are the driving force, with the power to use your past to work for you and not against you. It's time to take a breath, time to stand still and discard the thoughts which no longer serve you and only put back the thoughts which make you feel good. You are going to re-discover love with the absence of fear.

It's time to stop shining the light on the past because that's not where the future is.

I'm with you, I have your hand and I'm beside you all the way. I believe in you and by the time we finish this journey, the past will just be a distant memory and your future an opportunity to step more fully into your personal power.

Honesty is the best policy - how to recognise what isn't working in your life

Recap Exercise

- Use The Spotlight Process to track your thoughts
- Create an inventory of those negative, fearful beliefs and emotions which limit you, especially connected to the relationship with your mother
- Observe and question what you have come to believe about your relationship with your mother
- Keep a diary or journal to record any painful feelings, the situations in which these feelings arise and the self-talk which makes you feel unhappy. Use EFT to resolve these feelings and emotions
- Once you notice a thread of thought, examine whether the thoughts are propelling you forward towards joy and happiness, or whether your thoughts are holding you back from a happier relationship?
- Be aware from now on, when you think or behave in a way which may be limiting you. The words in your head create thoughts, those thoughts create feelings, the feelings create actions and actions create results (negative or positive)
- Let go of the beliefs no longer serving you using The Spotlight Process and EFT

AIDING YOUR OWN RECOVERY – LIMITING BELIEFS AND HOW TO CHANGE THEM

The Elimination Diet: Remove anger, regret, resentment, guilt, blame and worry. Then watch your health and life improve - Charles F. Glassman

What is a limiting belief?

You will unconsciously organise your actions and behaviour depending on your beliefs. Your beliefs are guiding principles and maps of how you make sense of the world. Some of your beliefs are not true and are simply thoughts which lead to your learnt behaviour and responses to people, events and life circumstances.

A limiting belief is a mental block stored in your mind, which limits your ability to achieve goals you set for yourself. A limiting belief acts as a barrier stopping you from achieving the success you desire and deserve, not only connected with the relationship with your mother but, in fact, with many other aspects of your life. A limiting belief is a repetitive, habitual thought which you think over and over again. It is my intention to guide you so you discover what negative beliefs you have about your mother and relationships generally. Your limiting beliefs create your perception, through self-talk and the internal dialogue you run inside your head. You can talk yourself into doing or not doing something and what you believe in, influences your behaviour and performance.

You may find yourself staying in the safety of your comfort zone, if a belief creates F E A R (**F**alse **E**vidence **A**ppearing **R**eal). Look carefully and you will see a limiting belief is nothing more than a thought you believe to be true. The word 'beLIEf' itself includes the word LIE and until we explore our beliefs, perceptions and judgments, we will not be aware of what lies we have been telling ourselves.

As with judgements, limiting beliefs are nothing but patterns of thoughts. Just because your experiences in the past may have been true, it does not necessarily follow they will continue to be true. You may find yourself building up walls of protection, trying to keep yourself safe from disappointment and heartache when in fact, it is these very walls which confine you and may stop you from having amazing relationships with yourself and others.

The conversations you have inside your mind, may build on existing limiting beliefs, as you find yourself replaying the limiting beliefs over and over. Limiting beliefs can affect every part of your life, your work, your well-being, your relationships and it is those beliefs we form about love in our early years, which impact our lives later on.

The limiting beliefs you have formed may be based on old fears, old hurts or old stories that have no relevance in the present moment. You may be blocked within certain areas of your life because of the beliefs you are running. These beliefs do not just influence how positive or negative a relationship will be, our limiting beliefs impact all areas of our lives. Those limiting beliefs will collapse the moment you stop feeding them and you can achieve this through the use of EFT and The Spotlight Process as detailed in this chapter.

Limiting beliefs and lifetime issues

In childhood we form many beliefs. In fact, childhood represents a huge percentage of our overall life experience. The experiences we have growing up, contribute to our inner dialogue. We may tell ourselves we are at fault in some way for whatever went wrong in our early years, even though this is based on false information or a misguided perception. Limiting core beliefs are the driving force in our lives and reflect our deepest vulnerabilities and pain. We are reacting from the younger part of ourselves. Our limiting core beliefs distance us from believing we are lovable and open to receiving love. Operating from the negative parts of ourselves, we cannot see the positives and the opportunities available to us.

Working through these beliefs, will bring more balance to your life and allow you the opportunity for personal transformation. This chapter supports you in gathering together the negative messages you heard about yourself growing up, the abuses, the traumas, and the conflicts. We have these kinds of experiences growing up and we are effected in different ways. Giving a voice to our feelings and experiences, no matter how old we are, gives us a new sense of liberation, a feeling of empowerment and an opportunity to put the past in the past once and for all.

Discovering limiting beliefs, behaviours, thoughts and emotions

Core beliefs can be represented as a table. At the top of the table, is the limiting core belief. This is held up by the table legs which are formed from family conditioning, societal conditioning, emotional events, upset and trauma. Your core beliefs may also have many other beliefs underlying them and supporting the core belief.

Here is a list of limiting beliefs you may have formed about yourself, life and relationships. Life issues related to core beliefs, come from the perception of success, love, belonging, self-worth, control, security, reality and reason. Core beliefs grow stronger rather than weaker (as we filter for evidence to back-up the false belief).

Read through this list and record which limiting beliefs are true for you:

I'm unlovable	I can't do it	I'm flawed/imperfect
I'm unwanted	I'm different	I don't matter
I'm bad	I'm unforgivable	I must be approved of

Something bad will happen	Something must change for me to be ok	I'm not strong enough
The world is dangerous	I'm helpless	Life is hopeless
People take advantage	I must be perfect	I must be in control
I don't belong	I'm not good enough	I can't trust anyone
I'm a failure	I'm insignificant	I'm shameful
I'm a mistake	I'm helpless	I'm not special enough
I'm invisible	I'm guilty	I'm not interesting
I'm unworthy	I'm undeserving	I'm worthless
I'm incapable	I'm misunderstood	I'm abandoned
I will be betrayed	I'm unproductive	I'm unattractive
I'm incompetent	I'm a failure	I'm a victim
I'm a burden	I'm dumb	I'm used
I'm alone	I'm bad	I'm guilty
I'm sinful	I'm confused	I'm trapped
I'm unlovable	I'm powerless	I'm inferior
I'm separated from a higher power	I'm un-teachable	I'm vulnerable
I'm stupid	I'm weak	I can't get it right
I'm vulnerable	I'm unsuccessful	I'm ugly
I can't say 'no'	I can't stand up for myself	I don't belong
I should not be here at all	I'm afraid	I'm fat
I'm unattractive	I'm left out	I don't deserve to be loved

Global Issues

Global issues relate to people who you may have had negative experiences with in your life and who have contributed negatively to your concept and beliefs about yourself

Mother/Father	Religious Institutions/ Societal influence	Brothers/Sisters
Extended family/step family	Teachers/School/ College	Other relationships

The good news is, beliefs aren't permanent and can be changed

Beliefs are nothing more than empowering or limiting thoughts. The beliefs we choose to give our attention to, guide our actions, behaviours and circumstances. Our core beliefs were developed at a time when we were children, when we had minimal ability to reason and think rationally for ourselves. The beliefs handed down to us were formed by our mother, other caregivers, mentors, teachers, environment and culture. Core beliefs form the picture we paint of ourselves, a portrait of our own abilities, our worth, flaws, strengths and our relationships with others and with the world. Our beliefs establish the limits of what we think we can, or can't, achieve.

We behave in ways consistent with our beliefs and values. Our beliefs impact on much of what we do, the thoughts we think, our feelings and our physical symptoms. We delete, distort and generalise information by forming an intricate filter of opinions, emotions and memories and we only notice what we think supports the existing belief.

Our thoughts, assumptions and beliefs influence the way we feel and what we choose to do

A limiting belief is a thought, or series of thoughts stopping us from moving forwards in life. Limiting beliefs could be based on past personal experiences or through witnessing the experiences of others. Limiting beliefs also shape the form of our thought patterns, including irrational thinking. We all, at some point, experience limiting beliefs. Until we examine what it is we believe and change any limiting beliefs to a more empowering belief, we are stuck inside the prison of our own thinking.

Beliefs have the potential to be changed by cultivating awareness; we can choose what it is we want to believe. Challenging a limiting belief with awareness, effective questioning and using The Spotlight Process and EFT, may seriously improve a person's sense of self-worth, reduce fear, improve confidence, improve communication (internal and external dialogues) and open up all sorts of new and exciting possibilities.

What are your limiting beliefs?

To measure how true a limiting belief may be for you, there is a scale called The Validity of Cognition (VoC) Scale. This is an individualised measure of beliefs, developed by Francine Shapiro. Use the VOC Scale to check the percentage of your current self-limiting beliefs, rating them from a 0 when you have no belief at all and 100 when the belief feels completely true for you.

Read through the list below to identify which limiting beliefs are true for you and add your own limiting beliefs to the list.

- **Fear of not being good enough**
- **Fear of not being loved**
- **Fear of rejection**
- **Fear of separation or loss of relationship**
- **Fear of failure**
- **Fear of being controlled by another**
- **Fear of success**

You may be wondering right now how you can transform your limiting beliefs about your mother, so here goes:

Part of the process of changing limiting beliefs is cultivating awareness, so we can distinguish the difference between:

- **What we'd like to believe**
- **What we think we should believe**
- **What we truly believe.**

It is our limited and negative thinking which holds us back from the things we seek. Beliefs are often so unconscious we seldom question them.

With effective self-questioning, taking into account:

- **When the belief was formed**
- **Whose belief it is (is it yours or was it handed down to you?)**
- **How the belief limits you and what it stops you from achieving**
- **How the limiting belief may actually serve a purpose (secondary gain or payoff behaviour)**
- **If the beliefs you hold are still appropriate for you as an adult based on your current reality**

Each of us has a choice and by choosing empowering beliefs much can be changed in our lives for the better.

In order to change a limiting belief we need to change the internal picture and representation we have of ourselves, of others and the world around us. Over time, our creative subconscious mind recognises new pictures and beliefs as a new reality and selects information from a different perspective. Instead of looking through dirty windows at the same old dirt, we notice things we never saw before or experienced before.

If a limiting belief is based on a lie or is a belief formed by someone else's opinion, then it is time to change the belief. Challenging a limiting belief and working out where it comes from, will provide enormous benefits. Changing our beliefs offers a renewed sense of freedom and there is a willingness to take new risks once we decide to look at the world through new windows.

Read through the following questions and notice your responses. You might be surprised at how unkind the thoughts you have about yourself really are.

- **How many of your thoughts about yourself are critical, blaming, bullying, shaming, ugly, unloving, downright rude and uncaring?**
- **What do you say to yourself on a regular basis which is damaging and unkind?**
- **How often do you project into the future the idea relationships are pointless, that you're not good enough, deserving enough etc?**
- **Would you talk to a best friend or a child the way you talk to and criticise yourself?**
- **Would you tell that person they will never amount to anything, say they are useless, unlovable, worthless, stupid, ugly, shameful, inadequate?**

Chances are you would not say these things or others like them to another person and so it's high time you stopped speaking about yourself in a limiting way. It's time to start loving yourself and giving yourself the time, attention, love and care you deserve.

The benefits of changing your limiting beliefs will be worth the commitment you make to yourself. Your future is in your hands now and if you want to make the rest of your life the best of your life, EFT and The Spotlight Process will lead the way. For longer standing emotions and limiting beliefs, patience and a willingness to use EFT regularly, will aid your progress towards overcoming more traumatic experiences. Our main problems and limiting beliefs, come from the perception of our level of success, love, belonging, self-worth, control, security, reality and reason. Once we realise the stories and movies we play in our minds are outdated and unhelpful, we know which areas to work on, transforming them through the use of EFT.

When you are ready to learn more about the science behind limiting beliefs, take a look at *Transform Your Beliefs, Transform Your Life: EFT Tapping Using Matrix Reimprinting by Karl Dawson and Kate Marillat.*

Remember, there is never any blame. Whatever you discover which has shaped your beliefs (if you felt unloved, unimportant, ignored or rejected by your mother) it doesn't mean she didn't love you, it was purely the meaning and belief you placed on an event or series of events and experiences with the knowledge you and she had at the time.

We forget as adults many of the beliefs we formed in childhood are outdated, destructive and are often completely wrong. Joking aside, I would like to remind you of some old, outdated, beliefs you may have moved on from already:

- Father Christmas
- The Tooth Fairy
- Monsters under the bed
- Fairy tales and other stories

Understanding beliefs and past conditioning

At this point in your life you may have many different beliefs about love and relationships running. When I say running, I mean running like movies, running through your mind or running like taped conversations playing over in your head or an endless series of thoughts, feelings and emotions moving through you.

These movies represent a constant flow of negatives (the voice of our inner critic/voice of doom, like a parasite eating away at us from the inside. We replay over and over the same movies and the same story, until the story becomes engrained. The movies or inner stories then become the default behaviours we respond to when presented with a situation like one we have experienced before and triggers off what we believe to be true. Most of what we react to has very little to do with a new experience and everything to do with past experiences (old movies)

What's blocking you from love?

It is crucial to ask yourself whether there is any benefit in keeping hold of limiting beliefs about the relationship with your mother. It might seem like an odd question to ask. However, we may hold onto something which limits us as it has a 'pay off' or secondary gain, a benefit of some sort. We may do this unconsciously without even realising it. More often than not, the things we say we don't want and don't like are things familiar to us. The feeling of familiarity and staying in our comfort zones can be appealing, even if we say we don't like something we feel safe in its sameness.

Think about the problem or limiting belief you would like to change. Use the VoC Scale to measure the percentage of each belief and how true it is for you - 0% being untrue and 100% being totally true for you. You may wish to also start tapping round your tapping points, using EFT, as you ask yourself the following statements:

- **Do I deserve to get over this problem?**
- **Is it good for me to get over this problem?**
- **Is it safe for me to get over this problem?**
- **Is it safe for others if I get over this problem?**
- **Is it possible for me to overcome this problem?**

- **Can I choose to allow myself to get over this problem?**
- **Am I willing to do what it takes to get over this problem?**

It is worth also noting your responses to the following questions

- **What are the negative aspects of you no longer having this problem?**
- **What would you lose if you didn't have this problem?**
- **What are the positive aspects of you not having this problem?**
- **What needs to happen to end this situation?**
- **What resources do you have or need to end this situation?**

As you read through *Mothers and Daughters,* there will be key points in the questioning I use and the information shared, will help you to examine your own beliefs, perceptions and judgements, aiding you to uncover the blocks which might be preventing you from finding love and enjoying happy and harmonious relationships.

POWER QUESTIONS

Your mind will answer most questions if you learn to relax and wait for the answer - William S. Burroughs

Questions like the ones posed here and throughout the book will offer you further insights into who your mother was, how you are like or unlike her and also how to express yourself more fully, releasing the pain from the past and discovering possibilities for the future of your relationships.

1. **What is your personal opinion of how a mother 'should' be?**

2. **What is your reality compared to your ideal?**
3. **Are you a mother?**
4. **If so, how often do you exhibit the qualities of how you think a mother should be?**
5. **When do you find yourself mothering in the opposite way to your experience, so as not to be like your mother?**
6. **In what circumstances are you like your mother?**
7. **What character strengths and weaknesses do you share?**
8. **What did your mother teach you about life, love and living?**
9. **Which negative emotions do you suffer from the most when you think of your mother? i.e. anger, guilt, sadness**
10. **What imagined fears are you still playing out? i.e. she will disapprove of me, reject me, punish me etc**
11. **How are you measuring your self-worth and lovability when it comes to your mother?**
12. **Is this an accurate measure?**
13. **What evidence supports your beliefs relating to self-worth and being worthy of love?**
14. **What have been your three most traumatic events in your life in relation to your mother and how have these events shaped you?**
15. **How do these experiences you have had with your mother hold you back in life?**
16. **In what ways have your experiences with your mother worked for you?**

17. What aspects of your childhood prevent you from feeling more at peace with yourself?

18. What resentments are you still carrying towards your mother?

19. What limiting beliefs do you have about your mother?

20. What limiting beliefs do you have about yourself? i.e. I'm not good enough, I'm not worthy etc

21. What limiting beliefs do you have about the relationship with your mother?

22. What limiting beliefs do you have about relationships generally?

23. What positive empowering beliefs would you like to have instead?

24. How will having these alternative beliefs support you in what you want to achieve?

25. In taking one positive action today which will improve how you feel about your relationship with your mother, how will making this choice benefit you?

Working through these questions and the other coaching style questions throughout *Mothers and Daughters* will continue to support you in understanding your mother and your relationship dynamics.

ENDING THE CYCLE OF PAIN

Rain after all is only rain; it is not bad weather. So also, pain is only pain; unless we resist it, then it becomes torment - I Ching

In addition to the choice of healing modalities offered in this chapter, helping you to break free from the cycle of pain, Chapter Four Mining for Gold, also offers various opportunities to heal your past through use of letter writing, poetry, candle ceremony and talking through your problems.

ART AS A MEANS OF EXPRESSION

Art is one of the greatest forms of human expression which you can use to release and convey your inner landscape. You might choose to experiment with artistic statements through painting, drawing, collage, mosaic, glass blowing, pottery, ceramics or textiles or, you might decide to create a nature garden or similar. Using art as a form of healing has so many benefits. Marion Dutton's wonderful book, *The Healing Art: The Ultimate Guide to Painting & Creative Therapy,* will offer plenty of guidance on using art as a form of healing.

WRITING AND JOURNALING

Writing and journaling are helpful aids to release emotional overwhelm. Whether you choose to purchase a special journal for writing, venting and expressing inner most thoughts and feelings is up to you. I personally write freehand with a good biro on A4 lined paper. I write uncensored without paying attention to spelling or grammar and keep writing until I feel a shift in emotion and a physical release. Julia Cameron details in *'The Artist's Way',* a process called 'Morning Pages', whereby each morning you write three sides of A4 paper to fully express how you feel. It is such a great way to unburden yourself, writing out all your concerns and fears, or simply using the writing as a means to clear your 'mental chatter' and prepare you for the day ahead.

When I've had a lot going on in my life or have been through a period of uncertainty, Morning Pages has been a wonderful outlet, enabling me to express my thoughts feelings and emotions without the judgment of others. As a reminder, Chapter Four offers a step-by-step guide to journaling.

CONNECTION WITH OTHER DAUGHTERS

As I conclude this chapter, I must acknowledge the chapter which follows. In Women's Words of Wisdom, you can read, a selection of daughter's experiences across the globe from completed questionnaires. What's shared in these pages, will not cover every eventuality in the mother-daughter relationship, though it is certainly my hope that by sharing the information passed to me, it will make you feel less alone in your own journey.

It is in finding connection with others who share similar experiences and those who strive towards common goals, which will open up our world even further. When we understand others and can empathise, we begin to understand our own story as well as our mother's.

Chapter 7

Women's Words of Wisdom

Women's Words of Wisdom

Mothers and Daughters would not be complete without the case studies and words of wisdom shared throughout these pages. It is with thanks and appreciation, through the openness of the amazing women, who were brave enough to tell their stories that we have an opportunity to learn about ourselves and in turn can begin to understand our mothers. The examples do not represent the whole range of mother-daughter relationships, they have been chosen to offer insights into some of the ways in which difficult relationships form and how those relationship dynamics shape our lives.

The case studies are from daughters aged 17 to 83, from different ethnic and socioeconomic backgrounds who have reached deep into the vaults of their childhood memories and willingly shared them with us. Many are also mothers, grandmothers or stepmothers. Some are daughters of foster mothers, adoptive mothers, stepmothers or have been daughters in a 'sibling carers' role. In some cases, I have changed the identity and detail slightly to protect those involved.

It was difficult to know exactly how to present the returned questionnaires. Not wanting to dilute individual experiences and to keep their voices intact, I am sharing an unedited selection which I hope will give you a deeper understanding of how each of these daughters' experiences have impacted their lives. Despite having gone through trauma and personal pain, these incredible women have honestly and openly shared their hearts and minds. Thanks to them, we can see we are not alone.

In Mothers and Daughters I contribute my own experience as a daughter and also as a professional supporting woman who helps others overcome relationship conflicts. Case studies include daughters who are also mothers and grandmothers who reveal how difficult it is at times to be 'a good mother' and how they, too, struggle with the challenges which come from being a woman and her expected role within the family.

What is shared may or may not be true for you. It is my hope that you gain an insight into the lives of other daughters as a whole and can take something from their experience which aids your own transformation.

The case studies also include those special moments daughters have experienced with their mothers. Even if these were few and far between, focusing on the positives and the gifts our mothers gave us, enables us to create new meaning in our lives.

With awareness, we can reframe our experiences and in doing so we stop searching outside of ourselves for love - knowing who we are is so worth loving regardless of the past. A willingness to open and share our stories heals not just our own wounds, but helps women across the world to heal.

Where questions have not been applicable the answer is sometimes shown as N/A. Some responses were left blank in which case I have added 'left blank'.

Q&A

Name: *Kim*

Age: *46 years young*

Are you a mother as well as a daughter? Yes/No if yes, how many children do you have what are their sexes?

No

What is your current personal relationship status: Single/ widowed/divorced/separated/co-habiting, second marriage etc:

I'm going through a divorce right now

Your mother's age as she is now if applicable:

Left blank

The age your mother was when she died if applicable (how old were you when she died?)

79 years

Your mother's Ethnic origin/Nationality/country of birth

Swedish, Sweden, white

Details of your Siblings, current ages and sexes:

A half brother (my mother's) 64 years

Details of your mother's siblings, age gap between them and your mother and sexes

No siblings

Are you part of a step family? If so do you have good relationship with them now?

No

Were you in care, adopted or fostered as a child/teenager?

No

If you were raised by your mother how did she raise you? I.e. single parent, with your father, with a step father, with aid of a grandparent?

Married with my father until I was 12, then they divorced and I came to live with my mother (just me and her)

Was your mother unavailable emotionally, physically or mentally ill and away from the family home for any length of time while you were growing up?

Oh yes (unavailable emotionally and mentally ill)

Did your mother use prescribed medications (for depression etc), recreational drugs, or alcohol to excess or have any addictions?

No

Was your mother ever physically violent or abusive towards you? *(Yes no is fine here if you want to keep the information brief)*

Yes, all the time. I can see now that I'm an adult that every time she got upset, sad, angry or any other "negative" emotion she abused me physically and verbally to get relief from her feelings.

What motivates you to share your experiences in relation to your mother?

I want others to know that it's not just in their family, that's there's nothing wrong with them nor something they did to deserve it and that's ok to talk about it openly.

Describe in a few sentences how you feel about your mother (feel free to use uncensored your experience)

A large part of me feels sorry for her and a small part of me still hates her for what she did to me and I think I will loath her until I come to terms with what she did and who she was and are able to forgive her completely. I can understand intellectually where she came from and why she behaved the way she did, but emotionally I'm still suffering from it.

When you think of your mother what emotions/feelings come up for you?

Anger, hatred, sadness, loathing, pity, grief, guilt, rage, rejection, helplessness, insecurity, sorrow, loneliness, disease, Invaded, controlled, no personal space and privacy that she (her presence dead or alive) can't penetrate.

What triggers or challenges bring up personal pain for you in relations to your mother? *I.e. perceived rejection, not feeling heard, not being considered, other people's anger, feeling unloved by a partner, seeing Mothers Day Cards, birthdays and celebrations etc.*

All of the above and a feeling of unworthiness, of not being good enough, deprived of my mother's love, deprived of my worth as a human being.

What were your unmet needs in childhood (regardless of the reason why) in relation to your mother?

Too many to count, I wanted/needed to be loved, seen and heard, made an important family member, respected as a person and not having my boundaries crossed all the time.

If your mother is alive what do you want from her now that you're not currently getting?

Left blank

How have your experienced your mother as you both age, what changes have you noticed?

I now feel sorry for her (I pity her) most of the time instead of going into 'how could you have done this and that to me'......

What do you believe about yourself or the world around you in relation to your experience with your mother?

I destroyed my mother's life and her happiness, I'm unlovable (getting much better now), I don't deserve happiness, no-one can love me, as soon as things start to get good something is going to happen that destroys it, I'm not worthy of respect, my boundaries are not important.

What is or has been your greatest fear in relation to you mother (for yourself and/or for her)?

That she's right, that I'm totally worthless and a burden to everyone who knows me (and that's why I don't have any friends who wants to spend time with me) and I'm never going to amount to anything and I'm going to self-sabotage anything good that comes into my reach.

How has your experience with your mother impacted other relationships?

I have a hard time trusting other people, I feel uncomfortable when I interact with people I know a little bit and I feel unsure and insecure in my social life. I have a hard time believing that people can like me, I feel disrespected and I have a hard time knowing when to say no and actually do it.

What beliefs do you have about relationships based on your own experience?

I don't deserve any good relationships at all, especially not a nice, good and kind significant other. It's hard to find friends who don't to use me.

What are your beliefs about 'women as mothers' in this era and how they should live their lives raise a family, have a career etc?

Of course women should be able to have careers of their own if they want to and they should be able to be stay-at-home moms too if they want to without being ridiculed for it. Without feeling as "bad mothers" for it whatever they choose.

What do you know about your mother's childhood and upbringing, her hopes, fears, beliefs about herself or the world around her?

Not much, she always used to tell me what a dreadful mean mother she had and how happy and grateful I ought to be to have such a kind mother as she and how thankful she would have been if her mother had been as nice as her (She used to say this every time she abused me.) But she never really talked about her upbringing and my questions about it went unanswered.

Reflecting on your past what stands out to you the most about your mother?

She really pitied herself, nothing was ever her fault, she was just a victim of others bad choices and bad luck.

What is your biggest regret when you think about your relationship with your mother?

That I didn't tell her how I felt about her and how she'd treated me as a child earlier.

If you were able to change your childhood what did you need the most from your mother that you never received? How would you have preferred your upbringing to be?

Of course I would want a "perfect" childhood with loving parents that saw me for me and told me I was valuable and knew the difference between me as a person and my actions, but..... I guess if I change anything I won't be the 'me' that I am today.

If you were able right now to say what you wanted to say to your mother, what would you say?

Why couldn't you see me? Why did you hate me so much?

How has your experience of your mother shaped you life to date (negative and positive aspects?)

I wrote this as an answer earlier but it goes here too. I have a hard time trusting other people, I feel uncomfortable when I interact with people I know a little bit and I feel unsure and insecure in my social life. I have a hard time believing that people can like me, I feel disrespected and I have a hard time knowing when to say no and actually do it.

I feel insecure of myself around other people, always on my guard, having a hard time believing anyone can like me and yet I want to be liked and respected really bad. I still feel unsure of me deserving love, attention and good things happening to me.

What did /has your mother taught you about being a woman, being a mother, life, love and living?

Being women meant you have to be nice, a good cook and have clean home so that you got married. And after you got married serve your husband 24/7. And don't get children, you'll regret that.

Depending on your relationship status with your mother if she is still alive how would you like the future of your relationship to be?

Even though my mother is dead I would like my future relationship with her to be a loving and kind relationship.

What gets in the way of not having the kind of relationship you've just shared?

I haven't forgiven either of us yet, but I'm working on that.

When you are with your mother do you find yourself reacting to her as an adult or as a child/teenager from the hurt part of yourself?

I reacted to her in both ways, sometimes as a grown up and sometimes as a little child.

If you were able to create you 'ideal mother' what would that be like for you? What would be her qualities, attributes, gifts, how would she be with you? What would she say to you right now?

She would love me unconditionally, know the difference between action and person, she would see herself as valuable, love and respect herself, know her boundaries and feel secure in her womanhood and of course be able to teach me all of those things.

What is the biggest thing you've learnt about yourself on your journey with or without your mother so far?

Maybe I'm not a bad person, maybe I can actually learn to love myself completely.

How do you meet your own needs now as an adult?

I'm trying to respect and listen to myself and my body.

What got you through your experiences?

I'm not through yet, but EFT, healing and self-help books.

What positive and negative traits do you have that your mother had/has?

I'm unsure about myself and my worthiness as a human being.

What things do you enjoy doing that your mother enjoyed?

Can't think of anything

Knowing that your mother gave you the gift of life, what are you most grateful for in recognition of this?

That I'm still alive

Using your past to make your future the best it can what skills and resources have you developed to use to your greater good?

I'm sensitive to other people's needs and emotions, I want everything I do to be perfect, I am good at being alone, I'm kind of independent of others, I'm really patient and I have compassion for others.

Please include any additional information as you wish that you feel is important for me to know.

My mother used to tell me when she abused me that I'd ruined her life and she wished me dead. She said that every time until I moved away from home when I was 15. When I was a little girl (4-6 years old I think) she showed me a special flower in our garden and told me that if I ate that flower I would die. So I did that to please her, but as you know I didn't die.

Q&A

Name: *Francesca*

Age: *53*

Are you a mother as well as a daughter? Yes/No if yes, how many children do you have what are their sexes?

Yes, son aged 30

What is your current personal relationship status: Single/ widowed/divorced/separated/co-habiting, second marriage etc

Divorced

Your mother's age as she is now if applicable:

85

The age your mother was when she died if applicable (how old were you when she died?)

N/A

Your mother's Ethnic origin/Nationality/country of birth

British

Details of your Siblings, current ages and sexes:

None

Details of your mother's siblings, age gap between them and your mother and sexes:

Several sisters older

Are you part of a step family? If so do you have good relationship with them now?

Yes, yes

Were you in care, adopted or fostered as a child/teenager?

Yes, in convent and foster care age 4-8

If you were raised by your mother how did she raise you? I.e. a single parent, with your father, with a step father, with aid of a grandparent

With step father who was often absent for work so partly as a single parent

Was your mother unavailable emotionally, physically or mentally ill and away from the family home for any length of time while you were growing up?

She was often distracted by her own needs: her own challenging relationship with my step-father. As well as this she spent a lot of time in a state of childlike abandonment due to the loss of her own mother, traumatic relationships in her past and was unable to fully comprehend what being a mother meant. She saw me almost like an accessory that she could be proud of when she felt like it and at other times I was in the way.

Did your mother use prescribed medications (for depression etc), recreational drugs, or alcohol to excess or have any addictions?

Not that I am aware of

Was your mother ever physically violent or abusive towards you? *(Yes no is fine here if you want to keep the information brief)*

Yes she had a bad temper and would fly into rages

What motivates you to share your experiences in relation to your mother?

To help others primarily and because we have a better relationship now. I understand her as a woman who was in a society that didn't support her needs. I forgive her for her mistakes because I am a mother who also makes mistakes and I understand that we are all doing the best we can with the tools we have.

Describe in a few sentences how you feel about your mother (feel free to use uncensored your experience)

Compassion, understanding of her past issues, understanding of her powerlessness as a woman in previous decades, sadness at her lack of assertiveness or ability to communicate her needs.

When you think of your mother what emotions/feelings come up for you?

Sadness, loss, depth of wisdom life understanding, compassion, pity and sometimes frustration

What triggers or challenges bring up personal pain for you in relations to your mother? *I.e. perceived rejection, not feeling heard, not being considered, other people's anger, feeling unloved by a partner, seeing Mothers Day Cards, birthdays and celebrations etc*

Her inability to be empathic, only seeing the world and myself through her own eyes. Seeing the difference between my mother and my step-mother. My step-mother has always been supremely strong and supportive and treated me as an individual in my own right. Understanding that my step mother was brought up in a very secure environment, completely different to my own mother's upbringing which was filled with insecurity and abandonment.

What were your unmet needs in childhood (regardless of the reason why) in relation to your mother?

Being allowed to be an individual my own person rather than only being there to keep her happy. My mother putting herself first.

If your mother is alive what do you want from her now that you're not currently getting?

Nothing, we are in a good enough place and I have acceptance of that (apart from her Alzheimer's which is very challenging)

How have your experienced your mother as you both age, what changes have you noticed?

My understanding of 'us' as women in the world and my sadness that she never felt as independent as I have done in my own life – I've had better opportunities in society that weren't available to her and considering that she did a great job.

What do you believe about yourself or the world around you in relation to your experience with your mother?

I used to believe I had to survive by myself and was distant from her. That she wasn't capable of being there for me. Now I believe that life 'is as it is' nothing is ever 'tidy' and I believe that she has loved me in the best way and the only way she knew how.

What is or has been your greatest fear in relation to your mother (for yourself and/or for her)?

For her: that she will end her life without ever having known true love, self-love, and the bigger picture of life – yet I also see that that is my journey, not hers, and that she has done exactly what she's meant to have done in this lifetime.

How has your experience with your mother impacted other relationships?

I used to leap into relationships or not trust at all. Now I have balance.

What beliefs do you have about relationships based on your own experience?

We're all doing the best we can. Life can be messy. Love is what counts.

What are your beliefs about 'women as mothers' in this era and how they should live their lives raise a family, have a career etc?

I think it's hard because along with opportunities women have the pressure of believing they have to be all things to all people. Society hasn't caught up with its own good intentions. I think women do a fantastic job whatever path they choose, we need to be more supportive of each other. Whether we have sons or daughters we need to instil confidence in them and that they are loved and good enough – that's all that matters at the end of the day.

What do you know about your mother's childhood and upbringing, her hopes, fears, beliefs about herself or the world around her?

She was brought up in Ireland on a farm, mother died when she was nine. Older sisters raised her and the other younger siblings. She was very alone in the world. Went to London and married the wrong man - my father.

Reflecting on your past what stands out to you the most about your mother?

Her vulnerability and inability to be strong for me or teach me that I could be strong for me, it took me decades to learn this by myself.

What is your biggest regret when you think about your relationship with your mother?

Sadness that she never really got it but then there are times when she says things and the spirit shines through and I wonder if perhaps she got it a lot more than I realised.

If you were able to change your childhood what did you need the most from your mother that you never received? How would you have preferred your upbringing to be?

More secure. My mother being a more confident person.

If you were able right now to say what you wanted to say to your mother, what would you say?

I love you, of course.

How has your experience of your mother shaped your life to date (negative and positive aspects?)

It's all been part of the big journey into wisdom. Awful messes and mistakes until my own middle age but great learning too. Learning about deeper understanding of women, her as a woman, society, and letting go of hurts.

What did /has your mother taught you about being a woman, being a mother, life, love and living?

She taught me love.

Depending on your relationship status with your mother if she is still alive how would you like the future of your relationship to be?

To continue on as the friends we've become in our understanding of being two women in the world.

What gets in the way of not having the kind of relationship you've just shared?

Her Alzheimer's but I'm so glad we got there before she became ill.

When you are with your mother do you find yourself reacting to her as an adult or as a child/teenager from the hurt part of yourself?

Occasionally I do slip into teenager mode, if I'm tired or stressed, but the majority of the time I remain the adult.

If you were able to create your 'ideal mother' what would that be like for you? What would be her qualities, attributes, gifts, how would she be with you? What would she say to you right now?

More like my step-mother: an inner strength; a mother who had a great childhood, was secure and confident in herself and so knew how to love me as a child and put my needs as a child before her own fears and desires.

What is the biggest thing you've learnt about yourself on your journey with or without your mother so far?

To love myself

How do you meet your own needs now as an adult?

Self-care, sense of humour, not taking life too seriously

What got you through your experiences?

A sense of knowing that there's something more, my soul

What positive and negative traits do you have that your mother had/has?

Sense of humour, I can be self-focused when I am in a childish mood

What things do you enjoy doing that your mother enjoyed?

Creative things, writing

Knowing that your mother gave you the gift of life, what are you most grateful for in recognition of this?

Life!

Using your past to make your future the best it can be, what skills and resources have you developed to use for your greater good?

Self-care, EFT, Matrix Reimprinting, self-acceptance, acceptance of mum

Q&A

Name: *Jude*

Age: *48*

Are you a mother as well as a daughter? Yes/No If yes, how many children do you have what are their sexes?

2 girls, age 19 and 14

What is your current personal relationship status: Single/widowed/divorced/separated/co-habiting, second marriage etc

Divorced

Your mother's age as she is now if applicable:

77

The age your mother was when she died if applicable (how old were you when she died?)

Left blank

Your mother's Ethnic origin/Nationality/country of birth

British

Details of your Siblings, current ages and sexes:

Sister age 52, brother age 50

Details of your mother's siblings, age gap between them and your mother and sexes:

Sister 71 – 6 year gap

1 sister died aged 56, 6 years ago, November

Are you part of a step family? If so do you have a good relationship with them now?

No

Were you in care, adopted or fostered as a child/teenager?

If you were raised by your mother, how did she raise you? I.e. single parent, with your father, with a step father, with aid of a grandparent. Please include what's relevant for you

Mother and father – still married

Was your mother unavailable emotionally, physically or mentally ill and away from the family home for any length of time while you were growing up?

Left blank

Did your mother use prescribed medications (for depression etc), recreational drugs, or alcohol to excess or have any addictions?

No

Was your mother ever physically violent or abusive towards you? *(Yes/no is fine here if you want to keep the information brief)*

No

What motivates you to share your experiences in relation to your mother?

Left blank

Describe in a few sentences how you feel about your mother (feel free to use uncensored your experience)

I always feel and felt that I had to make my mother happy, if she wasn't happy I felt sad and still do.

When you think of your mother what emotions/feelings come up for you?

That my mother never really supported me emotionally, I had to support her.

What triggers or challenges bring up personal pain for you in relations to your mother? *I.e. perceived rejection, not feeling heard, not being considered, other people's anger, feeling unloved by a partner, seeing Mothers Day Cards, birthdays and celebrations etc*

I was told I was not a planned child and I have truly felt I was always left out, although my mother would disagree with this.

What were your unmet needs in childhood (regardless of the reason why) in relation to your mother?

I felt my brother and sister were the favourites and definitely my sister was my father's favourite. I felt unsupported.

If your mother is alive what do you want from her now that you're not currently getting?

I want her to live her own life and release me from the caretaker role that I have got, once she is happy I can be.

How have you experienced your mother as you both age, what changes have you noticed?

I have felt very much tied to my mother most of my life, I am not sure if this is where the guilt has come from.

What do you believe about yourself or the world around you in relation to your experience with your mother?

I believe a lot of my insecurities have come from not feeling good enough. The toxic relationships I find myself in, I feel I am not worth much.

What is or has been your greatest fear in relation to your mother (for yourself and/or for her)?

My greatest fear is she will not be happy and I will always have the caretaker role and will not be able to be free until she is happy.

How has your experience with your mother impacted other relationships?

My relationships have more often than not been with narcissistic men, I never felt good enough, always looking for approval.

What beliefs do you have about relationships based on your own experience?

I have a low belief about relationships. I am very, very wary who I become involved with. I have trust issues.

What are your beliefs about 'women as mothers' in this era and how they should live their lives to raise a family, have a career etc?

No sure if this is a belief or how I have done it but I have given everything and left myself nothing - which I would not recommend.

What do you know about your mother's childhood and upbringing, her hopes, fears, beliefs about herself or the world around her?

My mother's upbringing was terrible, really abusive, she had low self esteem, her parents argued terribly, her father put his mother before his wife.

Reflecting on your past what stands out to you the most about your mother?

That she was sad but happy at times, she at times was frightened of my dad, she never spoke up if anything worried her.

What is your biggest regret when you think about your relationship with your mother?

That she was not able to show me emotional support and that I never felt free to live my life.

If you were able to change your childhood what did you need the most from your mother that you never received? How would you have preferred your upbringing to be?

I would have preferred to be on a level with my siblings, to feel wanted.

If you were able right now to say what you wanted to say to your mother, what would you say?

I would say, did you plan me, I know the answer.

How has your experience of your mother shaped your life to date (negative and positive aspects?)

I have a very negative view of myself, very low self-esteem and feel I always fail.

What did /has your mother taught you about being a woman, being a mother, life, love and living?

My mother has taught me nothing. I know how dreadful it is for me to speak like that.

Depending on your relationship status with your mother if she is still alive how would you like the future of your relationship to be?

I would want her to live her own life and be happy.

What gets in the way of not having the kind of relationship you've just shared?

Because my mother is not happy, it makes me feel responsible for her.

When you are with your mother do you find yourself reacting to her as an adult or as a child/teenager from the hurt part of yourself?

I react to my mother as a mother. I feel I am the adult and she is the child.

If you were able to create your 'ideal mother' what would that be like for you? What would be her qualities, attributes, gifts, how would she be with you? What would she say to you right now?

She would be happy, confident and make me feel safe and she is an adult and for her to tell me I'm perfect as I am.

What is the biggest thing you've learnt about yourself on your journey with or without your mother so far?

The biggest thing I have learnt is not to give everything up - I have needs too.

How do you meet your own needs now as an adult?

I really don't meet them, I have become an empty shell truthfully speaking.

What got you through your experiences?

I am not 100% sure how to answer this.

What positive and negative traits do you have that your mother had/has?

I can be negative but also very positive, I am not sure if I have traits, I just feel I have to keep going though life.

What things do you enjoy doing that your mother enjoyed?

I really like walking and the outdoors.

Knowing that your mother gave you the gift of life, what are you most grateful for in recognition of this?

I am not sure how to answer this.

Using your past to make your future the best it can what skills and resources have you developed to use to your greater good?

I have trained in Reiki 1 and 2, very proud for me, but I really live in the past, something I need to break.

Q&A

Name: *Jannine*

Age: *57*

Are you a mother as well as a daughter? Yes/No if yes, how many children do you have what are their sexes?

2 girls, 2 boys

What is your current personal relationship status: Single/widowed/divorced/separated/co-habiting, second marriage etc

Second marriage

Your mother's age as she is now if applicable:

78

The age your mother was when she died if applicable (how old were you when she died?)

Left Blank

Your mother's Ethnic origin/Nationality/country of birth

Scottish

Details of your Siblings, current ages and sexes:

Sister 63, sister 61, brother 59, me 57, brother 56, sister 54 (died as a child) brother 52

Details of your mother's siblings, age gap between them and your mother and sexes:

My mother is one of 12, 3 girls the rest boys. Not sure of ages etc, as I do not have a lot of contact with them.

Are you part of a stepfamily? If so do you have good relationship with them now?

My mother re married, never met the step family, they did not like their father.

Were you in care, adopted or fostered as a child/teenager? If you were raised by your mother how did she raise you? I.e. single parent, with your father, with a step father, with aid of a grandparent

I was fostered at 13 when both my parents left home. My brother and I looked after ourselves for about 3 months, then the neighbours called in the NSPCC. My parents were located and they had to come home for a meeting. We were supposed to be in our rooms. We all sat at the top of the stairs to listen about what would happen. My father chose to take my youngest brother, as his new partner only had a girl and she wanted my 'mother's baby' to spite her. My mother wanted the other boys, she only ever wanted boys. I listened as they both said that they did not want me.

Was your mother unavailable emotionally, physically or mentally ill and away from the family home for any length of time while you were growing up?

Unavailable emotionally most of the time

Did your mother use prescribed medications (for depression etc), recreational drugs, or alcohol to excess or have any addictions?

Addictions to men

Was your mother ever physically violent or abusive towards you? *(Yes no is fine here if you want to keep the information brief)*

My mother would beat me with the copper stick that she used for the washing. One time because I had heard my brother saying the work Fuck while outside. I used it indoors and she beat me so bad I could not sit down at school for a week. The teachers were horrified and called him in to speak to her, but nothing was done. She allowed my grandfather to be sexually abusive towards me as a child.

What motivates you to share your experiences in relation to your mother?

In my line of work I meet a lot of people carry the guilt of not loving their mothers. Just because someone gives birth to you. It does not make them a mother. You do not have to allow them to behave badly in our lives. We would not take this from anyone else, so why should we take this from anyone else. They need to heal and move on and to be able to forgive your mother and yourself for any part in this. You cannot blame your mother for your life forever. As an adult you are responsible for your life.

Describe in a few sentences how you feel about your mother (feel free to use uncensored your experience)

Sadly I have no feeling left for her. I used to be very angry at her for what she done in my life. I have through my work as a healer moved on and healed for all this. I forgave her and myself long ago, this enabled me to move on with my life and make my own choices about what I do. In some small way I am grateful for her as she has made me the strong woman that I am today.

When you think of your mother what emotions/feelings come up for you?

I feel sad that she has missed out on her grandchildren and great grandchildren, and all the great things I have done in my life. She has never met my wonderful Husband either.

What triggers or challenges bring up personal pain for you in relations to your mother? *I.e. perceived rejection, not feeling heard, not being considered, other people's anger, feeling unloved by a partner, seeing Mothers Day Cards, birthdays and celebrations etc*

None, due to the healing and letting go

What were your unmet needs in childhood (regardless of the reason why) in relation to your mother?

Just to be loved for being me and to be taught self love. It took me a long time to realize I was worth it.

If your mother is alive what do you want from her now that you're not currently getting?

Nothing at all, I was lucky enough to be gifted two very special women in my life who have stepped into her place for me.

How have you experienced your mother as you both age, what changes have you noticed?

According to my sisters, my mother has got worse as she has got older. She is even nastier now.

What do you believe about yourself or the world around you in relation to your experience with your mother?

I believe that I am a much stronger person because of what I went through. I will never allow her to define me at all. I chose to be who I am and what I will allow in my life.

What is or has been your greatest fear in relation to your mother (for yourself and/or for her)?

That she will find out where I live. She has done this before and written nasty letters to my husband and neighbours, with untruths about me and turned up on my door step at all hours. I have no contact with some of my family because they cannot be trusted to not tell her where I am.

How has your experience with your mother impacted other relationships?

When I was younger I was not good with people and never trusted anyone to love me. I would always push them away before they could get close, because I never believed that I was worth loving, because that is what my mother had told me. Thank God I have healed from that.

What beliefs do you have about relationships based on your own experience?

I believe there is good and bad in everyone. Love will heal a lot of things. You need to love yourself first, as you cannot pour from an empty cup.

What are your beliefs about 'women as mothers' in this era and how they should live their lives raise a family, have a career etc?

We should be able to do what the hell we want and not be judged on it. Support your 'sisters out there'.

What do you know about your mother's childhood and upbringing, her hopes, fears, beliefs about herself or the world around her?

Left Blank

Reflecting on your past what stands out to you the most about your mother?

My mother came from a large family, with lots of step brothers and sister. Her mother was quite a nasty woman and spent a lot of time 'working' at the docks. My mother just took over being a mother from where she left off.

What is your biggest regret when you think about your relationship with your mother?

She never learnt to change. I never want to be a mother like her. I never want my children to go through what I went through.

If you were able to change your childhood what did you need the most from your mother that you never received? How would you have preferred your upbringing to be?

I needed to be loved, you can put up with anything if you have love.

If you were able right now to say what you wanted to say to your mother, what would you say?

Why??? Why were you able to love the others and not me?

How has your experience of your mother shaped your life to date (negative and positive aspects?)

I have been able to help others with a greater understanding and compassion of what they are going through. I am very strong and don't suffer fools gladly.

What did /has your mother taught you about being a woman, being a mother, life, love and living?

*Love is everything in life, give it freely. Don't judge just others as you are a little F*** up yourself.*

Depending on your relationship status with your mother if she is still alive how would you like the future of your relationship to be?

I am very happy not to have my mother in my life at all. Sadly I will not even miss her when she dies.

What gets in the way of not having the kind of relationship you've just shared?

Nothing really as I have been lucky enough to have healed and moved on.

When you are with your mother do you find yourself reacting to her as an adult or as a child/teenager from the hurt part of yourself?

N/A

If you were able to create your 'ideal mother' what would that be like for you? What would be her qualities, attributes, gifts, how would she be with you? What would she say to you right now?

I don't see her. But my ideal mother shares my life, loves me for me. Picks me up when I am down, kicks my butt when I need it. Guides me and will just be there for me.

What is the biggest thing you've learnt about yourself on your journey with or without your mother so far?

I am in charge of how I live my life. I am the only one who can make me happy. I am worth it and I love me just as I am.

How do you meet your own needs now as an adult?

I just believe in me.

What got you through your experiences?

My guardian angel, I always know that someone was looking after me as well as some very special people gifted to me along the way. I am always grateful for them.

What positive and negative traits do you have that your mother had/has?

I hope that I have none of her traits at all.

What things do you enjoy doing that your mother enjoyed?

As I have had no contact with her for years. I don't know.

Knowing that your mother gave you the gift of life, what are you most grateful for in recognition of this?

Just that. The gift of life.

Using your past to make your future the best it can what skills and resources have you developed to use to your greater good?

I am a Reiki master healer, Psychic and therapist. I am also a laughter yoga leader. I have excellent people skills. I have become my own person on my terms.

Please include any additional information as you wish that you feel is important for me to know:

I gave my mother a chance to be part of my life again when my children were small. That did not last very long as she tried very hard to wreck my life yet again.

Q&A

Name: *Jo*

Age: *59*

Are you a mother as well as a daughter? Yes/No if yes, how many children do you have what are their sexes?

Yes

Three children, 2 boys 1 girl, Eldest boy was adopted out

What is your current personal relationship status: Single/ widowed/divorced/separated/co-habiting, second marriage etc

Divorced

Your mother's age as she is now if applicable:

N/A for my adoptive mother, 82 for my birth mother

The age your mother was when she died if applicable (how old were you when she died?)

Adoptive mother was 70 when she died

Your mother's Ethnic origin/Nationality/country of birth

U.K.

Details of your Siblings, current ages and sexes: 1 adopted brother 56

Two half siblings' sister 50 and brother 47

Details of your mother's siblings, age gap between them and your mother and sexes:

Both mothers had a younger brother with 5 years gap. Adoptive mother had a sister who was older and died at 9 months old.

Are you part of a step family? If so do you have good relationship with them now?

Left blank

Were you in care, adopted or fostered as a child/teenager?

Left blank

If you were raised by your mother how did she raise you? I.e. single parent, with your father, with a step father, with aid of a grandparent

I was placed in a closed adoption at 4 months old after being in foster care for the first 4 months. My adoptive mother raised me (with my adoptive father). She was careful to ensure people didn't think I was a spoilt child just because I was adopted so had a very firm parenting style. She wasn't very loving and I can't remember ever feeling a sense of love coming from her. She was quite cold emotionally.

Was your mother unavailable emotionally, physically or mentally ill and away from the family home for any length of time while you were growing up?

She wasn't away from the home but was definitely unavailable emotionally.

Did your mother use prescribed medications (for depression etc), recreational drugs, or alcohol to excess or have any addictions?

My adopted mother was prescribed amphetamines from the age of 18 which she took daily until she died. I suspect on reflection that she had a sort of amphetamine psychosis. She also had sleeping tablets to counter the 'speed.'

Was your mother ever physically violent or abusive towards you? *(Yes no is fine here if you want to keep the information brief)*

Her preferred method of punishment was shouting and smacking.

What motivates you to share your experiences in relation to your mother?

Whilst not wanting to get stuck in my story, my mother has a lot to answer for and sharing is a form of catharsis for me. I have gone out of my way to ensure that I don't berate her as I guess she did what she did because of her own conditioning etc.

Sharing with others can help validate the experience too for them and me.

Describe in a few sentences how you feel about your mother (feel free to use uncensored your experience)

I'm fucking cross with her a lot of the time and just writing that makes me well up. She was so wrapped up in her own shit that she didn't recognize how I was or how I felt or what I needed. My birth mother on the other hand is quite different although we don't see each other much.

When you think of your mother what emotions/feelings come up for you?

I get angry, incensed, teary, overwhelmed, frustrated.

What triggers or challenges bring up personal pain for you in relations to your mother? *I.e. perceived rejection, not feeling heard, not being considered, other people's anger, feeling unloved by a partner, seeing Mothers Day Cards, birthdays and celebrations etc*

I'm not really aware of the triggers or challenges if any. I try not to think about her. The only times it does crop up is when I read stuff that mentions people's relationships with their mothers.

What were your unmet needs in childhood (regardless of the reason why) in relation to your mother?

My adopted mum would always tell me how she stopped me sucking my thumb when they got me home, by swaddling me tightly in my cot. She took great delight in the fact that she nailed it when integrity mothers were worrying about thumb sucking and projecting teeth. She would also tell me that I was a willful and stubborn baby and that I would cry for attention. She said she left me to cry and I soon stopped.

I can't remember hugging and snuggling her. I can't remember her ever saying she loved me or was proud of me. I just felt I always had to do better. I was forever seeking her approval. She was very opinionated.

If your mother is alive what do you want from her now that you're not currently getting?

N/A

How have your experienced your mother as you both age, what changes have you noticed?

When I had my own children with my ex husband, she seemed much softer. She would hug them and play with them. She seemed more approachable.

What do you believe about yourself or the world around you in relation to your experience with your mother?

I believe that I am unlovable and unworthy. I know that's crap and I know that I'm neither. But at a deep level that's what I feel. That I need to seek approval for everything I do. I have to have permission even though I know it comes from myself.

What is or has been your greatest fear in relation to your mother (for yourself and/or for her)?

I don't want to die feeling that I'm unworthy. I don't want to be like her.

How has your experience with your mother impacted other relationships?

I'm rubbish at relationships. I sought 'love and connection' inappropriately from the age of 15, hence the teen pregnancy. I have a deep desire to be loved but can't actually allow it. I want to be that baby again but in different circumstances. I was married for 22 years but was just going through the motions. I didn't really feel deeply happy. I drank heavily and used recreational drugs to switch off from myself.

What beliefs do you have about relationships based on your own experience?

I'm not sure. I have a great knack of pushing people who love me away. I'm good at validating my own lack of self worth. I have developed relationships that have validated my belief that I'm nothing.

What are your beliefs about 'women as mothers' in this era and how they should live their lives raise a family, have a career etc?

I think mothers should do what's right for them I don't really have a view on it generally. For me I was at home mostly with the children as they were pre-school. I could work weekends or nights as a trained nurse so my ex husband was able to look after them.

What do you know about your mother's childhood and upbringing, her hopes, fears, beliefs about herself or the world around her?

My adoptive mother was brought up in Penarth in Wales; she was an only child after her sister died aged 9 months old. My mother was very, very bright. She had a Mensa IQ and worked in insurance until she married when she gave up a well paid role to be a wife as was expected in the 50's.

As a child she excelled at sports, particularly swimming diving and hockey. She won a scholarship to Howells school in Cardiff a very well respected public school.

He father was a boiler man on steam trains and her mother stayed at home. When she married she felt like the poor relation as she married into a middle class family. She never quite got over that and was bitter about how it made her feel.

As a teenager she never had periods and was taken to a top gynecologist to see why. She was told she had an infantile womb and that should she ever marry then sex would be difficult and so at 16 was put on steroids. Her weight ballooned and so at 18 she was prescribed Dexedrine to counter the weight gain. She remained on it her entire lifetime, save one period in hospital.

She was an avid reader and was not satisfied that her reason for not having children was just an infantile womb. She read an article in New Scientist (my dad's magazine) about the Androgen Insensitivity Syndrome. A rare disease that meant a woman had make chromosomes. It flicked a switch in her head and she asked the GP for chromosome count. He thought she'd lost the plot. However she was right. She should have actually been born a man. This affected her deeply as you can imagine. She was prone to depression as was my dad (he suffered manic depression and was in and out of mental hospitals).

When I became pregnant as a teenager I think that the way in which she responded to me was a direct reflection of her never coming to terms with the loss of her potential to be a proper woman or natural mother.

Reflecting on your past what stands out to you the most about your mother?

She was totally self absorbed.

What is your biggest regret when you think about your relationship with your mother?

That we never got to talk deeply about how either of us felt. That she never told me she loved me.

If you were able to change your childhood what did you need the most from your mother that you never received? How would you have preferred your upbringing to be?

Whilst my childhood wasn't particularly unhappy I'd have like more mother daughter connection with her. I wish she would have just stepped outside of her own story and into mine.

If you were able right now to say what you wanted to say to your mother, what would you say?

I forgive you.

How has your experience of your mother shaped your life to date (negative and positive aspects?)

It's made me be very open and honest with my own daughter. I brought her up to be precocious and strong. Not to fear anyone and do what makes her happy.

What did /has your mother taught you about being a woman, being a mother, life, love and living?

I'm not sure.

Depending on your relationship status with your mother if she is still alive how would you like the future of your relationship to be?

N/A with my mother, I have a nice relationship with my birth mother.

What gets in the way of not having the kind of relationship you have just shared?

N/A

When you are with your mother do you find yourself reacting to her as an adult or as a child/teenager from the hurt part of yourself?

N/A

If you were able to create your 'ideal mother' what would that be like for you? What would be her qualities, attributes, gifts, how would she be with you? What would she say to you right now?

My ideal mother would be approachable, honest, caring, open, loving. Full of fun and there when I needed her most.

What is the biggest thing you have learnt about yourself on your journey with or without your mother so far?

That I'm more resilient than I thought

How do you meet your own needs now as an adult?

I'm still trying to figure that out Wendy! I'm rubbish at fulfilling my own needs.

What got you through your experiences?

Ignoring them

What positive and negative traits do you have that your mother had/has?

Not sure.

What things do you enjoy doing that your mother enjoyed?

Adopted mum - Cooking and sports, birth mum - being in caring people centered work.

Knowing that your mother gave you the gift of life, what are you most grateful for in recognition of this?

For my birth mother I thank her for the qualities that she passes on to me.

Using your past to make your future the best it can what skills and resources have you developed to use to your greater good?

Tenacity and resourcefulness

Q&A

Name: *Lara*

Age: *47*

Are you a mother as well as a daughter? Yes/No if yes, how many children do you have what are their sexes?

Yes. I have 2 children. A boy and a girl

What is your current personal relationship status: Single/ widowed/divorced/separated/co-habiting, second marriage etc

Co-habiting

Your mother's age as she is now if applicable:

N/A

The age your mother was when she died if applicable (how old were you when she died?)

My mother 52, me 32

Your mother's Ethnic origin/Nationality/country of birth

Scottish

Details of your Siblings, current ages and sexes:

Sister 51

Details of your mother's siblings, age gap between them and your mother and sexes:

Brother. 2 years apart I think

Are you part of a step family? If so do you have good relationship with them now?

No

Were you in care, adopted or fostered as a child/teenager?

No

If you were raised by your mother how did she raise you? I.e. single parent, with your father, with a step father, with aid of a grandparent.

I was raised with my mother and father.

Was your mother unavailable emotionally, physically or mentally ill and away from the family home for any length of time while you were growing up?

My mother was loving a lot of the time but also distant too. She suffered from depression and took anti-depressants.

Did your mother use prescribed medications (for depression etc), recreational drugs, or alcohol to excess or have any addictions?

Only anti-depressants

Was your mother ever physically violent or abusive towards you? *(Yes no is fine here if you want to keep the information brief)*

No

What motivates you to share your experiences in relation to your mother?

To help you and because our relationship to our mother is always relevant

Describe in a few sentences how you feel about your mother (feel free to use uncensored your experience)

She was a quiet, loving, creative mother but she wasn't happy or comfortable in her life. Often she wouldn't listen to me. When she got angry which was not very often I took note. She wasn't really happy as a mother. There were lots of things she wanted to do.

When you think of your mother what emotions/feelings come up for you?

Sadness, love and pain

What triggers or challenges bring up personal pain for you in relations to your mother? *I.e. perceived rejection, not feeling heard, not being considered, other people's anger, feeling unloved by a partner, seeing Mother's Day Cards, birthdays and celebrations etc*

Not being heard, Mother's Day cards, Christmas, being a mother and being aware of the similarities between us and knowing what she was going through, my partner's mother, feeling uncomfortable, not feeling like a good mother.

What were your unmet needs in childhood (regardless of the reason why) in relation to your mother?

Not being listened to, being ignored.

If your mother is alive what do you want from her now that you're not currently getting?

N/A

How have your experienced your mother as you both age, what changes have you noticed?

N/A

What do you believe about yourself or the world around you in relation to your experience with your mother?

It's not safe to say what I think/ be me.

What is or has been your greatest fear in relation to your mother (for yourself and/or for her)?

I have feared that she would die.

How has your experience with your mother impacted other relationships?

I don't feel confident with my children. I am scared to speak out.

What beliefs do you have about relationships based on your own experience?

They're difficult and often uncomfortable.

What are your beliefs about 'women as mothers' in this era and how they should live their lives raise a family, have a career etc?

That there is little equality and women's role as a mother has not changed a great deal. I believe women should be able to work and have children but the reality is that it's difficult and the house and arrangements are left to women.

What do you know about your mother's childhood and upbringing, her hopes, fears, beliefs about herself or the world around her?

She had a very tumultuous childhood, alcoholic father, lost her mother at 8 years, lived with cold Victorian grandmother after this and her father disappeared. Her brother died when she was 10 years. I think she felt that life was unstable and bad things could happen unexpectedly.

Reflecting on your past what stands out to you the most about your mother?

She was kind and patient despite a hard life.

What is your biggest regret when you think about your relationship with your mother?

That I didn't share more of my thoughts with her

If you were able to change your childhood what did you need the most from your mother that you never received? How would you have preferred your upbringing to be?

To be listened to, to be allowed to be noisy and be myself, to be allowed to hurt myself physically without a panic.

If you were able right now to say what you wanted to say to your mother, what would you say?

I'm going to say what I really think. You were doing the best you could as a mum despite all you went through. I am experiencing the same problems you did. I wish you were here and I wish you could meet my children. I wish you could experience Matrix Reimprinting. I love you.

How has your experience of your mother shaped you life to date (negative and positive aspects?)

It possibly made me shy and be scared of the world and not feel able to express myself. It made me creative and created large learning curves.

What did /has your mother taught you about being a woman, being a mother, life, love and living?

It's hard to be a mum and I'm not very good at it. It's possible to get a job. Creativity is important.

Depending on your relationship status with your mother if she is still alive how would you like the future of your relationship to be?

N/A

What gets in the way of not having the kind of relationship you have just shared?

N/A

When you are with your mother do you find yourself reacting to her as an adult or as a child/teenager from the hurt part of yourself?

N/A

If you were able to create your 'ideal mother' what would that be like for you? What would be her qualities, attributes, gifts, how would she be with you? What would she say to you right now?

She would be my mother but she would be confident about herself and not so secretive. She would be expressive, bold and would do more of what she wants to do rather than trying to please. She would develop her singing and dancing and perform on stage. She would also write a book and short stories.

What is the biggest thing you have learnt about yourself on your journey with or without your mother so far?

That it's possible to transform negative patterns and that I have chosen this path and my parents.

How do you meet your own needs now as an adult?

By doing meditation, Matrix Reimprinting, dancing, creative stuff, speaking out when I can and getting help when I need it

What got you through your experiences?

Matrix Reimprinting, music, painting, writing and alcohol

What positive and negative traits do you have that your mother had/has?

Creative, full of ideas, low self-esteem, often lacking self-expression

What things do you enjoy doing that your mother enjoyed?

Singing, dancing, Painting, writing, exhibitions, theatre

Knowing that your mother gave you the gift of life, what are you most grateful for in recognition of this?

Grateful for healing the past with my family and being able to heal others

Using your past to make your future the best it can what skills and resources have you developed to use to your greater good?

Writing, Matrix Reimprinting, meditation

Q&A

Name: *Ruth*

Age: *54*

Are you a mother as well as a daughter?

No, I was unable to have children but have been a foster mother to fourteen children. Did try IVF four times but that did not work and I very nearly died in the process. After that I felt it was best to accept I would never have children. They are a gift and not a right. As it turned out, my marriage ended eight years later due to my ex-husband's gambling addiction.

What is your current personal relationship status?

Divorced from ex-husband but living with new partner, who strangely enough was my first boyfriend at school.

Your mother's age as she is now if applicable:

I don't know if my mother is alive, but as she was born in September 1940, she would be 75.

The age your mother was when she died if applicable (how old were you when she died?)

As above

Your mother's Ethnic origin/Nationality/country of birth

Born in England (white British) from Catholic family with Irish roots

Details of your Siblings, current ages and sexes:

I'm an only child. My mother was forcibly sterilised after she had me due to mental illness.

Details of your mother's siblings, age gap between them and your mother and sexes:

Patricia (2 years older), my mother Valerie, Raymond (18 months younger), Pamela (3.5 years younger), Angela (6 years younger), David (14 years younger), Stephen (17 years younger)

Are you part of a step family? If so do you have good relationship with them now?

No

Were you in care, adopted or fostered as a child/teenager?

Neither my mother nor father were deemed able to look after me (mother had mental illness and my father was a serving soldier) so I was put into the care of my maternal grandmother and was officially in her care (under social services/courts) until I was 16 when I left home. It wasn't until I went to court when I was 16 years old that I actually found out.

If you were raised by your mother how did she raise you? I.e. single parent, with your father, with a step father, with aid of a grandparent.

A bit of background: As my father was in the army, within three weeks of being born my father, mother and myself went to Germany (army compound) and I lived in Germany until I was three. My father was then transferred to Malaysia (first Seremban for two years and then Kluang until I was about eight years old). Soon after arrival in Malaysia, my mother had the first of a succession of nervous breakdowns and was hospitalised. Obviously my father was busy with the army, although I would see him regularly; therefore I was cared for by a Chinese-Malay nanny, of whom I have fond memories. When my mother was not in hospital she would be home but unfortunately had issues with drugs and alcohol and would forget to look after me, feed me, etc. A local Chinese man (who had lost his wife but had eight daughters) used to take me in and feed me. He used to be absolutely livid with my parents for leaving me to wander around Kluang, as you have to understand at that time it was a relatively small settlement on the edge of the jungle, which was dangerous.

When my mother's mental illness became more serious, we moved back to England and my father went through the courts to try to get custody but failed due to being a soldier, as the social workers felt that would not be a good lifestyle for me. My mother was hospitalised, so the social workers placed me with my grandmother in London, when she came out of hospital my mother came to live with my grandmother. However, that meant that a three bed roomed house contained my grandparents, my two youngest uncles, my mother (who by that time had met my 'step-father' who used to stay over) and myself. I ended up sleeping top to tail with the two boys. My mother used to help my grandmother to keep house but in essence it was my grandmother who was head of the household and who fed and clothed me.

My father, who was outraged that my grandmother was given custody of me, decided he would stop seeing me as he considered that if he came to visit my mother and grandmother would try to up the amount of money he was paying in maintenance. So I never saw or heard from him again until I was 42 years old, not even a birthday or Christmas card. I should mention that when he did make contact again, I quickly realised my father had major difficulties making any sort of social or emotional connections. He is now in a nursing home with dementia and Lewy-Body disease. Although my father says he loved me as a child, I am not sure he truly had any concept of what loving a child really means.

Was your mother unavailable emotionally, physically or mentally ill and away from the family home for any length of time while you were growing up?

Apart from what I've already mentioned, it's not clear exactly what my mother's issues were but she suffered from depression and was on all sorts of drugs. In addition, she had a tendency to 'act out' scenes in front of me as if 'miming', particularly if she was angry with someone. All a bit off the wall really. My mother never had any 'sense' of looking after me. For instance I went to the dentist with toothache and he was shocked at the size of the cavity in my tooth (it was enormous!) and he told her to make sure I had regular visits to the dentist to stop it happening again. Also, she never thought about whether I had a good diet, and expressed surprise when I said that I would like to eat fruit as I thought that would stop me getting so ill all the time with colds, etc. Also, my mother was unable to express love and emotions and I honestly have not one recollection of my mother ever having hugged me.

Did your mother use prescribed medications (for depression etc), recreational drugs, or alcohol to excess or have any addictions?

All of the above. She took Mogadon, Librium/Valium and an assortment of other drugs, could drink anyone under the table and my father later recounted that in Malaysia she would smoke cannabis or do cocaine.

Was your mother ever physically violent or abusive towards you? *(Yes no is fine here if you want to keep the information brief)*

My mother was never physically violent and rarely abusive, only a few times when she would swear at me calling me f&^ing lazy or whatever as I was growing up. In essence, my mother was relatively placid (or somewhat stoned on medications) which extended to not being able to stand up for herself against others, because she had been the victim of physically assault as a youngster from my grandmother, who had a filthy temper and treated my mother like a maid. In the house that was shared* *with my grandmother, although my grandmother was the one who cooked (that was her profession) and also took care of the finances (mostly down the pub!); my mother did the majority of the housework. It's a strange one really, because in a sense I suppose it gave my mother something to do, at a time when she was not up to working outside the home. My mother did say to me that she did not believe in physical punishment and I can see why, as my grandmother had a filthy temper and would regularly beat her children. I have an awful memory of my grandmother coming into the bedroom one night when I lived in London (the one shared with the two boys), and she literally beat them with a rounder's bat, as one of them had been in trouble at school (they both later ended up in borstal - small wonder).*

My mother did used to say to me every time she heard the song 'Stuck in The Middle With You' by Stealers Wheel she thought of her situation with me. I can understand why.

What motivates you to share your experiences in relation to your mother?

Because I want to share the message that sometimes what is termed 'a bad childhood' is often a gift that comes in a strange wrapping. In my own case, my ability to forgive both of my parents, particularly my mother, has enabled me to become the person I never realised I could be. In other words, my mother was in many ways my greatest teacher.

Describe in a few sentences how you feel about your mother (feel free to use uncensored your experience)

Many years ago I felt disappointment and anger at my mother but now I feel compassion for her. It sounds like a well trotted out cliché but I recognise that she did the best she could, with the level of self-knowledge and awareness that she had at that time. She was a woman of little or no self-esteem and therefore she was unable to offer me, in terms of love, support and the opportunity for emotional growth, what she had never experienced herself. It was her inability to be an emotional resource for me that provided me with the opportunity to go out into the world and discover ways to support myself and become independent. Plus, we're talking about the 1960s here, a time when it was considered acceptable to administer electric shock treatment (which my mother had a total of six times) and also she was sterilised because she was deemed unfit to have any more children, totally barbaric really.

When you think of your mother what emotions/feelings come up for you?

I feel regret that she had in many ways a wasted life. With the right level of support her life could have been different. I see now the importance of the choices we make in life, how our actions and inactions impact upon us, particularly when we are not aware of our power of choice. I also feel sad that she felt that she was better off staying with my step-father, who she knew had raped me as a young child (which is the reason I am unable to have children) and who had also married her bigamously, rather than be on her own. She made the decision to stay with him and cut contact with me altogether, hence why I have not seen her since I was 25 years old. I think it is a sad reflection that she perceived she had no 'choice' in the situation. Her parting shot to me was that when I get to her age (46 years old at the time) that I would understand her reasoning. I never did of course.

What triggers or challenges bring up personal pain for you in relations to your mother? *I.e. perceived rejection, not feeling heard, not being considered, other people's anger, feeling unloved by a partner, seeing Mothers Day Cards, birthdays and celebrations etc*

On Mother's Day and her birthday I do have a momentary sadness that we have no contact but on the whole I feel at least thankful that both she and my father brought me into the world. I think if there is one issue, then that is perhaps feeling regret that

I did not feel 'valued' as a child, but that is not entirely down to my mother, as obviously my father's actions were not helpful in that respect. However, the aspect of not valuing myself and not feeling valued carried on for quite some time.

What were your unmet needs in childhood (regardless of the reason why) in relation to your mother?

In all honestly where do I start? I was not cared for in a physical way with regards to being fed, looked after or my physical health being considered, nor did I received affection in the usual sense of hugs, cuddles or anything affirmative/positive said to me. In fact, my mother once remarked she was surprised I did so well at school and that she always expected me to become a pregnant teenager! She never took any interest in my school work at all. After I left home at 16 years (I left home the day I left school) after about six months I was admitted to hospital with suspected appendicitis. She would not travel to the hospital to sign the consent form for an operation as she did not want to miss a day off work and lose money (she had finally been given her own council home with my step-father and had found a job in a factory).

If your mother is alive what do you want from her now that you're not currently getting?

Nothing, I feel at peace with the situation, I have forgiven her, my step-father and my own father and I do not feel any 'need' of anything from her.

How have your experienced your mother as you both age, what changes have you noticed?

I am not sure how to answer that one.

What do you believe about yourself or the world around you in relation to your experience with your mother?

That my mother has in essence been my greatest teacher in terms of understanding where my own unconscious behaviour patterns came from and why I had such a difficult time valuing myself and moving my life forward. Without the experiences I have had, not only with my mother but the whole family, I would not have pushed myself to find healing and in doing so discovered a depth to myself, talents and abilities, which I would never have guessed I had. Yes, I still have issues in pushing myself forward sometimes, but at least I have the ability to self-reflect and work upon any issues as they come up. The issues I see in my mother are issues I have seen in myself and others, over and over again.

What is or has been your greatest fear in relation to you mother (for yourself and/or for her)?

I have no fears in relation to myself. I do wonder whether my mother will get to the end of her life and regret believing that she had no choice, because that belief led her to take actions and non-actions that ultimately I think would not have led to a good place for her.

How has your experience with your mother impacted other relationships?

I think when I was younger I entered into relationships very 'unconsciously', in terms of I never thought things through. I suppose I was not very 'streetwise' when it came to any of my relationships. Also, I tended to go along with what others wanted and especially when I was much younger never really had a sense of what I actually wanted to do.

What beliefs do you have about relationships based on your own experience?

That it is very important to be with someone who truly loves, values and supports you and who helps you become a better version of yourself and vice versa. Also, of course, it is most important to learn to love yourself because without that ability you cannot truly know love.

What are your beliefs about 'women as mothers' in this era and how they should live their lives raise a family, have a career etc?

I do not believe in 'shoulds' and actually feel it can be immensely beneficial to children to have strong, independent mothers, whether they choose to work or not or whether they choose to co-parent with another or not.

What do you know about your mother's childhood and upbringing, her hopes, fears, beliefs about herself or the world around her?

I think I have already covered this but if there is anything else specific you wish to ask, please feel free to do so. Basically they were a poor family, my grandmother worked three jobs to look after seven children but she was a very angry, frustrated woman and took her anger and frustrations out on her children. I believe my mother married my father simply as an escape route. Unfortunately, due to his own problems, he was unable to offer her emotional support.

Reflecting on your past what stands out to you the most about your mother?

That she was never really happy.

What is your biggest regret when you think about your relationship with your mother?

I feel sad for her that she felt she had no choice but to stay with a man who had raped her child in order to secure her future and therefore made the decision to sever her relationship with me. I regret the fact that I was unable to help her see she had the ability to make better choices.

If you were able to change your childhood what did you need the most from your mother that you never received? How would you have preferred your upbringing to be?

Positive affirmation and having someone to scaffold my development and confidence would have made a big difference to my life, particularly in my earlier years. I suppose in essence I am saying having a positive role model would have been important.

If you were able right now to say what you wanted to say to your mother, what would you say?

I hope you have been happy and your dreams have come true.

How has your experience of your mother shaped your life to date (negative and positive aspects?)

I think I have already covered this.

What did /has your mother taught you about being a woman, being a mother, life, love and living?

Bless her, she mainly showed me what not to be, and in many ways that is just as important. Other than that she did not score highly.

Depending on your relationship status with your mother if she is still alive how would you like the future of your relationship to be?

I am happy the way things are.

What gets in the way of not having the kind of relationship you've just shared?

Not applicable.

When you are with your mother do you find yourself reacting to her as an adult or as a child/teenager from the hurt part of yourself?

Not applicable.

If you were able to create you 'ideal mother' what would that be like for you? What would be her qualities, attributes, gifts, how would she be with you? What would she say to you right now?

An 'ideal mother' would be someone who is uplifting, affirmative, supportive, encouraging, motivating, able to handle her emotions, strong, independent yet able to be in a balanced relationship with others, emotionally aware, outgoing and have a purpose/ direction in life, In other words, a good role model, not just for her child but also for the women around her.

"You can do it" is what she would say to me and, of course, "I love you".

What is the biggest thing you've learnt about yourself on your journey with or without your mother so far?

That I am able to parent my inner child myself

How do you meet your own needs now as an adult?

I would love to say I take care of all my own needs perfectly as an adult but in truth there are many ways in which I do not. However, I am aware of them and able to turn things around with the use of EFT, hypnosis, meditation, etc., to a great degree, although having said that I do find my 'needs' are constantly changing! For example, at work I tend to 'settle' for working conditions that do not meet my highest expectations and also I tend to allow other things to get in front of the things that I want to achieve, such as building up a successful business. I find it difficult to allow other people to do things for me, simply because I have been used to dealing with stuff myself. But, on the whole, I think I do quite well, given the circumstances I have had to deal with, particularly in the last few years.

What got you through your experiences?

An extremely strong sense of spirituality, I was born remembering previous lives and was very strongly psychic. This led me to always seek for spiritual answers, although I suppose I was actually searching for other people like me. Also, a sense that there was 'something more' than the circumstances I had been born into. The ability to forgive and let go, to move on from things, once I make the decision that something has come to an end, I actually find it easy to get on with my life. I am also aware that I am incredibly adaptable, perhaps in part because I moved around a lot as a child. Books have also helped me through a lot! I have been an avid reader of psychology, astrology, healing, self-help and every form of spirituality from the age of ten and have been able to learn concepts and strategies that helped see my life from different perspectives. That is one of the reasons I wanted to offer my experiences, if they are helpful to you and your book, because books change lives.

What positive and negative traits do you have that your mother had/has?

Oh my I am the Cleaning Queen! Nothing grates on my nerves more than an unclean, untidy environment. It is actually a bit of a bug bear in the relationship I am now in as I live with Mr Untidy-Couldn't-Give-A-Damn-About-The-State-Of-The-Place. He thinks I have OCD. I, of course, consider him to have no standards!

I am forgiving, which can be a good thing but has not always served me well. I have 'toughened up' a tad on that one and am less inclined to put up with crap than even a few years ago but can forgive when it serves me to.

Not valuing myself and my skills and a lack of confidence has been an issue that on reflection I can see started with having a mother with very low self-esteem.

What things do you enjoy doing that your mother enjoyed?

Reading, writing and languages, my mother taught herself to speak German and I have always found it easy to pick up languages. I spoke five languages by the time I was five and although I have forgotten most of them it has given me the ability to 'make connections' linguistically quickly. I taught myself to speak French to 'A' level standard within three months just driving to and from work when my ex-husband and I bought a place in France ten years ago. My mother was top of her school for composition and so was I.

Knowing that your mother gave you the gift of life, what are you most grateful for in recognition of this?

I am most grateful for my life and also that I had an interesting start in life.

Using your past to make your future the best it can what skills and resources have you developed to use to your greater good?

The ability to pick up things quickly and adaptability, together with the desire to want to learn more about the world has propelled me out of the belief systems of my mother and her family.

Q&A

Name: *Cordelia*

Age: *66*

Are you a mother as well as a daughter? Yes/No if yes, how many children do you have what are their sexes?

Yes, I have two daughters

What is your current personal relationship status: Single/ widowed/divorced/separated/co-habiting, second marriage etc

Married

Your mother's age as she is now if applicable:

87

The age your mother was when she died if applicable (how old were you when she died?)

Still living

Your mother's Ethnic origin/Nationality/country of birth

Jewish

Details of your Siblings, current ages and sexes:

One sister aged 57, one brother aged 55

Details of your mother's siblings, age gap between them and your mother and sexes:

Mother eldest of several siblings (about 6 or 7), one of whom died, she had two older step-siblings.

Are you part of a step family? If so do you have good relationship with them now?

No

Were you in care, adopted or fostered as a child/teenager?

No

If you were raised by your mother how did she raise you? I.e. single parent, with your father, with a step father, with aid of a grandparent

With my father

Was your mother unavailable emotionally, physically or mentally ill and away from the family home for any length of time while you were growing up?

Emotionally unavailable

Did your mother use prescribed medications (for depression etc), recreational drugs, or alcohol to excess or have any addictions?

No

Was your mother ever physically violent or abusive towards you? *(Yes no is fine here if you want to keep the information brief)*

No

What motivates you to share your experiences in relation to your mother?

I think it is an important subject; rife with guilt and blame for many women.

Describe in a few sentences how you feel about your mother (feel free to use uncensored your experience)

I felt I brought myself up, from a baby. My mother felt like the child, and I the adult. It made me emotionally independent.

When you think of your mother what emotions/feelings come up for you?

Compassion

What triggers or challenges bring up personal pain for you in relations to your mother? *I.e. perceived rejection, not feeling heard, not being considered, other people's anger, feeling unloved by a partner, seeing Mothers Day Cards, birthdays and celebrations etc*

The fact that myself and my sister have had to carry her all our lives.

What were your unmet needs in childhood (regardless of the reason why) in relation to your mother?

Understanding and sensitivity

If your mother is alive what do you want from her now that you're not currently getting?

Her own spiritual growth

How have your experienced your mother as you both age, what changes have you noticed?

Initially I felt the black sheep of the family; she has grown to accept and appreciate me. We have a good relationship now.

What do you believe about yourself or the world around you in relation to your experience with your mother?

Blood is not necessarily thicker than water!

What is or has been your greatest fear in relation to your mother (for yourself and/or for her)?

That she would die not having enjoyed or appreciated her life.

How has your experience with your mother impacted other relationships?

It has taken quite a lot of my emotional and psychic energy.

What beliefs do you have about relationships based on your own experience?

You do the best you can to honour family relationships.

What are your beliefs about 'women as mothers' in this era and how they should live their lives raise a family, have a career etc?

It is good to accept support if it is available. I am not overly ambitious, but recognize that for many women this is an important part of their life and lifestyle.

What do you know about your mother's childhood and upbringing, her hopes, fears, beliefs about herself or the world around her?

Emotionally traumatic (repeats traumatic stories over and over again, as though they are in the present)

Reflecting on your past what stands out to you the most about your mother?

Although I would have liked more companionship and support, she managed not to do too much harm.

What is your biggest regret when you think about your relationship with your mother?

That I had to struggle so hard to make myself understood on any level.

If you were able to change your childhood what did you need the most from your mother that you never received? How would you have preferred your upbringing to be?

More spiritually focussed

If you were able right now to say what you wanted to say to your mother, what would you say?

You did your best.

How has your experience of your mother shaped you life to date (negative and positive aspects?)

Negative: having no support when rearing my own children hampered me.

Positive: harmlessness.

What did /has your mother taught you about being a woman, being a mother, life, love and living?

Many women are ruled by their emotions and hormones, and use their emotional power.

Depending on your relationship status with your mother if she is still alive how would you like the future of your relationship to be?

One of mutual respect

What gets in the way of not having the kind of relationship you've just shared?

We are getting there. Her emotions were always focussed on herself.

When you are with your mother do you find yourself reacting to her as an adult or as a child/teenager from the hurt part of yourself?

Adult

If you were able to create you 'ideal mother' what would that be like for you? What would be her qualities, attributes, gifts, how would she be with you? What would she say to you right now?

An Earth Mother, very sensitive - "You are doing well".

What is the biggest thing you've learnt about yourself on your journey with or without your mother so far?

My own tolerance, sensitivity and empathy!

How do you meet your own needs now as an adult?

My spiritual path; my awareness of myself as a 'Lightworker'

What got you through your experiences?

Early maturity, later the spiritual path

What positive and negative traits do you have that your mother had/has?

Positive: sensitivity (hers is mainly towards herself, but she has sensitivity to world suffering)

Negative: lack of energy.

What things do you enjoy doing that your mother enjoyed?

My mother is good at cooking, but did not enjoy it. I love cooking.

We dress similarly, and are both artistic, though she does not regard herself as artistic (comparing herself to her sisters)

Knowing that your mother gave you the gift of life, what are you most grateful for in recognition of this?

That she loves children and babies, she loves her own children, grandchildren and great grandchild.

Using your past to make your future the best it can what skills and resources have you developed to use to your greater good?

I do a lot of counselling.

Q&A

Name: *Cici*

Age: *34*

Are you a mother as well as a daughter? Yes/No if yes, how many children do you have what are their sexes?

No

What is your current personal relationship status: Single/ widowed/divorced/separated/co-habiting, second marriage etc

Single

Your mother's age as she is now if applicable:

64 years old

The age your mother was when she died if applicable (how old were you when she died?)

N/A

Your mother's Ethnic origin/Nationality/country of birth

Italian, she still lives in Italy.

Details of your Siblings, current ages and sexes:

I have one older brother who is 36. He lives in France.

Details of your mother's siblings, age gap between them and your mother and sexes:

My mum is an only child.

Are you part of a step family? If so do you have a good relationship with them now?

No step family.

Were you in care, adopted or fostered as a child/teenager?

No

If you were raised by your mother how did she raise you? I.e. single parent, with your father, with a step father, with aid of a grandparent

I was raised by both of my parents.

Was your mother unavailable emotionally, physically or mentally ill and away from the family home for any length of time while you were growing up?

No but she put on a lot of weight few years after having me and never lost it. Her mum did not look after her and she was raised by various people when she was little and so she had to come to terms with this burden.

Did your mother use prescribed medications (for depression etc), recreational drugs, or alcohol to excess or have any addictions?

Yes for medications but I am not too sure what. She has seen and still sees now a psychologist. No problems of drugs nor alcohol.

Was your mother ever physically violent or abusive towards you? *(Yes no is fine here if you want to keep the information brief)*

No

What motivates you to share your experiences in relation to your mother?

I want to help a lovely writer.

I think it is helpful for me as well to reflect on my relationship with my mum as it has got a great impact on my life and decisions even if I don't realise it most of the time.

Describe in a few sentences how you feel about your mother (feel free to use uncensored your experience)

I love my mum to bits as she has always wanted the best for me and she is a loving person who puts family first. However, I am disappointed to see she lacks courage in her personal life and lets her unresolved problems destroy her health. I have realised my mum is dependent on others in particular of my dad and their unhealthy relationship, too scared she won't find anything better. I feel there is a tight bond between us and if I don't meet her expectations in the role of the joyful giving daughter there is a guilt trip for me. I don't like my mother when she makes me feel bad about myself, that I should feel so grateful to have her compared to her own mother. I know my mum is unhappy but I can't do anything about it.

When you think of your mother what emotions/feelings come up for you?

I'm happy to see her but I have established some distance as she is too controlling and I want to protect myself.

What triggers or challenges bring up personal pain for you in relations to your mother? *I.e. perceived rejection, not feeling heard, not being considered, other people's anger, feeling unloved by a partner, seeing Mothers Day Cards, birthdays and celebrations etc*

I guess when I feel rejected by someone I am dating although I would feel it has more to do with my relationship with my dad.

What were your unmet needs in childhood (regardless of the reason why) in relation to your mother?

My parents had a dysfunctional relationship and I had to take sides listening to my mum and dad complaining about the other. It was not my role as a daughter.

If your mother is alive what do you want from her now that you're not currently getting?

I'd like her to be responsible for her life and not from others to do things for her or justify her own actions. I would like her to stop giving excuses for the status quo. I'd like to have fun with her, a bit of craziness and light hearted moments. I want her to get her health on track.

How have your experienced your mother as you both age, what changes have you noticed?

It was hard for my mum to let go.

What do you believe about yourself or the world around you in relation to your experience with your mother?

The fear of being abandoned, it is hard for me to live on my own and I feel very lonely at times. My mum has felt like this and still is.

What is or has been your greatest fear in relation to you mother (for yourself and/or for her)?

I'm scared she will die soon because of her poor health and that I did not help enough.

How has your experience with your mother impacted other relationships?

I have stayed in a long term relationship knowing full well it was not working out but I could not leave. I was dependent and it took a lot of time for me to break free.

What beliefs do you have about relationships based on your own experience?

I believe that you need to find yourself to attract the right person. Otherwise you will meet the wrong men thinking they will complete you and vice-versa; it will be a relationship of power and games. I know true love exists and I have met happy couples and they are my paradigm, not my own family.

What are your beliefs about 'women as mothers' in this era and how they should live their lives raise a family, have a career etc?

It is important for women to resolve their own issues with their families before being a mum as otherwise they will 'pass on' the parcel. I think there is a time for everything, women can do whatever they want but you can't have everything at the same time, you need to go with the flow.

What do you know about your mother's childhood and upbringing, her hopes, fears, beliefs about herself or the world around her?

She had a tough childhood. My grandma could not raise a child, she was not responsible enough. She must have been scared and withdrawn from what I gathered.

Reflecting on your past what stands out to you the most about your mother?

Preparing dinner for the whole family and stressing about it-feeding role and keeping up everything together even if the ship is sinking.

What is your biggest regret when you think about your relationship with your mother?

We did not talk about men and sexuality and it is a shame as it made it a taboo.

If you were able to change your childhood what did you need the most from your mother that you never received? How would you have preferred your upbringing to be?

More fun and adventure, less moaning, less judgments and negative comments

If you were able right now to say what you wanted to say to your mother, what would you say?

Don't be scared to be yourself, you are great the way you are. Don't put the others first and depend on them. It is never too late to break free.

How has your experience of your mother shaped you life to date (negative and positive aspects?)

Mostly positive as I have been looked after, I try not to repeat any pattern especially in my love life.

What did /has your mother taught you about being a woman, being a mother, life, love and living?

I know that the greatest joy for my mum was to have my brother and I. She has a positive outlook on life although she is averse to change.

Depending on your relationship status with your mother if she is still alive how would you like the future of your relationship to be?

A bit more carefree, less heavy conversations talking about my brother or other people - as it is pointless I am not going to change anything. I'd like to enjoy nice wine, restaurant, spa, cinema with her.

What gets in the way of not having the kind of relationship you've just shared?

The family burden…I don't know why things are complicated but it has always been the case.

When you are with your mother do you find yourself reacting to her as an adult or as a child/teenager from the hurt part of yourself?

Now I can say I see myself as an adult. I don't react and get upset; I analyse and give objective feedback when I feel the need to.

If you were able to create you 'ideal mother' what would that be like for you? What would be her qualities, attributes, gifts, how would she be with you? What would she say to you right now?

I have met my ideal mother! She is terrific! She has got a big family who gets together regularly. Everything is fun and cosy. I can say how I feel and what goes on in my mind without thinking twice, she is always caring and she loves her husband. Basically a person who can shine her love abundantly and feels grateful.

What is the biggest thing you've learnt about yourself on your journey with or without your mother so far?

What it means to be truly independent as a daughter. It does not mean to go abroad and be financially independent. I can see that I am an adult and that I love my mum although I don't agree on many things and that is fine.

How do you meet your own needs now as an adult?

My loving friends and nature

What got you through your experiences?

My close friends, two are my soul sisters, I know they will always be there for me which is reassuring.

What positive and negative traits do you have that your mother had/has?

I am very giving (which is not always a good thing!), a way to make others love you I guess.

I used to be a bit bossy but I don't know if it is relevant now.

We are both sociable and curious (arts, conferences, books)

What things do you enjoy doing that your mother enjoyed?

Travelling, learning languages, nice food and wine, dancing, acting/drama clubs

Knowing that your mother gave you the gift of life, what are you most grateful for in recognition of this?

I'm grateful for all the wonderful experiences I have had, the people I've met, the landscapes I have gazed at, the smiles, the sunbeams and the glittering sea.

Using your past to make your future the best it can what skills and resources have you developed to use to your greater good?

Take a step back, analyse and don't react little Aries!

More precisely the 4 Toltec agreements mean a lot to me. Be impeccable with your word, don't take anything personally and don't make assumptions, always do your best.

Q&A

Name: *Sam*

Age: *48*

Are you a mother as well as a daughter? Yes/No if yes, how many children do you have what are their sexes?

Yes, I have one lovely son age 13

What is your current personal relationship status: Single/ widowed/divorced/separated/co-habiting, second marriage etc

I've been single since my son's father left 9 years ago.

Your mother's age as she is now if applicable:

82 years old and looks many years younger. Also very active still.

The age your mother was when she died if applicable (how old were you when she died?)

N/A

Your mother's Ethnic origin/Nationality/country of birth

British / born in UK

Details of your Siblings, current ages and sexes:

I have one brother aged 46 (also adopted, but different birth mother to me)

Details of your mother's siblings, age gap between them and your mother and sexes:

My mother doesn't have brothers and sisters as she was an only child.

Are you part of a step family? If so do you have good relationship with them now?

N/A

Were you in care, adopted or fostered as a child/teenager?

I found information in my adoption notes that I spent the first month with my natural mother in hospital with feeding difficulties, then I was placed in care. I was fostered for a few months by a family then I was introduced to a different couple (my Mum and Dad) and was finally adopted by them when I was 13 months old. I have not had any contact with my birth mother.

If you were raised by your mother how did she raise you? I.e. as a single parent, with your father, with a step father, with aid of a grandparent

I was really bought up solely by my mother as she was left to cope on her own much of the time. My father was focused on his career as a Veterinarian Surgeon and running several Surgeries. When he wasn't working, he would prefer to spend his time networking in his Rotary club, attending Masonic meetings and lecturing at the Royal Veterinary College in London. Shortly after my adoption, my mother wanted to adopt another child from a "third world country" (my mother is not exactly pc, but her intentions were good!). My parents adopted my brother when I was around 2 years old. He was a 6 month old baby and took up most of my mother's attention. There was sadly not much involvement from grandparents, who on my mother's side said 'children should be seen but not heard'. My grandparents on my father's side were very involved with their other grandchildren (my father had a sister and a brother) but my brother and I didn't see them often.

Was your mother unavailable emotionally, physically or mentally ill and away from the family home for any length of time while you were growing up?

Sadly, my mother had always found it difficult to express affection, both verbally and physically towards me and to this day is extremely locked in emotionally. I've never seen her cry openly in all these years, just the odd grimace and watery eyes on the odd occasion. It's so very sad.

My mother's own mother died suddenly, shortly after my adoption, so I don't remember her, but I feel that my mother shut down emotionally following this tragedy, as they were very close. My mother's father was an ex military Officer who was very strict and as he became older, she visited him occasionally "out of duty" with me, but I was pretty much ignored while we were there.

Did your mother use prescribed medications (for depression etc), recreational drugs, or alcohol to excess or have any addictions?

I remember my mother taking Valium and other various medications to help her relax. She has never ever wanted to talk about her mental health to me, as she's always told me it's none of my business. She clearly suffered/suffers from anxiety and still has mood swings to this day, but she will never talk about it and will always laugh it off in denial if questioned.

Was your mother ever physically violent or abusive towards you? *(Yes no is fine here if you want to keep the information brief)*

My mother was very controlling and a bully as I was growing up...well actually right up into my adult life. It took me over 40 years to realise and accept that her issues were not MY issues!

My mother always wanted extreme control and there were many occasions when she demonstrated this control. When I was 14 years old, she had a large padlock installed up high on the bathroom door at home to prevent me from showering in the morning and making myself presentable for school. In her mind, she was concerned that I was spending too long making myself pretty for boys and not concentrating on my school work!?? My brother was away at boarding school, so it didn't affect him and my father just didn't get involved with conflict. On another occasion, I was marched into a hair salon straight after school to have all my long hair cut short, as a friend had used crimpers on it at break time…it was an 80's thing!!

What motivates you to share your experiences in relation to your mother?

I have done much work over the years on myself regarding the experiences and relationship I have with my mother. Our relationship was so toxic and unsupportive; it made me emotionally and physically ill for many years. I even attempted suicide on 2 occasions in my 20's. The last attempt left me in a coma for 3 days. That is all behind me now thankfully and I have moved forward with new knowledge and understanding about myself and my relationships, especially with my wonderful son who makes my light shine so much brighter.

I'm motivated to share my experiences and relationship with my mother, as I'm sure there are many other women and daughters who can relate to having toxic and controlling relationships with their own mothers. We all have the ability to change and take responsibility for our own emotions. We all deserve love and happiness and if our present situation and relationships aren't fulfilling this most natural and innate emotion, then positive action for personal change is required to find happiness and love elsewhere. I feel there is still some emotion attached to my mother, even though I have distanced myself, so this hopefully will be a cathartic process and give me new insight to heal further.

Describe in a few sentences how you feel about your mother

I don't like my mother much, as I had so much anger towards her growing up, but I've tried to forgive my mother for her choices and actions towards me. I do feel quite detached emotionally from my mother now after cutting the emotional cords from her. I can safely and quietly look into her world now when I choose to see her (not that often), but I'm not affected by her opinions, her negativity and her general presence as I used to be. I don't like the person who calls herself my mother and who remains unsupportive emotionally, but I still have a thin thread of love that is connected somewhere between us.

When you think of your mother what emotions/feelings come up for you?

Sadness is the dominant emotion. Sadness for the loss of connection and emotional support I wish I had. Sadness for not ever having a mother who I could trust, relax with and chat openly with. I can visualise a large hole in my tummy that I can see through and it's framing a scene of the ocean with a large coastal rock formation in the left foreground.

Wow, I guess I still have emotion to work on Wendy!!!! This feeling of sadness hasn't shown itself like this for a long time. It was anger and resentment that used to come up while working on issues around my mother. Actually there is also some frustration there.

What triggers or challenges bring up personal pain for you in relations to your mother? *I.e. perceived rejection, not feeling heard, not being considered, other people's anger, feeling unloved by a partner, seeing Mothers Day Cards, birthdays and celebrations etc*

Fear of rejection, separation and trust issues have always been huge for me, as these fears have prevented me from finding another partner and have distanced me from getting really close to people. It's all manageable though now but there's still stuff to be worked on. It's great to be given the opportunity to reflect honestly and openly with direct questions....so thank you!

Working on my issues surrounding my mother has not only helped me emotionally, but is also helping me to clear psoriasis that covered 75% of my body for over 25 years. As you may be aware, psoriasis is a separation issue in a Meta Health sense.

What were your unmet needs in childhood (regardless of the reason why) in relation to your mother?

I felt I was insignificant as my ideas and opinions were never truly listened to, as they didn't conform to my Mother's ideas. I so needed to be heard growing up and to be given the opportunity to make choices. I believed my opinion didn't matter at home or in school, so I started to rebel. Looking back, I also craved attention and unfortunately became the class clown in school.

If your mother is alive what do you want from her now that you're not currently getting?

I would love to have a normal close and happy relationship with her and feel the peace and protection from loving maternal cuddles. I've never experienced that from her.

How have your experienced your mother as you both age, what changes have you noticed?

I choose not to see or speak with my mother much these days to avoid any conflict, but when we do, it feels as if my mother listens to me a little more now and that I'm not the 'big idiot' that she believed me to be when I was younger. I also have a good understanding and better control of my emotions now, so can control the situation now in the sense that I can end the conversation with controlled positivity rather than slamming the phone down on her, walking off or shouting when the conversation heads in a negative direction. I see my mother as a victim of her own doing now and realise that her life and personal choices are very different to mine.

What do you believe about yourself or the world around you in relation to your experience with your mother?

I believe the world is a lonely place IF you don't have self-love or have experienced love. I believe that my opinion doesn't matter...but working on this one! I believe that people give up on me...still working on this too!

What is or has been your greatest fear in relation to you mother (for yourself and/or for her)?

Fear of not being understood and believed

How has your experience with your mother impacted other relationships?

I haven't been able to have long term relationships - the longest being 5 years. I always found a way to sabotage a relationship when it was going well in the fear that it was going to end and I'd be left on my own again, so I guess I subconsciously tried to end it first, but not always. I also used to be filled with jealously in relationships. I haven't had a relationship since my son's dad left us 9 years ago through choice, as my attention has been focused on being a good mother to my son to the best of my ability. I've done much thinking and self-healing during this time though and now my son is older, it's time to put myself out there again and make new connections.

I never understood and appreciated 'love' and happy relationships as I was growing up, as I didn't feel it at home and had no emotional guidance from either parent. I had to learn my own lessons the hard way. I saw little emotion between my parents, so they weren't great role models. They both had a huge amount of respect for each other, but they just seemed to be together out of duty.

I craved attention and expressed love as a physical love and unfortunately I became very promiscuous in my 20's searching for that elusive long lasting and loving relationship that I never found.

Thinking back, I found it very hard to make friends at school and never really had a best friend, as my mother was so disapproving of my choices. When I was 16 years old, I travelled to the USA on my own to attend school on a year exchange and it was only then I was able to form strong friendships with other girls and boys. My mother wasn't there to criticise and disapprove of my choices and I am still in contact with some of these now grown up men and women, 30 years later.

What beliefs do you have about relationships based on your own experience?

I still think that a relationship will end and I will be left on my own again if I get too close to someone.

What are your beliefs about 'women as mothers' in this era and how they should live their lives raise a family, have a career etc?

Women are multi-taskers and it is much more accepted in this era that a woman can juggle a career, as long as significant time is set aside to focus on being an attentive and hands on mother. I certainly don't think it's an ideal situation though to have multiple carers for a young baby or child, as it can be disorientating and unsettling.

I was a Director in a business with my son's father when my son was born and because of the heavy demands of the business, I regretfully decided to place my son in a day nursery from when he was 10 months old until he was 4 years old. I did feel very guilty, but also saddened to have missed out on a lot of interaction with him during key development stages and wish I could have spent 100% of my time with him. Although the nursery was a quality one with great facilities and experienced and attentive staff, looking back, nobody can replace an attentive loving mother's love for her child. I was in such a dilemma being aware that separation can develop into all kinds of insecurities for a child. I devoted the afternoons and weekends to my son during that time, so that was very precious time together.

What do you know about your mother's childhood and upbringing, her hopes, fears, beliefs about herself or the world around her?

Mum was an only child and she told me she spent much of her time reading and playing make believe games on her own. She wanted to be a teacher and achieved this dream by teaching, in her words, underprivileged boys in a 'special school' for many years. I think she underestimated the challenges ahead of her with these boys, but was able to maintain discipline and gain respect. She has spoken fondly in the past about a few boys she taught there and the relationship she had with them.

Mum was a very talented tennis player, but her early dreams of playing professional tennis were destroyed as she was told and believed she wasn't good enough to be a pro player, although she has many cups and trophies which she won in various tournaments.

Reflecting on your past what stands out to you the most about your mother?

Her strict and controlling nature, her anxiety, fear

What is your biggest regret when you think about your relationship with your mother?

I look back now and wish I hadn't rebelled so much, but I guess it was my way of trying to get noticed. I rebelled terribly against her and authority and found myself in a lot of trouble. I was unfortunately blamed and made the scapegoat for other people at school because of my naughty reputation, when I was completely innocent.

If you were able to change your childhood what did you need the most from your mother that you never received? How would you have preferred your upbringing to be?

Feeling LOVED...this is what I needed the most. I wish we could have been friends. She said to me when I was very young that we could NEVER be friends as she was my mother. I didn't live up to her expectations or fit her mould, so it felt like she didn't like me much. I so wanted her to like me...and FEEL loved by her. I wish she would have been open to family discussion and let me voice my opinion and feelings about situations, rather than being dictated to by her.

If you were able right now to say what you wanted to say to your mother, what would you say?

I feel so sorry for you mum, because you didn't know what being a mother really meant as you had never loved, or perhaps been loved in the way you wanted or understood it to be. You acted out the role of being a mother with your head but certainly not with your heart. Your heart is so closed and even to this day you choose to remain locked within a capsule of pain. It's written all over your face. It's so sad to see, but that is your choice. I'm walking away. I'm letting you go with love. I am free.

How has your experience of your mother shaped your life to date (negative and positive aspects?)

I found it hard to form lasting relationships and make friends, rather than just acquaintances when I was growing up. I now know this is because I was scared to get close to people because I believed they would leave me which was just too painful, separation from birth mother also perhaps.

Emotions were never ever talked about at home, which was hard for me as I'm such an emotional person and I constantly experienced my own outbursts of anger towards my mother and her consequent discipline. I lacked the understanding of relationships and I guess I was emotionally immature up into my 20's. Life would have been a lot easier I think growing up if my mother; actually both parents could have communicated more with me and listened to me constructively.

I was very needy in later relationships with boyfriends, putting the emphasis on the physical side of the relationship rather than the emotional.

I felt very angry and resentful towards my mum right up until about five years ago. The anger made me emotionally and physically ill and I was in and out of hospital over the years with stomach issues but no definite diagnosis. At 14 years old, I was dragged to the GP by my mother as she couldn't cope with our relationship and I was wrongly diagnosed with having a personality disorder (no medication or referral). I believed for years that I was seriously mentally ill by this label, which made me feel even more different than I already did to everyone else.

On a positive note...I've managed to break free from the cycle of misery with my mother and the labels that were stuck on me.

What did /has your mother taught you about being a woman, being a mother, life, love and living?

My mother is a true feminist and believes in strong capable women. This is partly because she was left to cope on her own with poor health and two small children so learnt to become independent as my father was rarely around. She has an iron determination and that is something I definitely have too when I put my mind to something.

I certainly didn't learn my maternal skills from my mother! Her parenting skills compared to mine are on opposite sides of the scales, she still thinks strict discipline is the best way to bring up a child.

Depending on your relationship status with your mother if she is still alive how would you like the future of your relationship to be?

Mutual respect and a show of appreciation for each other, a motherly hug would be lovely to have when we meet up. (She dislikes cuddles and kisses), but I love them! It would be a lovely refreshing change to get through a conversation with her without her making negative assumptions about me. Humour...I would love to be able to belly laugh with her about something mutually funny. I would love her to visit my home and allow me to cook a meal and just hang out with her.

What gets in the way of not having the kind of relationship you've just shared?

It always feels like one step forward and two steps back with her, as she doesn't want to believe people change (me) and she refuses to open herself up emotionally and discuss feelings. She has little belief in me and I've given up trying to explain to her how the Emotional Freedom Technique and Matrix Reimprinting has helped me enormously. She is personally terrified of getting in touch with her emotions and letting go and has sadly never wanted me or anyone else to help her.

When you are with your mother do you find yourself reacting to her as an adult or as a child/teenager from the hurt part of yourself?

I used to react to her as a hurt child/teenager, but now I react as an adult through new eyes, out of self love and self control.

If you were able to create your 'ideal mother' what would that be like for you? What would be her qualities, attributes, gifts, how would she be with you? What would she say to you right now?

My ideal mother would be open, warm, loving and funny with a joy for life and adventure. She would be stylish and take care of her appearance and love spending time with friends as well as me. She would love my company. We would giggle and laugh together and truly respect each other for the individuals that we are. We would travel and experience new countries and cultures together as a family with my son also included. She would say life is for living and support and encourage me to experience everything that life shows me.

What is the biggest thing you've learnt about yourself on your journey with or without your mother so far?

The only person I can rely on and trust is myself

How do you meet your own needs now as an adult?

My needs are not always met, but I accept that support, positive things and new opportunities will happen at the right time

What got you through your experiences?

My inner determination and soul purpose, I know I have guardian angels who keep me safe and protect me. There have been a few situations happen to me over the years where I know I have been protected when it could easily have gone tragically wrong, but I have been given extra time to keep learning and to 'get it right'. My beautiful son gave me the reason to truly love and is the light in my life.

What positive and negative traits do you have that your mother had/has?

I have my mothers' determination, I'm strongly independent, I lived far too long mulling over the past and blaming certain people around me which caused much anxiety and depression for many years.

What things do you enjoy doing that your mother enjoyed?

As I've got older, I appreciate nature and our environment much more than I used to. I've always loved animals, but I'm interested in plants and gardening that I know my mother truly feels at one with.

Knowing that your mother gave you the gift of life, what are you most grateful for in recognition of this?

I was adopted, so this isn't applicable, I am grateful to my birth mother though who I know suffered a huge amount, I am grateful to have all my physical senses and vision to experience this life and the opportunities, emotions and relationships that I will encounter during my time here.

Using your past to make your future the best it can be, what skills and resources have you developed to use to your greater good?

I'm a natural empath. I'm compassionate and love helping other people. By learning self-love and appreciation of myself, I've come out the other side in a positive light with a bright new energy I feel I need to share. I've freed myself from the disabling effects of anxiety and depression with EFT and Matrix and successfully continue to heal my skin issue with a natural holistic approach. I changed the old way I was looking at my life and the relationship I had with my mother and my perceptions of the things I was looking at began to change positively. I now intend to combine my personal experiences with my skills in holistic health, nutrition and energy psychology to help other people emotionally and holistically as a Mindset Coach enabling them to find an easier and healthier path to tread on their own journey.

Q&A

Name: *Alex*

Age: *71*

Are you a mother as well as a daughter?

Yes.

If yes, how many children do you have what are their sexes?

I have 2 children, one male and one female (and 5 grandchildren if that might be relevant?)

What is your current personal relationship status: Single/widowed/divorced/separated/co-habiting, second marriage etc.

Currently single by choice at present, whilst I heal my illness.

Your mother's age as she is now if applicable:

N/A

The age your mother was when she died if applicable (how old were you when she died?)

I was 52 when she died aged 81

Your mother's Ethnic origin/Nationality/country of birth

I was born in Egypt just before the end of WW2, because my father was stationed there, and my mother helped in the RAF stores. My father was British. My mother was British by nationality, because her parents were from Malta. But she was brought up in Turkey and learned to speak English after marrying my father who was in the RAF and stationed in Turkey during WW2. (It's complicated! Dad first encountered my mother at her parent's Pension she and her sister helped to run, and immediately fell in love with her, saying to himself, "That's the girl for me!" She didn't see it that way, at first, for she was already engaged to a Sergeant in the Army!! But luckily for me, true love won the day.

Details of your siblings, current ages and sexes:

I have a brother, now aged 65, and a sister, currently 68.

Details of your mother's siblings, age gap between them and your mother and sexes:

My mother had a sister and brother, but I don't know the age differences, sorry. There were also other siblings who died soon after birth, as often happened back in the early 20th century.

Are you part of a step family? If so do you have a good relationship with them now?

No

Were you in care, adopted or fostered as a child/teenager?

No

If you were raised by your mother how did she raise you? I.e. as a single parent, with your father, with a stepfather, with aid of a grandparent

In early childhood, from when I arrived from Egypt in late May 1945 I was mostly raised by my mother, as dad was in the RAF, and often posted away. He also was a crack shot, and often away in competitions shooting for the RAF, too. Soon after, my mother's sister came to live in the house next door but one to us, and my grand-mere, my mother's mother, came to live with my aunt, after Granpapaco died in Turkey. So a lot of my early childhood was spent with a maternal clan of wonderful women I could go to if I was unhappy with my own mother, or should she need a break from me!

Was your mother unavailable emotionally, physically or mentally ill and away from the family home for any length of time while you were growing up?

No, not emotionally unavailable; far from it! She was from the Mediterranean! And no, not unavailable physically, nor did she ever suffer from mental health issues.

Did your mother use prescribed medications (for depression etc), recreational drugs, or alcohol to excess or have any addictions?

No to any of those

Was your mother ever physically violent or abusive towards you? *(Yes no is fine here if you want to keep the information brief)*

Never, she'd swear in Greek or French, often telling us 'to go to the Devil/Hell' I'm guessing it was her way of venting any frustrations. But no, bless her; never ever did she harm us in any way. The first violence I ever encountered in my life was from my ex-husband, and I had no notion of how to deal with it, having never met violence in anyone before...

What motivates you to share your experiences in relation to your mother?

To support you, Wendy, in case this helps. And perhaps my mother makes an unusual case study with her very different background!

Describe in a few sentences how you feel about your mother (feel free to use uncensored your experience)

I loved her dearly, and still do. She would frustrate the hell out of me, sometimes, as I did with her, I know, but underneath was always an amazing bond of loving and highly expressive Mediterranean motherhood.

When you think of your mother what emotions/feelings come up for you?

Love, affection, fierce pride, and feeling deeply blessed to have chosen her as my mum.

What triggers or challenges bring up personal pain for you in relations to your mother? *i.e. perceived rejection, not feeling heard, not being considered, other people's anger, feeling unloved by a partner, seeing Mothers Day Cards, birthdays and celebrations etc.*

No pain, whatsoever. Oh, as a child, I did sometimes feel unloved, and unheard, of course, for she had 3 children just after the war, when rationing was operational, all washing was done by hand, and the only heat came from coal fires - and she managed a lot of the time on her own. BUT what I remember most about her was that despite there being 3 of us, she would ALWAYS, ALWAYS, be equally fair to each one of us. Dad would joke that he needed to get out his measuring tape to ensure not one of us got a fraction of an inch less cake than the others! She taught me so much about respect and fairness, as well as genuine love and warmth. I just wasn't in any way prepared for the way my ex-husband treated me, for his own family completely lacked the openness, warmth, expressiveness, and honesty that I'd been brought up with. It was a huge culture shock! (But one I learned from, of course, as I've already said to you).

What were your unmet needs in childhood (regardless of the reason why) in relation to your mother?

Of course, like any child, I wanted MORE of my mum, more time, more cuddles, just 'more'.

If your mother is alive what do you want from her now that you're not currently getting?

N/A

How have you experienced your mother as you both age, what changes have you noticed?

I certainly began to value and appreciate her far, far more, as I grew older. But I was always so proud of her, for everyone in my life loved her vitality and warmth. And her cooking, of course!

What do you believe about yourself or the world around you in relation to your experience with your mother?

Well, over the past 28 years, since I divorced a violent husband, I delved deeply into what I'd learned growing up, to explain how I'd ended up marrying him, and why it took me so long to see the truth, and leave him. Because I made a vow that this would NEVER happen to me again – and the only way to do that was to look at my own belief systems. What I did realise was that my mother, despite her incredible talents, warmth, humour and capacity to love, deferred to my father. I do remember her saying 'Mens know best' in her strong Mediterranean accent. My dad disagreed strongly, and always joked that she, not he, was "head" of the house! And we did laugh, for it was undeniably true. If she saw an injustice, she was the one to unhesitatingly go out and sort it – beautifully, with a twinkle in her eye and knowing that people would always succumb to her charming accent and way of putting things. Yet despite evidence to the contrary, I must have absorbed it, and learned not to fully trust in myself and my capabilities and talents, and to unwittingly see myself as 'less than' a man. Crazy, crazy, crazy! My parents were equals, and each had their own strengths that together made a special kind of magic.

And yes, here I am, at very nearly 71, highly trained, and very knowledgeable, also very self aware – yet I still doubt myself. I've managed to keep my vow to myself, and I've never had an abusive relationship since. Instead, I've had relationships in which I've blossomed and grown. And not only that, but I've delved so deeply BECAUSE of the anomalies of ending up in an abusive relationship, when there was no abuse whatsoever in my family of origin, I began to look at what defines abuse, and where it begins. That's the biggest gift I gained, for I've more than broken the chain of abuse that came from my ex-husband's side of the family. My children and grandchildren are as respectful of others as I learned to be. It's in the tiny things, as I learned, where abuse begins, in such subtle ways that most of society takes to be 'normal' and indeed, acceptable.

Now I just need to end abusing myself by disrespecting and avoiding trusting in myself – not in big, obvious ways, for I have learned to love myself. But it's that tiny glimmer of self-doubt that still slips in, unwittingly, unbidden, and that's what I have yet to fully heal. That's the challenge my beautiful mother gifted me. And I love her for it, for I wouldn't have had the amazing family I now have, without all of that learning. I'm blessed, and I know it. Now – down to healing myself!

What is or has been your greatest fear in relation to your mother (for yourself and/or for her)?

No fears whatsoever for her, or for myself. The first night in my new home, my sanctuary, the only fear I felt was being on my own in the dark! My children were both away, and it was the very first time I was completely on my own! But there's something incredibly nurturing about this little cottage that everyone who walks in notices that dispelled any fears I might have had. And I've always felt so safe here, since then. Yes, there did turn out to be ghost here, in this 230-year-old cottage, but that's another story!

How has your experience with your mother impacted other relationships?

Because I had what most would consider a really great and loving childhood, I absolutely had to look at myself when it came to understanding how I'd almost been killed by the man who said he loved me. The two differing family backgrounds just did not correlate. So I learned about me, and grew into more of me, and learned the value of intimacy (into-me-I-see). My mother never dared to look at herself, for she only saw her value through the eyes of others. When she was unwell with Cancer, she'd tell me how much she hated being forced to do nothing, and wondered why God was punishing her! Oh, I held her and reassured her. But she didn't grasp the truth, that just being herself was more than enough. I learned about co-dependency, and how it infiltrates our entire Western way of being in the world. How we all look outside of ourselves, when the truth is that it's all WITHIN. Bless her, my mum taught me passion, and to believe in the magic, and tried to teach me to believe in myself, but her behaviour gave her away, and it's exactly that that led me on to have amazing, loving, and equal relationships.

What beliefs do you have about relationships based on your own experience?

You can see that I didn't love or trust in myself, sufficiently, to be able to handle a highly manipulative and aggressive abuser, within a marriage. Outside of marriage, I'd never have tolerated what I did within it. My mother and my sister, and my whole family supported me in getting out. You could see the broken bones and bruises. They are obvious. But the deeper wounds of emotional and verbal abuse cut more deeply because we rarely 'see' it as abuse, in our Western culture.

Now, 28 years on, I refuse to allow anyone to talk deprecatingly about themselves, or another. I have phenomenal relationships, and people come to me for advice, even though currently I'm not working. And I can always help them see what's really going on for them. It's a talent I have and love doing just that. I wish my mother were still here to see just what I've achieved, on my own – standing on my own two feet. She'd be as proud of me as I am of her. I know it. For the greatest learning came from marrying a highly abusive man who appeared charm personified…

What are your beliefs about 'women as mothers' in this era and how they should live their lives raise a family, have a career etc?

My mother had a career, and always did something, even if it was simply helping people to learn French, even when I was young. Dad never stopped her. When all 3 of us were at Grammar Schools, mum decided she'd like to take up a nursing career she'd begun in Turkey, before she married dad. Dad called a family conference, and gave us all a chance to say how we felt about it. This was the early 60s – it was unheard of back then. We were told it meant we would all have to chip in with what had to be done in the house, and that included dad. And yes, all of us said to her do what you'd love to do, mum, we'll help and we'll be fine! And we were, despite it not being the norm, although times were beginning to change. So I do believe women have the right to choose – to stay at home and be a full time mother – or to mix both and have a career. It's our basic right, and one of many.

What do you know about your mother's childhood and upbringing, her hopes, fears, beliefs about herself or the world around her?

As I've said before, she assumed she wasn't enough, just being herself. Turkey's culture, certainly back then, from 1916 until the 1940's when she married, and despite mum coming from a Catholic community, was that women were the support system for their men. And that ran deep in her blood, in her subconscious. Yes, they got the vote before our suffragettes got theirs, but nonetheless, mum did not trust in herself to manage life entirely on her own. She deferred to the men in her life, and to her brother, as she was growing up.

Reflecting on your past what stands out to you the most about your mother?

What a mighty woman she was, in spite of everything.

What is your biggest regret when you think about your relationship with your mother?

None

If you were able to change your childhood what did you need the most from your mother that you never received? How would you have preferred your upbringing to be?

It was exactly how I needed it to be, for it's helped to grow me into the me that I am today.

If you were able right now to say what you wanted to say to your mother, what would you say?

I did say it all to her before she died. That I loved her, was proud of her, valued what she gave me, and valued her for who she was

How has your experience of your mother shaped your life to date (negative and positive aspects?)

I think I've already defined that.

What did /has your mother taught you about being a woman, being a mother, life, love and living?

She taught me how to love life with a passion, how to love my family and how to be FAIR – with everyone! She taught me laughter, and how to knit and embroider. She taught me who I am. She taught me love.

Depending on your relationship status with your mother if she is still alive how would you like the future of your relationship to be?

She might have died 19 years ago, but we now have an even better relationship than before. I often feel her presence...and love.

What gets in the way of not having the kind of relationship you've just shared?

Nothing, absolutely nothing

When you are with your mother do you find yourself reacting to her as an adult or as a child/teenager from the hurt part of yourself?

When she was still alive, we interacted as adults, though she did still try to 'fix' things for me!

If you were able to create your 'ideal mother' what would that be like for you? What would be her qualities, attributes, gifts, how would she be with you? What would she say to you right now?

She'd be Jeanne Novis, neé Caouki – just the same! She's my ideal mother and I wouldn't change her for anyone else, or try to make her any different. That's how much I love her.

What is the biggest thing you've learnt about yourself on your journey with or without your mother so far?

It's time to trust in myself, much, much more. And to keep on putting on myself first! Thank you, mum.

How do you meet your own needs now as an adult?

I learned to be my own best parent, 28 years ago, to love myself as if my life depended upon it, and to honour my needs by meeting them rather than kidding myself I didn't have any (as I had done within my marriage).

What got you through your experiences?

I'm guessing it's my mother's strength of spirit and depth of love, together with my father's quiet determination and integrity!

What positive and negative traits do you have that your mother had/has?

On the positive side, warmth and love, cheerfulness, honesty and directness

The remaining negative – I don't always see my own light, within this illness, just as she failed to see hers, within her marriage. It's time to trust in me and heal this illness once and for all.

What things do you enjoy doing that your mother enjoyed?

Dancing on tables and laughing loudly, having fun, being around our loving families, being creative with writing, just as she was creative with cooking, baking, sewing, knitting, crochet and so many more. Loving to dress up and look great, to wear a big hat whenever possible!, to care for people, and heal them, as she did, as a nurse and mother, and I do in my work with others, to commune with the unseen world, to have a depth of insight and wisdom that is pretty special. She always called herself a 'witch' because she picked up on stuff that no one else could know. I have that same gut instinct.

Knowing that your mother gave you the gift of life, what are you most grateful for in recognition of this?

This is difficult, for I'm deeply grateful for everything; however, if I had to choose just one thing, then it would be that she was so very DIFFERENT to all the other mothers. It's something my children often mention, and love about her. She stood out, in a wonderful way, like a feisty beacon of fairness and love.

Using your past to make your future the best it can be, what skills and resources have you developed to use to your greater good?

I've explained that, I think, already. Now it's down to me to trust totally in myself, (rather than some of the time) and heal this illness.

Please include any additional information as you wish that you feel is important for me to know:

I really don't think there's anything else! I consider myself one of the luckiest people in the world, even though I'm currently challenged by Fibromyalgia. But I've healed my body many times in the past, so I just KNOW I'll find a way to do it yet again so I can get back to doing more of all the things I love. And I'll value those all the more, too.

Q&A

Name: *Sue*

Age: *50*

Are you a mother as well as a daughter? Yes/No if yes, how many children do you have what are their sexes?

Yes, 1 daughter, 29 years

What is your current personal relationship status: Single/widowed/divorced/separated/co-habiting, second marriage etc

Divorced

Your mother's age as she is now if applicable:

81 years old

The age your mother was when she died if applicable (how old were you when she died?)

N/A

Your mother's Ethnic origin/Nationality/country of birth

White Caucasian, French, spent 35 years in South Africa, now back in France for 12 years

Details of your Siblings, current ages and sexes:

Only child

Details of your mother's siblings, age gap between them and your mother and sexes:

2nd eldest of 8 children (2 died in infancy in 1940) Brother 1 year younger, then sister deceased of cancer 4 years ago, 2 sisters and 1 brother all born within 8 years of each other

Are you part of a step family? If so do you have good relationship with them now?

No. Excellent relationship with all in-laws (mum, dad, sisters and brothers) for past 30 years

Were you in care, adopted or fostered as a child/teenager?

No

If you were raised by your mother how did she raise you? I.e. as a single parent, with your father, with a step father, with aid of a grandparent

With dad until I was 9 years old then parents divorced, I was very close to my dad

Was your mother unavailable emotionally, physically or mentally ill and away from the family home for any length of time while you were growing up?

Emotionally a little distant, cannot remember spontaneous hugs, kisses, intimate chats. Physically had everything I needed, food, clothes, schooling, secure home.

Did your mother use prescribed medications (for depression etc), recreational drugs, or alcohol to excess or have any addictions?

No

Was your mother ever physically violent or abusive towards you? (Yes no is fine here if you want to keep the information brief)

Got 1 or 2 smacks that I can remember only, raised her voice more.

What motivates you to share your experiences in relation to your mother?

Need to understand her more

Describe in a few sentences how you feel about your mother (feel free to use uncensored your experience)

Love more than like her. When I was younger found her irritable, we end up shouting at each other, I think she is selfish.

When you think of your mother what emotions/feelings come up for you?

Guilty, irritable, when together annoyed

What triggers or challenges bring up personal pain for you in relations to your mother? *I.e. perceived rejection, not feeling heard, not being considered, other people's anger, feeling unloved by a partner, seeing Mothers Day Cards, birthdays and celebrations etc*

She chose an abusive partner above me. Wouldn't believe me when i told her he was inappropriate towards me.

What were your unmet needs in childhood (regardless of the reason why) in relation to your mother?

No informal chats, didn't prepare me for periods, she gave me a book and some cotton wool

If your mother is alive what do you want from her now that you're not currently getting?

Nothing, don't want to drag up old feelings. She is old now.

How have you experienced your mother as you both age, what changes have you noticed?

We don't stay close and I see her twice a year. We speak on a weekly basis that is enough. She annoys me easily. Tolerate her more easily; I can put the phone down.

What do you believe about yourself or the world around you in relation to your experience with your mother?

Mothers always believe their children! Never believe the other person until proven otherwise.

What is or has been your greatest fear in relation to your mother (for yourself and/or for her)?

Don't want her to be alone. Feel concerned that we lost the close relationship when I was younger.

How has your experience with your mother impacted other relationships?

My role as mother is completely opposite than hers was to me.

What beliefs do you have about relationships based on your own experience?

I learnt to be emotionally available for my daughter. We are very close and have an open and honest relationship as all mums and daughters should have.

What are your beliefs about 'women as mothers' in this era and how they should live their lives raise a family, have a career etc?

They can be a working mother and a close mum to the children. Their children come first before all else. Mothers never leave their children, children leave their mothers as they grow, leave home, study etc.

What do you know about your mother's childhood and upbringing, her hopes, fears, beliefs about herself or the world around her?

Her mum was distant (8 kids) she was a selfish child (my aunts and uncles tell me so)

Reflecting on your past what stands out to you the most about your mother?

I was not always number one in her life.

What is your biggest regret when you think about your relationship with your mother?

Wish I was closer, we could chat more.

If you were able to change your childhood what did you need the most from your mother that you never received? How would you have preferred your upbringing to be?

She would have believed me. She should never have spoken ill of my father when I was younger, he was my world.

If you were able right now to say what you wanted to say to your mother, what would you say?

Nothing, she is too old and has health problems. Did confront her about 8 years ago, she had excuses. I thought she was selfish wanting a relationship that was not healthy for me.

How has your experience of your mother shaped your life to date (negative and positive aspects?)

Positive: I am a better mother! My daughter and I have an open, honest and close relationship. Negative: What's done is done, I can't dwell but we still clash.

What did /has your mother taught you about being a woman, being a mother, life, love and living?

She was a strong woman-so am I. I have always tried to be absolutely the opposite of what she is. I never ever wanted to be anything like her at all.

Depending on your relationship status with your mother if she is still alive how would you like the future of your relationship to be?

I'll chat with her on the phone, but won't go out of my way to visit. She's 81, still has strong views so I don't think our relationship will change.

What gets in the way of not having the kind of relationship you've just shared?

She had her chance and never placed me first at the time I needed her to, too late now. She doesn't listen to my advice; she expects things from me I'm not willing to forgive.

When you are with your mother do you find yourself reacting to her as an adult or as a child/teenager from the hurt part of yourself?

Child/teenager mostly, if I try to be the adult, she won't accept it.

If you were able to create your 'ideal mother' what would that be like for you? What would be her qualities, attributes, gifts, how would she be with you? What would she say to you right now?

Laugh a lot, casual chats; we could spend more than a day in each other's company without screaming at each other. I wouldn't feel irritated with her.

What is the biggest thing you've learnt about yourself on your journey with or without your mother so far?

To have an open, honest, fair relationship with boundaries with my daughter, I didn't have that with her.

How do you meet your own needs now as an adult?

I ensure that I am happy and place myself first before others, except when it comes to my daughter, but she is an adult, she looks after herself now.

What got you through your experiences?

Left home when I finished school and University, never stayed at my mother's for longer than a night, spent most of my time living with my dad.

What positive and negative traits do you have that your mother had/has?

She kept an immaculate home, I do too. I tend to have a sharp tongue, so have to think before I talk though not often. I've tried very hard not to copy any of her traits; I don't like any of them.

What things do you enjoy doing that your mother enjoyed?

Nothing

Knowing that your mother gave you the gift of life, what are you most grateful for in recognition of this?

I was cared for when I was young; she loves my daughter very much.

Using your past to make your future the best it can be what skills and resources have you developed to use for your greater good?

A lot of my skills I learnt in my nursing training. Sociable like my dad, love animals like my dad. Keep a clean home like my mother.

Q&A

Name: *Sheelagh*

Age: *64*

Are you a mother as well as a daughter? Yes/No if yes, how many children do you have what are their sexes?

No

What is your current personal relationship status: Single/ widowed/divorced/separated/co-habiting, second marriage etc

Living together

Your mother's age as she is now if applicable:

N/A

The age your mother was when she died if applicable (how old were you when she died?)

In her eighties, I was 53

Your mother's Ethnic origin/Nationality/country of birth

Irish/British

Details of your Siblings, current ages and sexes:

2 brothers age 62 and 53

Details of your mother's siblings, age gap between them and your mother and sexes:

1 elder brother, 5 younger sisters

Are you part of a step family? If so do you have good relationship with them now?

No

Were you in care, adopted or fostered as a child/teenager?

No

If you were raised by your mother how did she raise you? I.e. single parent, with your father, with a step father, with aid of a grandparent.

As part of a family unit, married to my father

Was your mother unavailable emotionally, physically or mentally ill and away from the family home for any length of time while you were growing up?

Yes, she was unavailable due to physical illness (problem after I was born and many miscarriages) and in my early teenage years. She was in a 'mental hospital' twice.

Did your mother use prescribed medications (for depression etc), recreational drugs, or alcohol to excess or have any addictions?

Not that I'm aware of, but she may have been on some kind of anti-depressant. She had ECT in hospital, barely drank alcohol.

Was your mother ever physically violent or abusive towards you? (Yes no is fine here if you want to keep the information brief)

No, but my father was abusive. However she did not always behave ''well'' to me and I believe she did not treat my younger brother well when he was a teenager/young man. My mother encouraged me to cook and shop for the household.

What motivates you to share your experiences in relation to your mother?

They are so complex and painful. I want rid but so far cannot be rid. Both my parents defined and limited me and I have struggled all my life to be strong and confident. Perhaps I can help others whose relationship is not the bed of roses society expects.

Describe in a few sentences how you feel about your mother (feel free to use uncensored your experience)

Numb, a baby crying far away whose cries go unanswered. I think she let me and my brother down remaining in an abusive relationship. I know rationally how difficult that was for her, but for me, the small child does not.

When you think of your mother what emotions/feelings come up for you?

Guilt that I was not the daughter I think she deserved. What a statement! I never felt loved by her although she said she loved me. I am crying as I write this, as I always do. Years of therapy and it still gets to me. Recently I have wondered why she kept becoming pregnant and miscarrying, when she already had two healthy children although I guess my youngest brother may not have been born. I am also angry at her for treating me as a mini-adult when I was a child. She treated me differently to my brother.

What triggers or challenges bring up personal pain for you in relation to your mother? *i.e. perceived rejection, not feeling heard, not being considered, other people's anger, feeling unloved by a partner, seeing Mothers Day Cards, birthdays and celebrations etc*

All of those (less so for cards) birthdays and when I don't feel heard or of importance.

What were your unmet needs in childhood (regardless of the reason why) in relation to your mother?

Someone to love me, cuddle me, keep me close. She could not breastfeed me, but did my brother, so that intimate bond never developed. Horrific sense of fear of rejection. Not being close to adults around me.

If your mother is alive what do you want from her now that you're not currently getting?

Left blank

How have your experienced your mother as you both age, what changes have you noticed?

Left blank

What do you believe about yourself or the world around you in relation to your experience with your mother?

That the world is often not safe, that I have to be strong and cannot rely on anyone, that I am alone and that is very hard to sustain.

What is or has been your greatest fear in relation to your mother (for yourself and/or for her)?

That she would abandon me and love them more. For her, I was afraid she was not happy and I couldn't help.

How has your experience with your mother impacted other relationships?

The fear of rejection has not had a positive impact.

She was kind and I am kind.

What beliefs do you have about relationships based on your own experience?

Quick sand! Beware! Trust and you get hurt. A lifelong struggle towards change and the light. I am not good enough and as a girl, the boy child mattered more.

What are your beliefs about 'women as mothers' in this era and how they should live their lives raise a family, have a career etc?

My mother had a career and I support mothers doing this. I am a lifelong feminist. My mother returned to work when I was little. She was a teacher. They should have a choice. But it was hard on me and if I had children, I would have stayed home with them.

What do you know about your mother's childhood and upbringing, her hopes, fears, beliefs about herself or the world around her?

Legend says her father was an alcoholic. Her mother brought the children up with the help of her mother.

Reflecting on your past what stands out to you the most about your mother?

That she was beautiful and very intelligent and I thought I could never be like her. She was unhappy and lonely living with my very difficult father.

What is your biggest regret when you think about your relationship with your mother?

That we never had the opportunity to repair our relationship, although I suspect she did not know how I felt.

If you were able to change your childhood what did you need the most from your mother that you never received? How would you have preferred your upbringing to be?

I wanted love and acceptance and for both of my parents to be there, physically and emotionally, if my upbringing had been like that, I might have been a happy and content child and adult.

If you were able right now to say what you wanted to say to your mother, what would you say?

I felt I was the mother in our relationship, as perhaps you were with your mother; can we change and reverse this now?

How has your experience of your mother shaped your life to date (negative and positive aspects?)

Find that very difficult to answer; I believe I carried on with my life without reference to my mother, as some bizarre coping strategy. Felt motherless for most of my life.

What did /has your mother taught you about being a woman, being a mother, life, love and living?

She was harsh when I became a teenager; she was seldom emotionally available to discuss my love life, etc. Although we often talked of her relationship with my father, again, I have no sense of my mother as a moral compass, guiding me; I just got on with it.

Depending on your relationship status with your mother if she is still alive how would you like the future of your relationship to be?

Left blank

What gets in the way of not having the kind of relationship you've just shared?

Left blank

When you are with your mother do you find yourself reacting to her as an adult or as a child/teenager from the hurt part of yourself?

Left blank

If you were able to create your 'ideal mother' what would that be like for you? What would be her qualities, attributes, gifts, how would she be with you? What would she say to you right now?

She would say "sorry" and hug me harder than anyone has ever done to me. I have no concept of an ideal mother for we are all human, perhaps 'The Mother in the Walton's'

What is the biggest thing you've learnt about yourself on your journey with or without your mother so far?

I am a survivor, had to be.

How do you meet your own needs now as an adult?

Loving and helping others, my partner and my beautiful cats with their unconditional love, being creative, developing and growing myself, my home and garden.

What got you through your experiences?

Sheer tenacity, guts, balls, being kind to others, empathy, intuition (trust your intuition, toughen up)

What positive and negative traits do you have that your mother had/has?

Genuinely, I do not know. I am told/I know I look very like her and sound like her. I have no "daughterly" sense of being like my mother, other than superficial.

What things do you enjoy doing that your mother enjoyed?

My garden, nature, I think of her as the season's change, art, especially painting and writing. In funny ways I replicate her.

Knowing that your mother gave you the gift of life, what are you most grateful for in recognition of this?

That I'm alive, I have an enhanced love of nature because of her. My empathy, kindness and intuition were developed due to circumstance and being her daughter. Today I thank her for giving me life.

Using your past to make your future the best it can be what skills and resources have you developed to use to your greater good?

My greater good is tied up in the greater good for all, for the planet. For me, I cannot separate this. I am an INFP on the Myers-Briggs Personality type indicator! Sometimes struggling, I use Mindfulness, my hypnotherapy skills, being creative and active as much as I can despite illness and depression.

Please include any additional information as you wish that you feel is important for me to know:

Thank you, Wendy!

Writing this has been hard, but quite therapeutic, healing. You see, my mother died very suddenly in January 2006, five months after my father's also sudden demise. Leaving myself and my brothers devastated and me robbed of any opportunity to reconcile with her and have a better mother/daughter relationship.

I became very ill some months later. I fought very hard to stay alive. Well, I am still here and my life is very different. I believe that I would not have been ill if my mother had not died when she did. I have kept my belief to myself until now (time to let it out). Perhaps one day I will write about it.

In the meantime, I hope you can read my writing and found something useful for your book here.

Love, Sheelagh x

With Thanks and Appreciation

It is with heartfelt appreciation that I share daughters' Words of Wisdom with you and it has certainly been a privilege to enter into their personal world. Without the sharing of these stories, the book would not be complete. They provide an insight into how we can all move on from the past into the beautiful and amazing women we are.

I hope in some way that reading through the experiences of other daughters, you have felt a sense of connection, hope, support and love. May your journey onwards unfold into something which allows you to be all of who you are and that you recognise the love you have within for yourself. Happiness is not a destination, it is a journey. My wish for you is you find moments of happiness to treasure along the way.

FLY FREE

Fly free, my daughter. Be what I could never be and leave the cage forever - *Nalini Singh*

My experience of my mother has shaped my life and who I am. I wouldn't change it for a thing. The circumstances of her life and mine, have guided me to this moment which is perfect for me. In completing *Mothers and Daughters* I have come full circle in understanding and transforming my relationship with my mother. I choose to look back on the laughs we shared, the things I learnt from her, especially learning the alphabet and our mutual love of animals, nature and baking. On her passing, I planted a commemorative rose called 'Blessings' and each day when I pass by the rose, I am reminded of the blessings in life and the life she gave me, the life I have lived and the life I have ahead of me.

It is my hope in sharing my words of wisdom; you as the child, teenager, adult and the beautiful woman within will go on to live a fulfilling and happy life with or without your mother's love. As you begin to understand your mother, your ancestry, your beliefs and who you are as a person beyond the role of daughter, true transformation begins. Not only are you changing as a daughter and a woman, the world over woman collectively are beginning to understand and transform the relationship they have with their mothers and ultimately themselves.

To all daughters everywhere, know you are the change. I salute you in coming this far, you are amazing.

Author End Note

Mothers and Daughters offers an overview across a number of topics connected with conflicting mother-daughter relationships, though it is certainly not exhaustive. It is beyond the scope of one book to include details which may be related to your personal experience. If there is something you would like to talk over which is particular to your personal journey, please do consider reaching out. You are welcome to contact me to discuss your needs and which means of support will be of benefit for you at www.mothersanddaughters.solutions

Appendix

After Care and support:

Take a bow. You have already taken transformational steps in understanding your mother and yourself in relation to her.

If you are wondering what to do next to fully implement your learning, take a moment and consider the following options available at www.mothersanddaughters.solutions

- You may wish to work with me on a programme of support privately to further the progress you have already made
- Download your free resources connected with the book
- Download the free and additional choice of self-help audio's
- Sign up to my newsletter
- Follow my blog
- Leave a book review on www.amazon.co.uk or www.amazon.com or contact me direct with your feedback
- Share the gift of this book with your mother, your daughter and others who you feel will benefit
- Continue to honour, respect and love all of who you are unconditionally
- Recognise your inner child. When she needs your love, be sure to listen to her needs, nurture and comfort her
- Use The Spotlight Process and EFT daily in your life
- Practice daily gratitude, giving thanks and appreciation for all you have
- Every day of your life you are blessed with 86,400 seconds, spend them wisely

Resources

- **Gary Craig** www.emofree.com for additional information about EFT and free EFT manual for further study
- **Karl Dawson** www.efttrainingcourses.net for forthcoming training courses and information about EFT and Matrix Reimprinting
- **The GoE** www.goe.ac The Guild of Energists The GoE - GoE.ac - The Guild of Energists was founded in 1998 and is a not-for-profit, world-leading professional membership organisation and provider of modern energy training courses, including in Energy EFT
- **EFT Universe** http://www.eftuniverse.com/ is a great resource aid for all things EFT including research and resources of all kinds
- **Silvia Hartmann** www.silviahartmann.com Creator of Energy EFT, Positive EFT and Energy in Motion (EmoTrance)
- **Curly Martin** www.achievementspecialists.co.uk Curly is in my opinion one of the best coaches on the planet, check out her training courses and range of bestselling books on coaching
- **Sasha Allenby** www.sashaallenby.com Author of Write an Evolutionary Self Help Book – The Definitive Guide for Spiritual Entrepreneurs. Sasha offers a range of coaching and mentoring programmes. Sasha has been a key player in helping me to write Find YOU, Find LOVE and *Mothers and Daughters.*
- **Anne Jirsch** www.annejirsch.com Anne is one of the world's leading experts and pioneers of Future Life

Progression. Bestselling Author of Instant Intuition, The Future is Yours, Cosmic Energy, Create Your Perfect Future

- **Kate Marillat** www.katemarillat.com Creativity Coach and Author of Transform Your Beliefs, Transform Your Life. Kate inspired me to begin my writing journey

- **Sharon King** www.magicalnewbeginnings.com Author of Heal Your Birth Heal Your Life. Sharon offers a range of training courses and workshops including Matrix Birth Reimprinting

- **Caroline Maidment** www.carolinemaidment.com offers a range of meditation CDs and is also an EFT Practitioner

References

Chapter 1

Arcana, Judith, Our Mothers' Daughters, The Woman's Press Ltd, 1984

Bassof, Evelyn, Mothers and Daughters, Loving and Letting Go, Penguin Books Ltd, 1988

Bowlby, Dr John, Attachment and Loss, Volume 1, Basic Books, 1998

Cozolino, Louis, The Neuroscience of Human Relationships, W.W. Norton and Company, 2006

Edelamn, Hope, Motherless Daughters, Second Edition, Da Capo Lifelong Books, 2006

Freud, 'Female Sexuality' essay, Collected Papers, vol 5, 1950

Friday, Nancy, My Mother Myself, Dell Publishing, 1987

Fuerstein, Laura Arens PH.d , My Mother, My Mirror, New Harbinger Inc, 2009

Redmond, Layne. When the Drummers Were Women, Crown Publications, 1 edition, 1998

Karlson, Kathie, In Her Image, Shambala Publications, Inc, 1989

Keaton, Diane, DVD, 'Because I said So'

King, Sharon, Heal Your Birth, Heal Your Life, SilverWood Books Ltd, 2015

Mahler, Margaret S, Pine, Fred, Bergman, Anni, The Psychological Birth of the Human Infant: Symbiosis and Individuation, BasicBooks, Inc, 1975

Montagu, Ashley, Touching, Harper Perennial Library, 1971

Rich, Adrienne, Of Women Born, W W Norton and Company, 1976

Wallin David, Attachment in Psychotherapy, Guildford Press, 1st Edition, 2015

Wassamer, Julie, More Than Just Coincidence, HarperTrue, 2010

Chapter 2

ACE Study http://www.cdc.gov/violenceprevention/acestudy/index.html

Bandler, Richard and Grindler, John, Frogs into Princes: Introduction to Neurolinguistic Programming Revised edition, Eden Grove Editions, 1990

Edelamn, Hope, Motherless Daughters, Second Edition, Da Capo Lifelong Books, 2006

Freud, Female Sexuality essay, 1931

Herman, Judith, MD, Trauma and Recovery, Basic Books, 2015

Holocaust Exposure Induced Intergenerational Effects on *FKBP5* Methylation http://www.biologicalpsychiatryjournal.com/article/S0006-3223(15)00652-6/abstract

Jung, C.G., Psychology and Education, Translated by R.F.C. Hull, Princeton Legacy Library, 1969

Keller Pringle, Mia, Dr, The Needs of Children Hutchinson, 1989

Lipton, Bruce, PhD, Biology of Belief, Hay House, 2011

Miller, Alice, For Your Own Good, Farrar, Straus and Giroux, 3rd Revised ed., 1983

Scaer, Dr Robert , The Body Bears the Burden: Trauma, Dissociation and Disease, 3rd Edition, Routledge, 2014

Watts, Terence, Warriors, Settlers, Nomads: Discovering who we are and what we can be, Crown House Publishing, 2000

Chapter 3

Banyan, Calvin D, The Secret Language of Feelings, Banyan Hypnosis Centre for Training and Services Inc, 2003

Cameron, Julia, The Artists Way, Pan Books, 1993

Chapman, Gary, Campbell, Ross, The Five Love Languages for Children, Northfield Publishing, 2012

Dawson, Karl, Allenby, Sasha, Matrix Reimprinting using EFT, Hay House, 2010

Fry, Wendy, Find YOU, Find LOVE: Get to the heart of love and relationships using EFT, Milton and Fry Publishers, 2014

Jeffers, Susan, Feel the Fear and Do it Anyway, Century Hutchinson, 1987

Hay, Louise L, You Can Heal Your Life, Specialist Publications, 1984

Marshall, Fiona, Losing a Parent, Sheldon Press, 2011

Notre Dame Professor and Psychologist Darcia Narvaez http://psychology.nd.edu/

Nova, Jenbella, The Meaning of Negative Emotions A-Z, Strategic Book Publishing and Rights Co., 2013

Dutton, Marion, The Healing Art: The Ultimate Guide on Art and Creative, Create Space Independent Publishing Platform, 2016

Chapter 4

Adams, Kathleen, Journal to the Self: Twenty-two paths to personal growth, Warner Books, Inc, 1990

Capacchione, Lucia Ph.D, The Creative Journaling Process, Swallow Press, 2015

Commins, Patricia, Remembering Mother, Finding Self, Health Communications Inc, Deefield Beach, 1999

Edelamn, Hope, Motherless Daughters, Second Edition, Da Capo Lifelong Books, 2006

Lawler KA, Younger JW, Pieferi RL, Billington E, Jobe R, Edmonson K, Jones WH, A Change of Heart: cardiovascular correlates of forgiveness in response to interpersonal conflict , Journal of Behavioural Medicine, electronic version, 2003

Lawler KA, Younger JW, Pieferi RL, Billington E, Jobe R, Edmonson K, Jones WH. The unique effects of forgiveness on health: an exploration of pathways, Journal of behavioural medicine, electronic version, April 2005

Swick, Jessie, Please Just Listen, poem, freely available on the internet

Zahn-Waxler, Carolyn, Developmental Psychology, American Psychological Association, 1998

Chapter 5

ACE Study http://www.cdc.gov/violenceprevention/acestudy/index.html

Chapman, Gary, Campbell, Ross, The Five Love Languages for Children, Northfield Publishing, 2012

Hay, Louise L, You Can Heal Your Life, Specialist Publications, 1984

Herna , Bert, Affirmations and Self Talk, Kindle edition, e-book

King, Sharon, Heal Your Birth, Heal Your Life, SilverWood Books Ltd, 2015

Pert, Candice, Molecules of Emotion: The Science behind Mind-Body Medicine'' Simon and Schuster Ltd, 1998

Chapter 6

Craig, Gary, Flint, Garry. A, Emotional Freedom: Techniques for dealing with emotional and physical distress, NeosolTerric Enterprises; Revised ed., 2001

Craig, Gary, The EFT Manual (Everyday EFT: Emotional Freedom Techniques, Energy Psychology Press; 2 edition, 2011

Dawson, Karl, Allenby, Sasha, Matrix Reimprinting using EFT, Hay House, 2010

Hartmann, Silvia and Craig, Gary, Classic EFT Tapping Collection: Comprehensive Guide to Emotional Freedom Techniques, Dragon Rising, 2016

Picture Credits

Cover photo: Idea from and original design vikncharlie at Fiverr, modified by Richard McMunn, Book Publishing Academy

Logo: Design by daydreamer94 at Fiverr

Illustrations: Amy Branton https://www.pinterest.com/freehearteft/living-from-the-heart/ Amy is also a skilled EFT and Matrix Reimprinting Practitioner www.freehearteft.co.uk

SUE Scale: Guild of Energists with kind permission to share from Silvia Hartmann

Bibliography

- Adams, Kathleen, Journal to the Self: Twenty-two paths to personal growth, Warner Books, Inc, 1990
- Arcana, Judith. Our Mothers' Daughters, The Women's press, 1984
- Bandler, Richard and Grinder, John, Frogs into Princes: Introduction to Neurolinguistic Programming Revised edition, Eden Grove Editions, 1990
- Banyan, Calvin D, The Secret Language of Feelings, Banyan Hypnosis Centre for Training and Services Inc, Tustin, 2003
- Bassoff, Evelyn, PdD, Mothers and daughters: Loving and Letting Go, First Plume Printing, Penguin Group, 1989
- Bowlby, Dr John, Attachment and Loss, Volume 1, Basic Books, 1998
- Capacchione, Lucia PhD, The Creative Journaling Process, Swallow Press, 2015
- Cameron, Julia, The Artists Way, Pan Books, 1993
- Carlcon, Kathie. In Her Image: The unhealed daughters search for her mother, Shambhala Publications, Inc, 1989
- Chapman, Gary, Campbell, Ross, The Five Love Languages for Children. Northfield Publishing, 2012
- Chernin, Kim. The Woman Who Gave Birth To Her Mother: Tales of changes in women's lives, Penguin Books, 1998
- Cleese, Alyce Faye, Bates, Brian. How to Manage Your Mother: Understanding the most difficult, complicated and fascinating relationship of your life, Arrow Books, 2003

- Cozolino, Louis, The Neuroscience of Human Relationships, W.W. Norton and Company, 2006
- Commins, Patricia. Remembering Mother, Finding Self: A Journey of love and Acceptance, Health Communications Inc, 1999
- Cori, Jasmin Lee. The Emotionally Absent Mother: A guide to self-healing and getting the love you missed, The Experiment, LLC, 2010
- Craig, Gary, The EFT Manual (Everyday EFT: Emotional Freedom Techniques, Energy Psychology Press; 2 edition, 2011
- Craig, Gary, Flint, Garry. A, Emotional Freedom: Techniques for dealing with emotional and physical distress, NeosolTerric Enterprises; Revised ed. Country, 2001
- Crawford, Christina. Mommie Dearest, Morrow, 1978
- Danu, Morrigan. You're Not Crazy - It's Your Mother, Darton, Longman and Todd Ltd 2012
- Dawson, Karl. Marillat, Kate. Transform Your Beliefs, Transform Your Life. EFT Tapping using Matrix Reimprinting. Hay House, UK. 2014
- Dawson, Karl. Allenby, Sasha. Matrix Reimprinting using EFT. Hay House, UK. 2010
- Dodd, Ray. The Power of Belief. Hampton Road Publishing Company, Inc. Charlottesville, 2003
- Dutton, Marion, The Healing Art: The Ultimate Guide on Art and Creative, Create Space Independent Publishing Platform, 2016
- Edelman, Hope. Motherless Daughters: The legacy of Loss, Da Caopo Press edition, 2006

- Fisher, Annabel. The Healing Game: Transforming Chronic Illness Using EFT, Different Maker Press, 2015
- Freud, 'Female Sexuality' essay, in Collected Papers, vol 5 (1950)
- Friday, Nancy. My Mother My Self, Dell Publishing Group Inc, 1987
- Fry, Wendy, Find YOU, Find LOVE: Get to the heart of love and relationships using EFT, Milton and Fry Publishers, 2014
- Fuerstein, Laura. My Mother My Mirror: Recognising and making the most of self-inherited Images, Canada Raincoat Books, 2009
- Fuller, Tina. It's My Turn: How to gain freedom from a manipulating and self-centred parent, Lulu.com, 2013
- Hammer, Signe. Daughters and Mothers: The relationship explored, Hutchinson and Co, 1975
- Hartmann, Silvia. Positive EFT. DragonRising, 2013
- Hartmann, Silvia and Craig, Gary, Classic EFT Tapping Collection: Comprehensive Guide to Emotional Freedom Techniques, Dragon Rising, 2016
- Hay, Louise L, You Can Heal Your Life, Specialist Publications, 1984
- Herna , Bert, Affirmations and Self Talk, Kindle edition, e-book
- Holden, Robert. Loveability. Hay House, 2013
- Jeffers, Susan, Feel the Fear and Do it Anyway, Century Hutchinson, 1987
- Jirsch, Anne. Cafferky, Monica. The Future is Yours. Piatikus, 2007

- Johnson, C.J, PsyD. Wombology: Healing the primordial memories and wounds your grandmothers daughter gave to you, iUniverse, 2009
- Jung, C.G., Psychology and Education, Translated by R.F.C. Hull, Princeton Legacy Library, 1969
- Katie, Byron. Loving What Is. Random House, 2002
- Keller Pringle, Mia, Dr, The Needs of Children Hutchinson, 1989
- King, Sharon, Heal Your Birth, Heal Your Life, SilverWood Books Ltd, 2015
- Krasnow, Iris. I Am My Mothers Daughter: Making peace with mom before it's too late, Basic Books, 2007
- Lipton, Bruce. Spontaneous Evolution: Our Positive Future and a Way to Get There from Here. Hay House, 2009
- Lipton , Bruce, PhD, Biology of Belief, Hay House, 2011
- Mahler, Margaret S, Pine, Fred, Bergman, Anni, The Psychological Birth of the Human Infant: Symbiosis and Individuation, BasicBooks, Inc, 1975
- Martin, Curly. The Life Coaching Handbook. Crown House Publishing Ltd, 2001
- Manning, Martha. The Common Thread: Mothers and Daughters and the power of empathy, HarperCollins, 2002
- Marshall, Fiona, Losing a Parent, Sheldon Press, 2011
- McBride, Karyl, PhD, Will I Ever Be Good Enough?: Healing the daughters of narcissistic mothers, Atria, 2008
- McKay, Matthew, PhD. Fanning, Patrick. Prisoners of Belief. New Harbinger Publications, Inc., 1991

- Miller, Alice. The Drama of Being a Child, Virago Press Ltd, 1986
- Miller, Alice, For Your Own Good, Farrar, Straus and Giroux, 3rd revised edition, 1983
- Morris, Gillian, EFT for Everyone, Zento Publishing, 2016
- Nova, Jenbella, The Meaning of Negative Emotions A-Z, Strategic Book Publishing and Rights Co., 2013
- Perin, Margo. How I Learned to Cook and other writings on complex mother-daughter relationships, Penguin Group, 2004
- Pert, Candice, Molecules of Emotion: The Science behind Mind-Body Medicine'' Simon and Schuster Ltd, 1998
- Redmond, Layne. When the Drummers Were Women, Crown Publications, 1 edition, 1998
- Shaw, Marléne Rose. Out of Fear Into Love, Angel Ink, 2016
- Scaer, Dr Robert. The Body Bears the Burden: Trauma, Dissociation and Disease, Haworth Medical Press, second edition. 2007
- Secunda, Victoria. When you and your mother can't be friends, Dell Publishing,
- Streep, Peg. Mean Mothers: The Legacy of Hurt, HarperCollins, 2009
- Tannen, Deborah. You're Wearing That: Understanding mothers and daughters in conversation, Random House, 2006
- Watts, Terence, Warriors, Settlers, Nomads: Discovering who we are and what we can be, Crown House Publishing, 2000

- Williams, Sue. Believe You Can, Believe You Can Books, 2015
- Williamson, Marianne. A Woman's Worth, Random House, 1993
- Zahn-Waxler, Carolyn, Developmental Psychology, American Psychological Association, 1998

DVD's & CD's

- Because I Said So, 2007, Michael Lehmann
- Diving Secrets of the Ya - Ya Sisterhood, 2002, Callie Khouri
- Fly Away Home, 1996, Carroll Ballard
- Georgia Rule, 2007, Garry Marshall
- Gypsy, 1990, Mervin LeRoy
- Mothers and Daughters, 2004, Hannah Davies, David Connelly
- Mothers and Daughters , 2016, Paul Duddridge
- My Sisters Keeper, 2009, Nick Cassavetes
- Mildred Pierce, 1945, Michael Curtiz
- Postcards from the Edge, 1990, Mike Nichols
- Spanglish, 2004, James L. Brooks
- Terms of Endearment, 1983, James L. Brooks
- The Blindside, 2009, John Lee Hancock
- The Joy Luck Club, 1993, Wayne Wang
- What Babies Want, An exploration of the consciousness of infants, Debby Taikawa, 2004
- Warming the Stone Child: Myths and stories about abandonment and the un-mothered child, Clarissa Pinkola Estes, PdD, 1990, Sounds True (CD)

A further dedication to my mother Jeanette

Thank you mum for teaching me the following:

Learning manners and respect for others

Remembering to say please and thank you

Learning the alphabet ~ eventually!

Learning how to tie my shoe laces

The importance of being kind to animals

How to pot a plant

How to be organised and keep a clean and tidy home

How to write a letter

How to make lemon meringue pie (yours is still much better than mine)

To appreciate nature

Thank you for bringing me up, I know at times life wasn't easy for you

Most of all, thank you for giving birth to me

They say 'we pick our mothers before birth' and even though at times life has been challenging for both of us, my experiences with you have been perfect for me and without them this book would not have been written.

Thank you for being my mum,

Wendy x

About The Author

Wendy first became interested in emotional health and wellbeing after overcoming many challenges in her personal life. Through exploring her past, changing her limiting beliefs and working through her own demons, Wendy has gone on to train extensively to support you in transforming your relationships.

Wendy reaches out from her heart to yours through the contents of this book in the hope she can support you as you turn around any limiting beliefs you may have about your relationship with your mother and significant others. It is the choices you make from now on, that will ultimately lift you up or keep you down.

Wendy offers support and guidance as a relationship consultant and therapist using a range of healing modalities: EFT (Emotional Freedom Technique), Matrix Reimprinting, Hypnotherapy, Life Coaching, NLP (Neuro Linguistic Programming), Picture Tapping Technique, Spotlight Process, Energy in Motion, Matrix Birth Reimprinting, Matrix Life Purpose, Future Life Progression, Positive EFT and Reiki.

Wendy is a member of The British Institute of Hypnotherapists (BIH). She is registered with the International Coaching Institute of Coaching and Mentoring (IIC&M), member of The Guild of Energists (GoE) and The EFT and Matrix Reimprinting Academy (EFTMRA).

Wendy has a practice based in Surrey, United Kingdom and she also works internationally over Skype and runs workshops worldwide. For additional details on Wendy's services visit www.mothersanddaughters.solutions